March 1, 1981

Dear Bruce & Karen;

Our best wishes
to a great couple &
new friends!
"Duncan" sends his
regards!!

Sincerely,

Bob & Anne

Woolf

Behind Closed Doors

Behind Closed Doors

Bob Woolf

With the editorial assistance of Mickey Herskowitz

Introduction by Roger Kahn

New York   *Atheneum*   1976

Library of Congress Cataloging in Publication Data
Woolf, Bob.
    Behind closed doors

1. Woolf, Bob.   2. Lawyers—United States—
Correspondence, reminiscences, etc. 3. Professional
sports—United States. I. Title.
KF373.W6A32   344'.73'099   75-41850
ISBN 0-689-10712-9

Portions of the Introduction have appeared in a different form
in *Esquire* magazine.

Published simultaneously in Canada by
McClelland and Stewart Ltd.
Manufactured in the United States of America by
The Book Press, Brattleboro, Vermont
Designed by Harry Ford
First Edition

To my family

My wife, Anne, who presented me with three lovely children: Stacey, Gary, and Tiffany, as well as the title of this book.

My mother, Anna R. Woolf, and the memories of my father, Dr. Joseph R. Woolf, and my brother Irving Woolf.

Acknowledgments

I would like to thank Mickey Herskowitz of the Houston Post, Will McDonough of the Boston Globe, Chuck Corn of Atheneum Publishers for their advice and assistance; and a special thanks to a tireless and overworked secretary, Angelica Joan Francesca Leone, better known as Jill.

Introduction

Roger Kahn

I N A simpler time, which to be sure is any time past, a forgotten outfielder named Gene Hermanski spent a summer bashing line drives against the right-field wall of the Brooklyn Elysium known as Ebbets Field. Hermanski drew a salary of $7,500 a year. That winter he walked into a so-called contract negotiation, a heart full of hope inflating his sturdy chest. "This year," he announced to a newspaperman named Bob Cooke, "the family's getting away from meat loaf. I really got a case for steak." Hermanski strutted into the office of Branch Rickey, a man with a Puritan distaste for money in other people's hands, and while Cooke waited in an anteroom a classic old-time sports negotiation began.

"Well," Cooke said when Hermanski emerged, his face wrinkled into a wide grin. "I guess you got your raise."

"Nope," Hermanski said, "but he didn't cut me."

Today, a quarter century later, playing professional sports no longer condemns the athlete to a marginal livelihood: it is his ticket to hundreds of thousands of dollars a year. According to one of my favorite and most accurate sources, the average National Basketball Association jump-shooter earns about

$100,000 a season. In baseball, where Hermanski's old salary no longer buys an assistant trainer, thirty players make over $100,000. Even in professional football, the most tightly organized and in certain ways the most penurious of our major sports, there are twenty-five players up in that bracket.

You cannot explain such change of circumstances by mere inflation. The very nature of American sports has been revolutionized, changing from a glamorous peonage in which the owners got to make the money and the players got to sign the autographs (Veblen's psychic income) into something that resembles in a vague and even disquieting way the old Hollywood star system.

I've seen some of this developing and heard still more about it during many pleasant hours with an attorney named Robert G. Woolf, who numbers three hundred athletes among his clients. Bob Woolf is an intense, black-haired, solidly built man who at forty-seven has mastered the most remarkable of all legal tricks. He is a lawyer who does not talk like one.

Since 1964, when a strapping, handsome pitcher named Earl Wilson came calling at his office after an automobile accident, Woolf has built a consistently expanding, innovative practice. "Earl kind of reminded me of a cross between Jim Brown and Harry Belafonte," Woolf says, "and when we talked we discovered we had a lot of attitudes in common. One day we found ourselves discussing methods by which an athlete could defer income and that I guess is where the whole thing began."

In his most remarkable coup, Woolf represented Derek Sanderson, a good but surely not great center for the Boston Bruins at a time when both the Bruins and the Philadelphia Blazers, an entry in the new World Hockey Association, coveted Sanderson's services. "I sat in a room," Woolf recalls, and a kind of boyish wonder brightens his eyes, "in which money suddenly seemed to lose all meaning. These people simply had to have Derek."

Woolf arranged for a $2,650,000 five-year contract and Sanderson proceeded to bomb in Philadelphia. Woolf negotiated a million-dollar release from the Blazers and Sanderson returned to the Bruins, where he revived. He now employs a chauffeur to drive his Rolls and it may be suitable at length to ask, Where have you gone Gene Hermanski? A grieving country misses you. (Or maybe unsuitable. The meter is imperfect.)

I caught up with Woolf one typical Saturday after he had made business trips to seventeen cities in eleven days. He was reworking early drafts of a then embryonic memoir which he planned to call *Behind Closed Doors,* and arranging a weekend at the Sidney Hill Country Club for several guests and his soft-eyed wife Anne, whose charm grows on you as the charm of a good and faithful woman always does.

Woolf lives in Chestnut Hill, near Boston, and there, amid a clatter of children and television sets, he seemed more relaxed than I had seen him for some time. "The Matuszak thing is done," he announced, by way of explanation.

John Matuszak was then a lineman out of the University of Tampa whose hair flared wildly and whose measurements would have given pause to King Kong. Height: 6 feet 8 inches. Weight: 290 pounds. Waist: 34 inches. Chest: 54 inches. Disposition gentle, except when dressed in a football uniform. Then he became a tackle of such fierce demeanor that he was chosen first in the 1973 National Football League draft. As a sensible young behemoth, Matuszak reached a great paw toward a telephone and called Woolf.

Drafts are designed to equalize—that is, the last-place team picks first—and Matuszak was fated to play for the Houston Oilers on plastic grass, under the Lucite heaven of the Astrodome. Sid Gillman, a tough, old-time sports bargainer, opened negotiations with a tough, old-time manager's letter. He volunteered a sub-$50,000 bonus to Matuszak, presumably the most valuable of all graduating college football players, and a starting salary of less than $25,000. Gillman closed on a note that would have done Branch Rickey proud. This was the first, best and absolutely final offer.

Because he does his homework and equally because he had represented a dozen first-football-draft choices, Woolf concluded that Gillman's offer was significantly out of line. But because Woolf possesses a sense of pragmatic psychology, he recognized that charging at Gillman would be pointless. A stubborn, gifted man had taken a position. There was nothing to be gained by butting heads, except mutual concussions.

How then to move? Woolf discovered that he and Gillman both were to be honored in late spring at a Boston banquet. Phone calls to Houston. Could attorney Woolf arrange for a car to meet Mr. Gillman at Logan Airport? No? Already arranged? Well, perhaps he and Sid could find a few moments alone to chat. This was not a Sanderson situation, or anything of the sort. There was nothing to worry Gillman, really. But John Matuszak was a nice boy and all attorney Woolf wanted for his client was a fair offer. A secretary reported that Mr. Gillman's Boston schedule was so heavy he'd have no time to see Woolf. Patience, Woolf told himself, patience.

The Toronto Argonauts are a mainstay of the Canadian Football League, and what a boon it would be to Canadian pride to expropriate the N.F.L.'s number-one draft choice. Woolf decided to visit Toronto on hockey business. While there, he spoke to John Bassett, a former newspaper publisher who owned the Argonauts. Lightly, or as lightly as one could, he dropped the name of John Matuszak into the conversation.

Bassett was interested. "I don't want to bring John up here unless you're really serious," Woolf said, "because John really is willing to play for your team."

Curiously, after Matuszak flew into Toronto, wirephotos of him there flashed into every major American city, including Houston. Within twenty-four hours Gillman, no longer quite so busy, was telephoning Woolf. Matuszak presently signed with the Oilers for what Woolf describes as "a fair and significant improvement" over Gillman's original first, final and best offer. Such bargaining skills are not without worth. Woolf himself concedes to an income well in excess of $250,000 a year, and although he is essentially an unostentatious man, he does own the only Cadillac I have seen with separate telephones for front and rear passengers.

Spending time with him can be somewhat harrowing. Like many surpassingly successful men, Woolf feeds on work. It seems to strengthen him. He budgets minutes and appears to enjoy negotiating six contracts at once, while planning three business trips and talking on the phone to a famous client— Calvin Murphy, Jim Plunkett, Carl Yastrzemski—about a prospective speaking engagement. Urgency is the word. Urgency moves Robert Woolf.

Although he is no intellectual, I don't believe I have encountered a quicker mentality, nor one more troubled by concepts of fairness in a rather Talmudic sense, as such concepts troubled the philosopher Hillel. If the old peonage was unfair, the pendulum has now swung too far the other way, Bob Woolf insists. That question worries him. The idea is not to create a star system that brings disorder and sorrow to sports as some suggest the old star system did to Hollywood. Fairness, Woolf says over and over. Fairness. The man who owns a franchise, that man bargaining across the table, has a right to a decent profit. He's taken the risk.

I don't mean to suggest that Woolf's concern for the capitalist facing him precludes his getting the best possible contract for his client. It does not. Indeed, one of the risks of owning a franchise is having to bargain with Bob Woolf. But he has no sympathy for athletes who jump contracts, nor any inclination to shove a struggling franchise into the hands of receivers. He looks tirelessly for devices—deferred-income programs, special bonus arrangements—that will keep the franchise in good health and the athlete in grocery money for the next three or four decades.

Woolf comes out of Portland, Maine, where his father Joseph was a physician of such dedication that once he advertised for any of the Portland sick to call on him without charge. The stock market crashed and with it the profits of Dr. Woolf's practice. There were seven in the family and Bob recalls an ebb when everybody had to live in one room above a cafeteria. On certain nights, he says, he can still recall the scent of second-rate cooking from the floor below assaulting his nostrils.

But the family stayed together and moved to Boston and times improved. Woolf graduated from that ruby of public education, Boston Latin School, attended Boston College on a basketball scholarship, and graduated from Boston University Law School. It is a mark of his urgency that he insisted on taking the bar exam before graduation. He passed. After that, he built a general law practice good enough to bring him $100,000 a year. Then Earl Wilson's auto accident opened a golden new world.

"Secrets?" he was saying at his home in Chestnut Hill. "Nothing all that deep or that profound. I work hard, but I love sports. You know that. You've seen me at games. So when I can help an athlete to a decent contract, and see that he makes sensible investments and looks past the age of thirty and even thirty-five, I get a thrill.

"And I'm a fan. I know it sounds ridiculous, but when I think of myself, a kind of ordinary college athlete, sitting with the most important men in sports, that thrills me too."

"But Bob," I said, "representing three hundred athletes, you are one of the most important men in sports."

He looked, unblinking. "Maybe, and is that a good thing?"

I think it is, but then I trust Bob Woolf's sense of fairness and proportion. I think so, and don't really know. There will be other months, other decades of sports boom in which to consider what shape the athlete-owner-attorney triangle assumes. It is, to be sure, a triangle of gold and I think most of us are growing weary of the relentless emphasis that the press and television lay on the money side of sports. But as you will see across the pages of *Behind Closed Doors*, Woolf's life in sports is not merely a financial report. It's been a journey among heroes and rogues and robber barons, a journey filled with excitement and joy and wonder about who's going to win the game tomorrow and why somebody lost today.

That he has been able to make his journey in a Cadillac with two telephones is not an unmixed blessing. We were riding outside Boston once when the phone in the front seat rang. A hockey player had a problem and it had to be solved right then.

Woolf listened patiently and made a few suggestions in the traffic. When the call ended, a bemused look crossed his face.

"These constant demands on your time bother you?" I asked.

"Not at all," Woolf said. "That's what I'm paid for." He smiled briefly. "I was just wondering why, if he wanted to get me in the car, he felt he had to make the call collect."

Preface

OVER THE DOOR at the University of Buffalo Law School, where not too long ago I addressed a group of students, a large inscription reads:

> The first thing we do, let's kill all the lawyers.
> William Shakespeare, *King Henry IV*

I have thought this was the motto of the owners and general managers in major league sports around this country, who couldn't be expected to embrace the attorneys crashing the executive office and clubhouses. Management and sports attorneys are natural opponents, but it's been my experience that the front office thinks of its team as family, and although family I may never be, as attorney and personal confidante for the players, I was solving problems for management. I took on their headaches, and in spite of the dollar tenseness at contract time, I was there—on their turf—to help, not hurt, the team. The sports attorney has become much more than a necessary evil. And I found in the inner sanctums of the sports world untold dimensions of human drama.

In this book, you'll see behind the closed doors of sports from my vantage point. In the past decade, a deluge of books has taken the fan into the locker rooms, barrooms and bedrooms of the athlete. Others, not nearly as many, have dealt with the upper echelon of a particular sport, like Bill Veeck's writing about baseball. But in *Behind Closed Doors*, I reveal yet another level of the sports world. The cases and issues of these stories I feel will be relevant to sports history in its most critical era.

But most important, these experiences are about people, their emotions, their lives and their destinies that unfolded before me as I represented over 300 of the top athletes in the country. With them, I enjoyed great thrills, and endured deep depressions. I regret nothing, except, perhaps, not having helped even more athletes, and not having told our stories candidly and sooner, so that others—like them—and like me—might not make the same mistakes.

Contents

Illustrations

Don Shula and Darryl Carleton

With Johnny Bucyk of the Bruins in a triumphant moment

Pete Varney gets the press treatment.

With Luis Tiant and his father at Tiant Sr.'s seventieth birthday party

Strolling with Russ Francis (Cary Wolinsky)

Joe Namath, Derek Sanderson and Bob Woolf at the opening of Bachelors Three (Fred Vytal)

Derek Sanderson with Allan King and Buddy Greco on the Johnny Carson Show (Time Inc.)

Harpo Gladieux, Jim Plunkett, Danny Simons and Bob Woolf

Behind Closed Doors

1

Dirty Derek

———

I WATCHED UNEASILY as he propped his feet on the polished surface of my desk, his legs crossed at the ankle. A cigarette dangled from his lip—a *weed*, he called it, an expression I had not heard since the '50s.

The performance was characteristic, I would learn later, for this young hockey player I was meeting for the first time. I recognized the name, Derek Sanderson, but knew almost nothing else about him. The more we talked, the better I liked it that way. You had the feeling that he was doing an impression at a party, and you were supposed to guess who it was. Bogart? Charles Bronson? James Dean? Maybe something of all of them.

Sanderson was doing most of the talking. "I don't need you right now," he confided, "but in a couple of years I'll be the biggest guy you'll handle."

"Oh yes?" I answered, while I shuffled the papers on my desk and thought about firing the secretary who let this cocky, fresh-looking belligerent into my office to waste my time.

"That's right," Derek continued, undaunted by my obvious lack of interest. "I'm going to make a million dollars. And when

I do, you'll need me."

About that time, what I didn't need was more aggravation from a freewheeling character. I was in the middle of several Ken Harrelson escapades and was not in the market for any new "swingers." Harrelson was then at the peak of his Boston Red Sox glory.

This was the spring of 1968, and Ken Harrelson happened to be in an adjoining office making a phone call.

"Hawk," I called out, switching on the intercom, "step into my office, will you? I want you to meet your hockey counterpart."

I didn't think that I would ever have a client who could match the flamboyance of Harrelson. But they were, indeed, a pair. The Hawk was warm, open, spectacular. Sanderson worked at being colorful and, in time, was amazed at how well he succeeded. Derek, I soon discovered, was the biggest put-on since Orson Welles. He would worry about the mentality of anyone who would take Derek Sanderson seriously.

That day in my office, he had just walked in from the street, unannounced. He was coming off a glittering first season with the Boston Bruins and had been voted rookie of the year in the National Hockey League. But I wasn't really into hockey at the time and I wasn't appropriately impressed.

Time would prove Derek right, up to a point. I grew to like him. His mother loves him. His father thinks he's super. As for the rest of the world . . . it's a tossup.

Yet, Derek was a prophet. He did make a million, and more. He did become one of the biggest clients. But, did I *need* him? You can figure out as you read on.

All it took to bring Derek the biggest contract in the history of sports was five years of almost daily phone calls, any time of day or night; visits to jails and hospitals; journeys in and out of love affairs and movies; frequent fence-mending jobs with his employers; steady denials of explosive statements he made in the press; countless retirements and threatened lawsuits.

I could sum it up now by saying that at times he has been the most exasperating athlete I ever met; and at other times, behind all the nonsense and flim-flam, one of the most appealing. He is every family's wayward child. Somehow, after each new scrape and misadventure, you come to feel more affection for him. Astrology fans may find it significant that he was born at the stroke of midnight. In fact, half the records at the Niagara Falls General Hospital show his date of birth as June 15, 1946, the other half as June 16. A true Gemini, maybe this explains why he seems like two different people.

There were times when I gladly would have strangled Derek. One night during his second season in the league, I received a phone call from the Boston police, notifying me that they had him locked up at Station 7 in East Boston, near Logan Airport.

The story I unraveled later was this: Derek had gone to the airport that evening to pick up a well-proportioned friend, as so many of his friends are. Her flight was late in arriving, the terminal was crowded and, in his own style, Derek decided to park his car right in the middle of the main traffic lane outside the front entrance. A state trooper—the state police patrol the airport in Boston—was writing out a ticket when Derek emerged with the young lady on his arm.

"If this is your car, this is for you," the trooper informed Derek as he handed him a ticket.

"Thank you," said Derek, taking the ticket and tearing it to shreds and scattering it to the winds in front of the disbelieving officer of the law.

The trooper was naturally disturbed, particularly since Sanderson neglects to carry such trivial credentials as a driver's license or identification on his person. Sanderson was taken into custody. It took me only three hours to convince the law that they shouldn't throw away the key.

But for every instance that he gives you that tough-kid-from-Niagara Falls routine, there are just as many when he shows the decency in him. I have heard an endless line of players who swore they were going to take care of their parents when they made it—but Derek was one of the few that I know of who ever did. He didn't say in the end, "Here's a thousand or two, Mom and Dad." When he signed a record-breaking contract —$2.65 million with the Philadelphia Blazers—he saw to it that his parents got $100,000. And he made sure that the money was guaranteed to them, *before* he agreed to any other terms.

But that's getting ahead of the story, because to really understand Derek, you have to go back to the beginning, rough as it was.

When I first met Derek that day in my office in 1968, he was making $10,000 a year. He was a skinny kid who pictured himself as a dead-end type. His manners were abrasive. His attitude was arrogant.

If I had misgivings when I met him, they were multiplied a few weeks after our introduction when my wife and I invited him to attend the press photographers' ball in Boston. Harrelson was being honored there and, in just a short time, Derek and Kenny had become fast friends, kindred spirits.

As we entered the ballroom, I took Sanderson aside and decided to play a little game with him. Derek was devoid of any of the common courtesies at the time, such as "thank you" or "you're welcome." So I resorted to some strategy.

"Every time you say the right thing at the right time tonight," I offered, "I'll give you a point. Every time you don't say thank you, or you're welcome, I'll get a point." No prize was involved, but I was counting on Derek's competitive instincts.

He really tried that night, and still lost by a score of 18 to 6, which gives you an indication of how much social polish he had.

About this time, though, Sanderson started to build his own image. The writers and the sportscasters liked him. And why not? I've seen him give fourteen interviews after a game, to fourteen different writers, and each one would be different, contradicting the previous one. Then the next day he'd deny it all, or claim he was misquoted. There was something about having people hang on his every word that Derek found comic.

It was obvious from the start that he lived for the moment. He loved to say controversial things, to shock people, to stir up mischief. There had been no one like him in the conservative world of ice hockey.

That summer, holed up in the Hawk's apartment, which he had subleased, Derek was host to writers from every medium. Of course, they were properly impressed by "his" luxury apartment, and "his" fifty suits hanging in the closet with matching accessories; and "his" closed-circuit TV with a control panel convenient to a circular, leopard-skin bed, where he entertained some of Boston's fairest ladies.

We really didn't plan it, but almost spontaneously this twenty-one-years-old roughneck from the Canadian side of Niagara Falls, with one season under his suspenders, was becoming the most colorful character in hockey. "This has to be it for me," I recall him advising me, as he has countless times. "I'm on the same team with Bobby Orr, the greatest player in hockey. I'm on the same team with Phil Esposito, and he's the greatest scorer in the game. If I'm going to make it, I'll just have to be the most colorful guy in the game."

He was and is. His sense of style combined with the force of his personality made him a trend-starter. Hockey didn't have long hair until Sanderson came along, and after Sanderson, players habitually checked their reflections in the glass panels as they skated past the end zones. Sanderson sported the first modern-day NHL mustache. He was the first to insult the revered league president, Clarence Campbell, calling him a stuffed shirt.

And he wanted to be the first in the game to wear white skates, emulating the footwear of a fellow who was to become his business partner in Boston, Joe Namath. To which his coach, Harry Sinden, responded: "I'll let you wear white skates if you play in a pink hat to go with them."

Yet in less than a year, the entire Oakland hockey team, owned by Charles O. Finley, was shod in white.

And as far as sport historians can tell, Derek was also the first player in the buttoned-down NHL to give the crowd what is politely referred to as an obscene Italian gesture—the old flex-your-arm salute. Not untypically, he made his move in Chicago, on national television, right in the camera's eye, throwing the Bruin front office into shock. "I don't know what all the excitement is about," said Derek, in his mock-choirboy manner, when we were called on the carpet. "It must mean something different in Chicago. Back home, in Niagara Falls, when we do that it's just a way to say, 'Hi, how are you?'"

One way or another, he was a hard man to ignore—especially for women. Once, WBZ, the largest radio station in New England, ran a Date Derek contest. Women had to write in why they wanted to have a date with him, and the station would pay for 103 of them—103 is the WBZ spot on the dial—to be his guests at Bachelors III in Boston, where, at the ripe old age of twenty-two, he was keeping things going for Namath.

Over 13,000 ladies applied for a date, and the pressure, on Derek and the station, became so intense that they had to pick a seventy-three-year-old grandmother, Mabel Hocking, as the grand-prize winner so there wouldn't be any repercussions. Mabel spent a pleasant evening at the club and Derek treated her with great courtesy and respect.

I don't quite know what it is about Derek and women. They go crazy over him. I suspect that he is so deliberately obnoxious and arrogant, at times, that he brings out the motherly instinct in women and they tell themselves, "He can't be that bad. There has to be some good in him and I'm going to bring it out."

Admittedly, Derek has let more than a fair share of them try.

In that league I would have to rate him ahead of Namath, considering that in the early stages of his career Derek didn't have the funds to support his endeavors. He had to do it on charm. Joe has charm, too. But money helps.

Part of Derek's charm, I think, is that he says exactly what he feels, and lives the way most of us wish we could. He is the kind of guy who, even when he is sober, tells the boss what he thinks of him.

Derek had signed a three-year contract coming out of junior hockey which paid him $10,000, $12,000 and $14,000. About halfway through it, he started chirping to anyone who would listen: "I'm getting paid peon's wages. I'm paid like a common laborer. I'd be better off picking fruit."

His public grousing was disconcerting to the Bruin management, but it threw Derek into the limelight. In 1971 he was featured in *Life* and *Time,* and was on the cover of a number of other magazines, and appeared on the Johnny Carson, Dick Cavett and Merv Griffin shows. It was the complete media blitz. Bobby Orr, Bobby Hull, Gordie Howe, Rocket Richard, all of the great ones, had never gotten this kind of exposure for hockey. Yet here was this kid, with less than three years in the league, who had never scored 30 goals, who had yet to receive a single vote for the all-star team, commanding all of this attention while putting together an autobiography with noted hockey writer Stan Fischler that would turn into a sports best seller.

I remember Johnny Carson, who enjoyed Derek and still does, asking him one night on his show what he planned to do when his career ended. "Well," said Derek, "after watching you in action tonight I think I'll come back and take this job away from you."

At one point, he flew to Montreal to make his debut as a film actor, or so we thought. His part was to be a hockey coach —type casting—who visits a small Canadian town scouting local talent and winds up having the movie's female lead fall in love with him.

I reviewed Derek's portion of the script and found it harmless, if not exactly the kind of material that would make the world forget Laurence Olivier. When the filming was completed, Derek and I proudly accepted our invitations to attend a private screening, at which the stars of this epic would appear.

We were not very far into the movie before my heart sank and my stomach got queasy. *It was a porno flick.* I couldn't believe my eyes. While Derek's scene was clean, nothing else in the movie was. The scene in which he met his "love interest" was preceded by one in which she slept with ten or eleven guys— forgive me, but I lost count.

Fortunately, I had an escape clause in the contract. I wasted no time in getting his sequence cut; all the while Derek was feigning shock and insisting he had no knowledge of the movie's actual content. There are times when I think he has great acting talent.

But the Bruins management didn't find Derek so entertaining. "How can one guy get into so much trouble?" Milt Schmidt, the general manager, used to ask me. Milt was the all-time hall of fame center in the NHL and held Clarence Campbell in almost reverent regard. When Sanderson knocked Campbell, and called him a stuffed shirt, Milt all but blew the roof off the Boston Garden.

When the time came to sign a new contract, Derek conducted his own negotiations in the press, which didn't do much for my efforts with management. Bud Collins, of the Boston *Globe*, wrote a humorous article suggesting that Bruin fans send in twenty-five cents each to help pay Sanderson's new salary.

Finally, the Bruins held a press conference and aired their side of the story, including how much salary and bonus money they had paid Sanderson over the years. During the 1970–71 season he received $14,000 in salary and a $10,000 bonus. By the standards of the sport it amounted to a reasonable sum, but to Sanderson that wasn't the point. In their special Olympian style, whenever the Bruins tried to do the right thing by him, they made it sound like a favor, when Sanderson felt he had earned it.

Salary details in sports—the particular figures on a contract—were just not divulged by a team, short of a court order. I had never heard of it before, or since. Campbell added to the uproar by telling the hockey press in Canada that Sanderson was getting paid what he was worth and he quoted the figures.

None of this made the job any easier for Sanderson's attorney, so we hassled and haggled right down to the last minute. Finally, at 2 P.M. on the afternoon of the opening game of the 1971 season, we reached an agreement. The figures were written into the contract but Sanderson wanted one more thing. "I'm taking that contract back," he announced, "unless I can play tonight."

"You're not playing tonight," snapped Schmidt. "You're not physically ready to play. You'll come to the game and watch. You won't dress or play."

"If I don't play, I don't come," said Sanderson, and with that he stalked out of the office.

About two hours later, I called Schmidt at his home trying to cool things off, when he informed me: "Bob, if Derek Sanderson isn't at the Boston Garden tonight, I'll trade him within a week. And I mean it."

Milt Schmidt never says anything he doesn't mean. And to this day—or until he reads this book, if he ever does—Sanderson didn't know about the above conversation.

I tore out of my house and drove down to Bachelors III where he was holding court. As I said, I didn't tell him about the trade threat because he was a born rebel, and Schmidt's ultimatum would be like filet mignon to his palate.

It was the only time in my career that I ever became openly enraged at a client. Derek had never seen me lose my temper before—or since—and it stunned him. "Okay, Bob," he said, reluctantly, "I'll go. But I don't like it. This is humiliating."

So Derek went to the Garden that night, sat out the game, worked himself back into shape and went on to play on two Stanley Cup champion teams in three years. On the way to the second cup, we started hearing rumors about, and getting feelers from, the upstart World Hockey Association. The new league was being put together by the same entrepreneurs who established the American Basketball Association. Although I wasn't enamoured of some of the people who started it, the more I considered the potential owners in each city, the more respect I gained for the league, and I foresaw that it might become a reality.

Our first contact came in December of 1971, when Herb Martin of Miami called to say he had the rights to the WHA franchise in Miami and wanted Sanderson for his team. When I met Martin for the first time, at the "57" Restaurant in Boston, I understood why he so wanted Derek. They were soul brothers. Martin was colorful and flamboyant. He brought with him a mutual friend, Bob Halloran, the top TV sportscaster in Miami.

Martin owned merchandise marts in Miami and Dallas, and had special coins minted, with his name on them, that he handed out to new acquaintances. He was then constructing a new sports arena in Miami to house his Screaming Eagles, as the team was to be called, and he wanted Sanderson's name on the marquee. This was the gimmick on which the WHA would build its future. Each team wanted to poach one superstar from the NHL, so that it would have at least one box-office attraction.

So Sanderson was the man selected for Martin's Miami team. "What would it take," Martin asked at that first meeting, "to get Sanderson away from the Bruins and down to Miami?"

"In the first place, Herb," I said, "I don't think Derek will ever leave. He loves Boston and the Bruins. Despite what he says, he loves this team. But I'll tell you this much. He won't leave for anything less than $250,000 a year."

The figure was strictly a wild stab by me. Maybe I'd been hanging around Derek too much, and wanted to see if I could shock someone myself. But Martin didn't blink. "That sounds fair," he said, nodding. "We'll take care of that okay. But it will have to be long-term, something like ten years."

"You mean a package of $2.5 million over ten years?" I asked incredulously.

"We can manage it," Martin assured me. "He'll be worth it to us in the long run."

At this point, the WHA and the Miami Screaming Eagles were just bull's wool and ozone. The league hadn't been officially formed, and, as it turned out, when the time did come to put up the money, Martin couldn't produce it. Construction of his arena, half-finished, was about to be halted by the city because of zoning problems. You can't play hockey without ice.

Derek, intrigued initially by Martin's offer, didn't seem at all disappointed by this turn of events. Life in Boston was going too good for him. He was now a partner in three of the swinging singles places in town—Daisy Buchanan's, Zelda's and the Great Gatsby's. These bars, because of Sanderson's affiliation, were prosperous.

Someone asked Harry Sinden during the Team Canada–Russia hockey series if he could think of any way to stop the Russians after they had stunned the Canadians with three wins and a tie in their first five meetings. "If I could just get their team into Daisy Buchanan's for one night," said Sinden, "*that* would take all the pep out of them."

After Martin failed to meet the ante in Miami, the franchise was switched to Philadelphia and an attorney named Jim Cooper.

Cooper was a hockey enthusiast. He'd go anywhere to watch a game. When the chance came to get his own team, Cooper talked his friend Bernie Brown, who ran a successful trucking business, into backing the team financially while Cooper would run the hockey enterprise. Brown had never seen a hockey game and didn't know Derek Sanderson from Howie Morenz. But as a businessman he just wanted to diversify, and Cooper made a WHA franchise sound like a good investment.

Cooper approached me about Sanderson in an unusual way. He telephoned and said he wanted Ron Plumb, a Bruin farm-hand who was also one of my clients. But he told me he was going to show his good faith in dealing with Plumb, so he could get at the bigger plum—Sanderson. "I want Derek for Philadelphia," he vowed, "and we're going to do anything to get him."

Recalling similar statements by Martin, I was skeptical. Cooper erased some of my doubts, however, by coming up with $60,000 a year for Plumb, who just the year before had drawn a salary of $10,000 at Oklahoma City.

About this time, Derek was itching to go to Europe, and I thought the timing was perfect. There was extensive coverage of him now in the media, and he was getting advice from all directions. So Derek left for parts unknown on the Continent. This didn't deter Jim Cooper. He wanted to get everyone together and close the deal immediately, even if it meant chasing Sanderson around Europe to do it.

"Listen, Jim," I said, stalling, "I don't even know where Derek is. I can't tell you what country he's in, much less what hotel he's staying at."

"That's all right," said Cooper. "We'll find him. I'll get Johnny McKenzie"—another Bruin star he had just hired as a player-coach—"and the three of us will go over there and find him and get this contract settled."

Somehow I prevailed upon Cooper to ease the pressure and wait until Sanderson returned to the States for his audience. Our first meeting with Cooper was at my house, but before that, I sat down with Derek and urged him not to act like a smartass. "I'm impressed with Cooper," I told him, "and I think he means business. Just this once, try not to be obnoxious. We're talking astronomical sums. Something good could come of this."

Exactly how, or what, I couldn't be sure, because at that point Sanderson had no notion of leaving the Bruins or the Back Bay scene. But, obligingly, he turned on the charm for Cooper but gave no indication that he would leave the Bruins.

Two days later, Cooper called back and asked me to meet him at his oceanside home in New Jersey. I visited him on the weekend and, instantly, he caught me off guard. "Tell me, Bob," he said, "what will it take to get Sanderson away from the Bruins? How can I do it?"

This was a twist, a reversal of roles. Usually, the attorney assumed the role of coercing the owner.

"Make him the highest paid athlete in the world," I told Cooper. "If you do that, he might bite. Otherwise, if it isn't anything sensational, he won't do it. The idea of making more money than any other player in sports would make him flip."

Cooper agreed, and before the day was over we had outlined a package for about $2 million. This was the package to end all packages. In putting it together, I wanted it to be perfect. I drew from every contract I had ever experienced or heard about, using every possible clause that would be beneficial to Derek. After several calls and one more trip to New Jersey, we worked out a deal worth $2.65 million.

Derek was going to start at $500,000 for the first year because, somewhere in our research, we had discovered that Pele, the great soccer star, was reputed to be the highest paid athlete in the world at $400,000. We spread the rest of the contract over a number of years so the tax burden would be less. In addition, the Blazers agreed to hire Derek's father as a scout, for four years and $100,000.

I worked hard to make the contract airtight. If he was injured after he signed, and never played a game, Derek would be paid every cent. If, after five years, he decided he didn't *want* to play anymore, he could become a scout at $100,000 a year for the remainder of the contract.

There was, I hoped, no way he could lose—but he still hadn't said he wanted to, or would, leave the Bruins.

I had no intention of stringing Cooper along. He was straight and open and I liked doing business with him. "This will be our last negotiation," I said, when I left Atlantic City. "I'll talk to Derek and see what he says. But I must also tell you we're continuing to negotiate with the Bruins."

Meanwhile, back at Boston Garden, the Bruins were having their dynasty taken apart brick by brick. This team that had won two Stanley Cups in the past three years, and in those three years had won more games than any team in hockey history, was being ravaged by the World Hockey Association.

Gerry Cheevers, their fine goalie who had just clinched the Cup for them months before by shutting out the New York Rangers, 3–0, in the final game, had jumped to Cleveland. Ted Green defected to the New England Whalers. John McKenzie joined the Blazers, along with Plumb, who was considered the best young defenseman in the organization and a Bruin star of the future.

Up to now, the Bruins had treated the WHA as a joke, and they were paying for that attitude. Before Cheevers was ever approached by the Cleveland team, the difference between signing or losing him was a trifling $5,000 a year.

Sanderson was just as close. They had, in fact, verbally agreed to a salary of $80,000 during negotiations that had not directly involved me. The Bruins had a disconcerting habit of telling their key athletes, at contract time, "Hey, you don't need anybody to do *your* thinking. *We're* all grownups. *We* can work this out." And, then, when anything goes wrong, my telephone rings and the voice of management on the other end says, "Bob, come on down and let's get this straightened out."

So they had persuaded Derek to make his own deal, which he did, with myself not actively engaged. It would have quietly worked that way, had not the Bruins begun to haggle over clauses, taking this away and holding that back. Consequently, the actual signing was delayed. The result was that it would cost them, again, when Cooper moved in.

Still, I was determined to avoid a repetition of a bitter scene that resulted between John McKenzie and the Bruins. Hurt when he wasn't one of the fifteen players protected that spring in the annual draft, McKenzie just fled for Philadelphia and never gave them a chance to make a counter offer. Hockey is the only sport that allows existing franchises to draft players from each other. It was apparent, from their statements after the fact, that the Bruins would not have matched Philly's package. Yet they had the alibi that McKenzie never gave them a chance, and the feeling spread around Boston that Johnny was a traitor.

So, I would give the Bruins every chance to compete, for several reasons, the most important being our mutual respect, mine and Derek's, for Weston Adams, Sr. This man *was* the Bruins. His father had founded the franchise in the late 1920s, and Wes was in control—except for a half-dozen years—from the early 1940s on.

The team had plunged into the NHL cellar in the years when Wes Adams was not in charge, foundering there until he regained control of the board again in the early 1960s. Having made millions away from hockey, he eagerly returned to this labor of love, personally scouting all of the young men who would come along to win those Stanley Cups.

I had bumped into Mr. Adams many times on airplanes, as he sat alone in the economy section, going over his notes on some youngster he had spotted in a remote corner of Canada. He was the man who found Derek Sanderson cavorting in a Junior "B" League, signed him for the Bruins and came to think of him as "one of my boys." He called him "my ugly duckling with the look of a hawk."

This personal attention he lavished on the Bruin farmhands caused other, bemused executives around the NHL to comment: "Every scout dreams someday of becoming an owner. Weston is an owner who wants to be a scout."

By the time we set up a meeting with Mr. Adams, Derek had not yet indicated to me whether he wanted to jump or stay. He was impressed, even excited, when I recited the details of Cooper's offer, but he remained noncommital.

But it was then that I discovered another of Derek's curious traits. While he can be rational, almost cagey, in private, he has a habit of making his decisions in public. My first inkling of what he was going to do came, typically with Derek, from the newspapers. On my desk one morning was a Toronto newspaper, and the headline over Milt Dunnell's column read, "Sanderson to Jump to WHA."

The column went on to quote all the important figures in the contract. "I'm going," Sanderson had told Dunnell, an old friend whose kindness he was repaying in the best coin he had, giving him the story. He was so proud of the offer he had to tell someone. I am convinced that Derek talked himself into jumping to the Blazers by giving the story to Dunnell. Up to that point, he had never said to me or anyone else that he was going, or that he was seriously considering it. Despite the headlines, I was still somewhat skeptical.

The announcement created a furor in Boston, and in that atmosphere we kept our appointment with Weston Adams, Sr. The Bruins sent a limousine to fetch us at my office, and we were transported in style to his home overlooking beautiful Marblehead harbor, just north of Boston.

Outside, a sudden turbulent rainstorm contrasted sharply with the subdued meeting inside. I covered the history of Derek's dealings with the WHA, from Herb Martin up to the present, as Mr. Adams listened, attentive and silent. When I finished, he looked at Derek as a father would a son who told him he was about to marry a streetwalker. But there was no bitterness in his voice. "Derek," he said, "if the money's there you have to take it. You'd be a fool not to. You'll never have another chance like it in your life."

As we prepared to leave, Mr. Adams fetched an umbrella, so we wouldn't get soaked on the way to the car. We shook hands in the doorway and I could feel his sadness. His team, what he thought would be a hockey dynasty, was crumbling. As we stood there, with the rain pelting the sidewalk, he asked me in a very gracious way for a small favor.

"Bob, you represent another boy I love, Gregg Sheppard. Please, if there is any possible way, save Gregg for my Braves."

"Mr. Adams," I vowed, "if there is any way it can be done, Gregg Sheppard will stay with your organization."

Luckily for me, I was able to fulfill that pledge. For some reason, the World Hockey Association misjudged the talent of Gregg Sheppard, who had been the most valuable player in the Central League the previous year. The Bruins, and Mr. Adams, expected Sheppard to move up to their Boston Braves farm club in the American Hockey League, but in short order he was their rookie of the year, and considered by many the best rookie in the big league that season. Ironically, Gregg Sheppard would take Derek Sanderson's place as the third-line center, and prime penalty killer for the Bruins.

Jim Cooper lived up to his promises. It was all there in the contract, which Derek signed in front of 5,000 people in Philadelphia's John F. Kennedy Square. The Blazers wanted to do it up right, with a modest piece of showmanship, so they had a Brinks armored car standing by as the principals signed this historic document. As he surveyed the crowd—mostly women —an overwhelmed Jim Cooper announced: "I'm issuing a challenge right now to the Philadelphia Flyers to play us in a game in January, and the loser has to leave town." Thank heaven no one took him up on it, or the Blazers' stay in Philly would have been even shorter than it was.

Meanwhile, though we still faced several court battles with the NHL over his leave-taking, Derek started to set up house in Philadelphia. He was in the process of purchasing a 28-room mansion, with quarters for a maid and a valet; and now that he was a millionaire, he decided that a $32,000 Rolls Royce, with chauffeur, should replace his sports car. Moreover, he began making arrangements to rent a train to bring a thousand of his close friends from Boston to Philly for a housewarming.

But the good times didn't last long. The Blazers were hit by a plague of bad luck. Their opening night—which they celebrated by handing out pucks to the first-nighters—was a disaster. The icemaking machine broke down and the game had to be canceled.

To pacify the crowd—and what a diplomatic *faux pas* this was—Cooper asked Derek to make a speech to the disgruntled customers, who were heaving those free pucks at anyone who ventured onto the iceless rink.

"All I can say," soothed Derek, reverting to form, "is that I hope no one gets hurt leaving the parking lot. The parking here stinks. I couldn't even park my own car."

The statement produced another salvo of pucks. At that point, the fans would have liked nothing better than to drag Derek around Philadelphia on the end of a rope, behind his new Rolls.

For the next two months, every move Derek and the Blazers made would be the wrong one. The team was besieged by injuries, including a back ailment that hampered Derek. The team with the biggest payroll in hockey, possibly in all of sports, couldn't win a game.

Bernie Brown, the Blazers' silent partner, suddenly found his voice. In short order, he got rid of Cooper and made known his intention to send Derek packing. On the day he emerged from the shadows, Brown held his own team meeting and made a speech to his employees that rivaled Patton addressing the Third Army. "Look, you bastards," he told them, "if you think you're going to put the screws to me, you've got another think coming. I made my money the hard way and I'm not going to let a bunch of guys laying down on the job blow it for me. From now on, either you produce or you're gone."

Derek's aching back, which caused him to be hospitalized, was only one of a series of items that contributed to Brown's petulance. But the event that really unraveled him—one of the zaniest things I've ever heard in sports—involved his goaltender, Bernie Parent.

Admitted to a Philadelphia hospital with a hockey injury, Parent was ready to be released, and to play again, when he decided that, quite inexplicably, as long as he was there, he might as well have a minor operation often performed on male babies at birth. It is called a circumcision. Bernie Parent had a circumcision, which led to complications that would keep him out of the lineup for another month.

In a way that I prefer not to dwell on, the surgery of Bernie Parent came to symbolize all of the problems and failures of the Philadelphia Blazers.

So the pressure was incredible, and the high-priced Derek Sanderson was catching most of the heat. Brown regarded him, in charitable moments, as a fraud who wanted to retire with an injury. The injury clause in his contract gave Derek full pay if he was unable to play again.

By the time Derek was out of the hospital, Phil Watson, a

man who had earned a reputation around hockey as "Fiery Phil," had moved in as coach. Derek declared himself ready to play, but Watson ignored him. The Blazers issued a statement that Sanderson was not yet physically qualified to play, and soon I caught the drift of the squeeze play taking shape. They wanted to unload Sanderson, and void our contract on the grounds that he was hurt before he ever reached Philadelphia, and had therefore signed the contract under false pretenses.

Derek was on the phone to me three and four times a day. "Bob, they're trying to drive me mad down here. Watson is really on me. If he doesn't get off my back I'm going to deck him right in the dressing room."

I came out of my chair at that one. "Belt him just once," I warned, "and you breach the contract for insubordination. That's what they're trying to get you to do. You just take all their guff, and I'll get this straightened out."

As exasperating as he could be, I knew Derek wanted to play. He was prepared to play. And even during this period of unpleasantness, his better instincts showed through. He had discovered a gang of kids hanging around the arena after the games, playing a form of shadow hockey and looking for loose pieces of equipment to rip off. Derek adopted them. He paid their way to the games, 12 to 15 of them, and dug into his own pocket to outfit them with sticks and gloves and other accessories. He called them "my gang" and he spoke their language.

The Blazers were letting him practice, but they did not allow him to dress for the games. In one two-day span he scored nine goals in scrimmages, and still he wasn't allowed on the ice in competition.

I appealed to the league office to intercede, and was quickly brushed off by the commissioner of the moment, Gary Davidson. Mr. Brown, he said, was the man I had to see. The question that must soon be resolved was whether the case had to be settled in court. My position was clear: The World Hockey Association was not backing up a commitment it had made.

In the meantime, of course, Derek was not exactly blameless. He was acting like an original member of the Spoiled Rotten Generation, and the acrimony with the Blazers fed on itself. Where I kept hoping he would show me some maturity, he would come up instead with a wisecrack. Yet watching TV one night, I laughed out loud when Derek said, during an interview, "Bernie Brown wakes up in the morning and, instead of reading the newspaper, he studies my contract, trying to figure a way out of it."

I began to prepare my case on the chance that we would, indeed, all wind up in court. I had Derek fly discreetly into Boston, where three of the top doctors in the country examined his back. All gave him a clean bill of health. I kept their statements on file, if it became necessary to refute the Blazers' charges.

At that point, in all honesty, I felt some sympathy for the team's management. It was a question of survival. They wanted out of a contract, a contract they really could not afford, but were confused about how to do it.

A week after I had slipped Derek into Boston, I flew to Miami to meet with Bernie Brown at his home there. He turned out to be a decent fellow, well meaning, a man who had never seen a hockey game in his life until he bought a team, and who now felt he was being misused. "I don't want that guy on my team," he said bluntly. "I don't think it would be good for the team to have him around. What kind of settlement can we make?"

So it was to be divorce, as far as Brown was concerned. Over the next three days we worked out the terms. For a figure in the vicinity of $1 million, Philadelphia was to be free of Derek Sanderson. It wasn't bad pay for play in *eight* regular season games.

Just as important as the financial settlement was Derek's status as a free agent, which would give him the opportunity to return to the Bruins, play elsewhere in the NHL, or play anywhere in the World Hockey Association.

But our delight was shortlived. The Bruins, using the instant Telex communications now employed throughout pro sports, sent wires to every National Hockey League team warning them, in effect, that Derek Sanderson was still the property of Boston and any team daring to talk with Bob Woolf would be charged with tampering.

At the same time, Bernie Brown decided to bring in a new general manager, Dick Olson, who also worked for him in the trucking business. This move did not bode well for the liberation of Derek Sanderson.

"Wait a minute, Bernie," Olson was to tell him. "This doesn't make any sense. If we're going to pay all that money to a guy who's supposed to be a helluva hockey player, we ought to get some use out of him. Why should we pay him *not* to play?"

The new general manager had an influential ally in Mrs. Brown, a lovely and elegant woman, who like so many others just didn't believe that Sanderson could be as disagreeable as everyone said he was.

When it became apparent that the Blazers were wavering, Derek felt like a man who was released from San Quentin, only to find the law waiting at the gate to put him back in the slammer on another charge.

"Bob," he assured me, "there is no way I'm going back to Philadelphia. They can take the contract and . . . !"

I was inclined to agree with Derek, except that he had too much to lose. If he now refused to play, he voided the contract. This was no time to duck an issue. We had to find a way for Olson, and the Browns, to get back that old feeling for him— contempt.

"Have the kid come down to Miami for a few days," said Brown reluctantly, "and we'll talk this thing out. Maybe if I meet him in different surroundings I'll get to like him."

I hoped not. Now here I was, rooting against my own client's lovable disposition. How ridiculous could one deal get? I was soon to find out.

2

The Other Derek

———

WE MET at the airport in Miami. Derek Sanderson was in a grumpy mood, and that suited my strategy fine. We found two seats in the terminal while we waited for his bags to appear, and I briefed him.

We did everything but chalk the plays on a blackboard. "Listen," I primed him, "there's only one way we can win. You have to be your usual self. Be obnoxious. Really turn it on. You have to make them hate your guts."

Bernie Brown and his wife were waiting for us at their luxurious apartment on the shores of Miami Beach, down the street from the Fontainebleau Hotel. The tension was our own creation, but a fortune was at stake. I continued to instruct Derek in the taxi as we cruised along the freeway, toward a meeting that would serve as a final gesture of reconciliation. It was crazy. Brown didn't want Derek, but at the last minute he felt obliged to salvage a little more value for his money. Derek certainly didn't want the Blazers, or Philadelphia, and we had to convince Brown that getting rid of him was cheap at any price.

For once, I wanted Derek to do his thing, and the idea excited him. He was given the role every actor dreams about—a chance to play a character so well drawn he thinks he is playing himself. It was like handing Raymond Massey a stovepipe hat.

The Browns received us warmly, meeting us at the door with their twelve-year-old son, who hoped to get Derek's autograph.

We were barely inside the room, hardly into the small talk that courtesy requires, before Derek bellowed, "Bob, for crissakes, I got to get the hell out of here and play some golf." His characteristic cigarette was stuck between his lips, Bogart-like, just off center. He swung a golf club he happened to have with him, as he began an imaginary round in the middle of the Brown's living room.

It was an Oscar-winning performance. Derek refused to be drawn into the conversation. He ignored every attempt at friendliness. He preferred to direct his more poignant remarks to the charming Mrs. Brown, telling her in Mr. Brown's presence how "none of the guys" in Philly could stand her husband, all the while flicking the ashes from his cigarette on her new rug. The stricken expression on her face showed that her hopes for Derek's salvation had fled.

We stayed not much more than an hour. Our good-byes were strained as they saw us politely to the door. No decision had been reached. The Browns wanted to think it over for a night. However, as I left their building, I had the feeling that my client's final performance in Miami would not warrant any curtain calls.

The next day an exasperated Bernie Brown phoned. "Bob, I'm sending you a trophy. Any man who can put up with that character deserves an award."

The divorce was final. Brown felt that if his luck held up he might never see Derek again, and the feeling was shared by Sanderson. For a long while after that drama, I felt guilty about having resorted to histrionics, but I knew in the end that it was to everyone's advantage. With all the friction between management and the team, and the innuendo that Sanderson had faked an injury, there was nothing in Philadelphia for Derek except hostility.

"Getting out of Philadelphia," he would say (only to deny it later), "is like getting out of Vietnam."

Over the weeks that followed, the issue was occasionally raised of the morality of any athlete receiving a million dollars for *not* playing hockey. I heard various reactions. My feeling was that we didn't initiate either transaction. The Blazers had chased us to sign, and then were just as anxious to have Derek unsigned. Either way it was what they wanted.

In February of 1974, I appeared on the "Tomorrow" show, whose host, Tom Snyder, kept addressing me as "sir." I asked him why. "Listen," he said, "anyone who can get a guy a million dollars not to play, I call 'sir.' " Whatever the reaction, I felt the agreement was fair. For all sides.

Others in hockey still wanted Sanderson. Contrary to popular belief, there is never a tight market for those described as problem players. Either they are wanted by weak teams that have little to lose, or else by a coach whose ego tells him he can succeed where some other self-styled psychologist has failed.

Walter Kaiser, the president of the Chicago Cougars of the WHA, called and offered over $100,000 if Derek would just play the rest of the season. Then they would allow him to become a free agent again. The WHA office kept calling, asking me not to let him go back to the NHL because they were negotiating with a new buyer for the New York Raiders. A deal could be worked, it was suggested, to make Derek a part owner.

But, Daisy's, Zelda's and the Great Gatsby's were beckoning from Boston. So was Harry Sinden, the team's former coach, who had returned to become the managing director of the Bruins.

Derek, meanwhile, remained on a vacation he could now well afford in Miami Beach. He had informed his friends he was uncertain he would ever play again, and whiled away his time shooting a few rounds of pool each day with Johnny Carson and Ed McMahon at Le Club International. I was at my winter home in Hollywood, a half-hour up the road, and we were on the phone every day.

"I don't want to play anymore this year," he said, when I called him with the daily report on the various offers, including some surreptitious ones from NHL clubs. Three different teams in the NHL called me, wanting to know if Derek would go to their city if a deal could be worked out with Boston for his rights. If they were caught it would have meant a heavy fine from the league office, and the loss of their first-round draft choice the next season.

The astounding thing was that so many teams still felt he was worth the risk, though he had played hardly at all that year and had still not reestablished himself as a super talent. But what always intrigued hockey people about Derek is this: no one ever came up bigger in the clutch. He is a marvelous team player; if there was such an event as a hockey decathlon, where each contestant had to skate, forecheck, backcheck, face off and score, etc., he would win it. He is a great athlete, an opinion often expressed by his teammates and other competent observers who hope that in time his personality will allow him to prove it.

My own strong feeling was that Derek should return to hockey as soon as possible. I don't like to see any athlete not playing. Inactivity erodes talent and undermines self-respect. It is hard for an athlete in any sport to lose a year and come back and still play up to his capacity. I didn't want Derek to waste his talents.

At this point, I was saved by another stroke of luck. One day in March, while Derek was at my home in Hollywood, filming a segment for CBS's "Sports Illustrated" show, Harry Sinden called from Boston to chat with me. In the midst of our conversation he asked to say hello to Derek.

I walked out to the backyard, where the TV crew was at work, and left the two talking on the phone. The next thing I heard was Derek, yelling through the kitchen window: "Bob,

I'm flying to Boston to practice with the Bruins, okay?"

"Whaaaat?"

"Yeah. Harry just asked me to come up and practice with the team tomorrow and I think I will."

I nearly keeled over into the flower bed. He didn't even have a contract and here he was going to work out with the team. I thought, what if he gets hurt in practice? How much are they going to pay him? What about the Cougars and the Raiders and those other NHL teams?

But back we went to Boston, to play more of the waiting game. The Bruins had been very conservative about salaries and benefits long before Harry Sinden came back to a position of power, and Harry was not interested in altering that tradition.

For two weeks Derek skated and practiced, while I argued with one of my former clients, Sinden, about money. My other problem was Derek. He wanted the Bruins. He had never stopped loving the city or the team. Even when he was in Philadelphia, he used to call some of his former teammates to find out how things were going. He itched to get back in the groove. He wanted to be number one again among the swinging singles set of Boston.

I still contended that Derek was a free agent, able to sell his services on the open market. But I had to be practical. The Bruins had frightened off a lot of teams with their warning, and Derek was now pushing me to get him back to his old club.

The Bruins, meanwhile, were having their miseries on the ice. The team had gone sour, and the situation became almost catastrophic one night when they were ruined on their own ice by the Rangers, as Derek and I sat watching the game on TV in his new penthouse apartment overlooking Boston Harbor.

Sanderson was outraged at seeing his pals blasted by their old rivals, the hated Rangers. As he worked himself into a lather, I decided on impulse to call Harry Sinden at the Garden after the game and invite him to the apartment, immediately. Harry was ripe. We negotiated until three in the morning, and finally agreed to a deal. For a six-figure, one-year contract. It wasn't exactly what I *felt* was right for Derek, but it was close, and knowing how much Derek wanted to play, we agreed to the terms.

Two days later, it appeared there might be a hitch. "The deal isn't final," Sinden told us, "until Mr. Adams okays it. He wants to talk to Derek."

At the time, Weston Adams, Sr., was in the hospital, seriously ill. I had heard rumors that he was dying of cancer, and I was apprehensive about seeing him. We had to promise to tell no one about the meeting, or even that Mr. Adams was in the hospital.

As soon as we walked in the hospital room, and I saw the look in Mr. Adams' eyes, I had the feeling that we were there because he simply wanted to see Derek again. The meeting went well. We reviewed my negotiation with Harry, and laughed together about Derek's escapades. In the end, Mr. Adams approved the contract and welcomed Derek home. It was a visit we both enjoyed, a memory we both cherish. Not long after that, he passed away, and as we walked away from the funeral, Derek and I talked about what we had felt in that hospital room. We knew, then, that all Mr. Adams really wanted was to hear Derek say that he wanted to come back.

For Mr. Adams, it was his role in the reenactment of the story of the Prodigal Son. There was no question that he would take him back, but he needed to hear him ask. Derek understood that. He felt the loss deeply, because to him Wes Adams had been one of the people who counted.

That, we thought, would mark the beginning of a turnaround. Derek was reunited with the Bruins, happy again, ready to fulfill the faith and affection that a dying man had for him.

But the 1972–73 season ended in a somber way for the Bruins in almost every respect. They were knocked out of the Stanley Cup playoffs in the first round. Phil Esposito suffered a serious knee injury and, though Derek played well in the playoffs, it couldn't make up for all the things that had happened to the team throughout the year.

I was never more relieved to see a season end. It had been one continuing circus, and with Sanderson there are six rings in perpetual motion compared to the usual three. We had no inkling then that 1973–74 season would be even worse.

With Derek, only half the action is on the ice, and sometimes less. He is one of those who can't say no to people, usually deferring that chore to me, which is why I am constantly swept up in his zany adventures. Odd characters move in and out of Derek's life like stagehands, darkly rearranging the props and furniture. There have been many, but for sheer brass, the fabulous Darrell Tishman wins the prize.

You have probably never heard of Darrell Tishman—which isn't, of course, his real name—but he goes down in my book as one of the great operators of the con game.

One night in October I was at home, sleeping soundly, when the phone rang. "Bob, this is Darrell Tishman. I just wanted you to know that I'm over at Derek's apartment and I have his car. Derek was hurt tonight in the game, but everything is all right. He's going to be fine and we didn't want you to be alarmed."

After being assured the injury was a minor one, I rolled over and went back to sleep, still not sure what to make of it. I had never heard of Tishman, and I thought I knew all of Derek's friends, at least by name. My interest was aroused again the next day when I received a second call.

"Bob, I'm with Derek in the Mass. General Hospital. I just want you to know I'm bringing in new doctors and nurses for him. I don't like the way they're handling him here. Oh, by the way, I brought his Cadillac around today and it has a few dents in the fender. I'm ordering a new Lincoln Continental. A guy with Derek's style shouldn't be riding around in a beat-up car."

Now my antenna was beginning to twang. The Mass. General Hospital is one of the finest hospitals in the country, and Derek's car was brand new. "Darrell," I said, "just who the hell are you?"

"You must know my family," he said, breezily. "The Tishmans. We're in the real estate business. We own the Tishman Buildings in New York and Los Angeles. I've been a friend of Derek for years and, don't worry, I'll see that he's treated right around here."

The third day I got a call from Sanderson from the hospital. "Bob, Darrell wants to go down to New York to see the Mets play in the World Series. Could you get a couple of tickets for him?"

I said, well, yes, okay.

The next day: "Bob, this is Derek. Say, *who the hell is Darrell Tishman?*"

I said, "Are you kidding? He's your friend, not mine. He was at your apartment. Drove your car. He says he's known you for years."

"Bob, can I tell you something? I never laid eyes on the guy until four days ago. He showed up at the hospital and said he was a friend of mine, and I was under sedation, and too embarrassed to say I didn't remember him. Then he started telling me all the great things he was gonna do for me. I thought, 'Wow, I got a live one,' so I kept him around to do errands for me."

Tishman did more than run errands. He skipped town with $500 of Derek's money in his pocket, and his new Cadillac. The police finally found the car in Providence, Rhode Island. Tishman? He was never heard from again.

That was one of the few light moments in a 1973–74 season that would include more than the usual quota of sudden turns and twists, and would find Derek in the minors, suspended and, eventually, bound for New York.

Right away in the fall, things went wrong. Derek had looked forward to starting off with a new deck, and forgetting his sorry experience in Philadelphia. But he was injured in training camp, came back, began to play well and rehurt himself.

As Derek again began to round into shape, the Bruins decided to send him down to the minors to get the playing time he needed to speed the process. Derek's pride was stung. He had never played a minute in the minors and he was damned if he'd go there now. He'd quit first.

I met with him in Harry Sinden's office and, between us, we reasoned with him. It was, after all, for his own good. Harry assured him he would be recalled within ten days, or sooner, if he got his timing back. Derek was a sober young man when he left Harry's office. It is always a poignant moment when a player, who has been on top, is sent down to prove his talent.

The night he was to appear for the first time for the minor league Braves, in the Boston Garden, Harry and I both worried up to the last minute that he'd show. We walked into the auditorium and found a crowd of nearly seven thousand on hand, instead of the usual eight hundred or so who would have turned out for a match between the Boston Braves and Providence Reds. But Sanderson did show and in typical fashion, he had a sensational night, scoring a couple of goals, killing penalties, checking all over the ice.

I walked into the locker room after the game. Derek was surrounded by reporters. He was exultant. "I *love* it here," he roars. "I never want to go back to the Bruins. I love it. No more flyin'. We got a bus, and we get to drive to Hartford and New Haven. Bob, I love it!"

Did my hearing need to be checked? Was this the same Derek Sanderson who three times had walked out of Sinden's office and threatened to retire from hockey, rather than face the embarrassment of being shipped to the minors?

The newspapers, even *Sports Illustrated*, had jumped on the story, sparing no hearts and flowers. Some of the local writers were saying he just wasn't good enough anymore, which was simply untrue. The club line was that he was being sent out to get in condition. My own guess was that in some oblique way they were disciplining him. The romance, I began to sense, was already over.

Derek had not been getting along with his coach, Armand (Bep) Guidolin. This would be the source of his season-long problems and, eventually, a showdown Derek would lose.

But Derek's game came back to him during his week to ten days in the minors. He was playing loose and easy, with his old flash, and attendance figures soared throughout the league. Then Sinden kept his word and recalled him to the Bruins.

With the season grinding on, and Derek back where he belonged, I thought, I flew to Florida in January, 1974, to open our home in Hollywood. A few days later, Derek stunned me with a call to tell me he had been suspended.

Suspended? I couldn't believe it. He had scuffled in the locker room with Terry O'Reilly and later missed a team plane. He was grounded for the rest of the season—including the playoffs—and slapped with a $2,000 fine for the fight with O'Reilly. There was no doubt in my mind that the fine had no legal basis. When I pointed out that no such penalty had been assessed against Terry, the Bruins management quickly back-tracked, said the fine was for missing the flight, and then dropped it altogether.

I was inclined to call up Bernie Brown and tell him I wanted that trophy he had promised me. If I hadn't earned it by then, I was going to now. Derek had gone through all the emotional states, anger, disbelief, self-pity, defiance and numbness.

And Derek had had it with the Bruins.

"To hell with it," declared Derek. "I'm going to Hawaii. Get me to New York. I want to play for the Rangers." And off he went.

So while Derek was vacationing in Hawaii, I went back to work. First, I had to meet with Harry Sinden to discuss the suspension, which I strongly felt was illegal. I knew Harry had been put in a tight position. He had to back up his coach. Derek and Bep had been snarling at each other all season, until Derek had, stupidly, issued an ultimatum: either he goes or I go. And there he went. Naturally, Derek had the last word, which was to predict that Guidolin wouldn't be back the next year. The prediction proved true.

I thought grounds existed to take the suspension to court,

but it seemed more prudent to use that threat as a bargaining lever. I agreed to accept the suspension, on the condition that we were free to speak with any club, and make any deal we wanted. Harry went along, although he made it clear that they would prefer to see him land with one of the newer, weaker teams, St. Louis, Oakland or Washington. He would take a dim view of Derek going to one of their top rivals, for example, the Rangers. I decided not to press the point then.

Now, I felt the kind of stimulation a gambler must feel when he steps off the plane in Las Vegas or Monte Carlo. We were back in action. The Bruins had twixed—cable-ese for their instant telegraph system—the message to all the teams that I had their permission to discuss a deal for Sanderson. The calls started pouring in, and I was suddenly overbooked for lunch, hurrying off to meetings, putting calls on hold.

Derek remained in Hawaii, living it up. One day, I walked into my office around eleven in the morning and found three urgent phone messages from him. Before I could return his call, the fourth one had come through. He had a problem. He wanted me to call the manager of his hotel in Hawaii, and complain about the lack of hot water in his room. It was pure Derek.

In the meanwhile I was trying hard to give everyone a fair appraisal of the situation. The Bruins, for reasons of their own, put out the story that Derek had lost it all, his talent, his touch, his desire. And I countered by telling people I didn't think that was so, but if they wanted him they would have to gamble. The record was clear. He was suspended toward the end of a terrible season. He had hardly played enough in two years to win a varsity letter.

All this time, I knew the team he wanted was the big one in New York. And, curiously, the Ranger coach, Emile Francis, The Cat, has always had an affection for him, even in the days when the New York crowds were unfurling banners that read "DEREK IS DRECK," and booing his every move. I had represented a few of the Rangers, including Vic Hadfield and

Bruce MacGregor. Whenever we met, Emile made it a point
to ask how Derek was doing, always adding that he would love
to have him on his team.

In a curious way, I decided, Sanderson wanted to play for the
Rangers because Emile Francis, an extraordinarily decent man,
reminded him of his father, Harold. And they did look somewhat alike, sharp, almost pinched faces, not big but with hard,
wiry bodies. They even sounded alike in a direct, artless way.

Harold Sanderson is a colorful man who once collected and
saved the hockey stitches out of Derek's face. He kept them in
a box, 164 stitches. He devoted his life to his son. Harold
worked a night shift in a factory, in Niagara Falls, Ontario,
so his days would be free to spend with his son on the practice
rink he had built in their own backyard. He has the same wild,
put-on humor as Derek, and the original toughness. Derek is
fond of regaling strangers with tales of his tough childhood,
and the rough neighborhood he escaped. The truth is, he grew
up in a pleasant, middle-class residential area, in a one-family
house. Pampered by a charming, Scottish-born mother, Caro-
line, who still has her brogue, and a doting older sister, Karen,
who to this day keeps a scrapbook about Derek.

So what can you say about a hockey player, a Bolshevik
at heart, who wants to play for a team because the coach re-
minds him of his father?

The Rangers, of course, were interested. And just when we
needed it most, we got yet another break. A realignment of the
league placed the Bruins and the Rangers in different divisions,
with different paths to the playoffs. Harry Sinden's last objection to making a deal with New York had been removed.

I told Emile that I thought Derek was changing, growing
up, and if anyone could influence him it was The Cat; "He
has great respect for you. He has confidence in you. And New
York, well, he thinks the city is magic."

I was walking on eggs by the time Derek left Hawaii and
returned to Boston. We sat down in my office. "You understand, don't you?" I said. "If it goes through, if we get you to

New York, this is the last time we go to the well. There are no more rabbits to pull out of the hat."

He nodded.

"Okay," I said. "Just sit tight."

I laughed even as I said that. I was always telling Derek to sit tight and, almost instantly, he would wander off into some new situation comedy. Sure enough *Oui* magazine called, while he was waiting out his suspension in Boston, to offer $10,000 if Derek and his girl friend would pose for a nude layout. I declined, as politely as I could, and later told Derek about it, for laughs.

But he got that faraway look in his eyes and said, thoughtfully, "Well, hell, Bob, I'm not doing anything right now."

I got firm. "Forget it. There is *no* way I'm going to let you pose for a nude layout."

A day or so after that, Derek phoned. "Bob," he said, "I've been talking it over with my girl and I think we've found a way to do it."

I said, "How? How in the world can you even consider it?"

"We've been *practicing*," he said, a note of triumph in his voice, "and it's okay. Her hand just fits over it. Her hand is big enough!" To this day, I don't know if he was kidding or not.

I congratulated both of them and excused myself to take another call. While we didn't accept this offer, Derek did manage to do several "Banacek" episodes with George Peppard, and even sneaked my wife and myself into some of the scenes.

The negotiations to get Derek to New York were delicate ones, because strong resentment had begun to build on both sides and I was in constant fear that Harry Sinden might change his mind and veto the deal. But, finally, it was done, in a complicated, prearranged, three-team maneuver. The Rangers left Jim Neilson, a twelve-year veteran, unprotected in the draft. The California Seals exposed Walt McKechnie. The Seals claimed Neilson. The Rangers took McKechnie, then dispatched him to Boston for Sanderson.

A press conference was called during the '74 draft in

Montreal to announce the three-part trade, which wound up with the Peck's Bad Boy of ice hockey bound for Broadway. When Derek got up to speak, he said a chestful about the Bruins and Harry Sinden. He told the press that Harry, who had coached him as a rookie in Boston, had let him down, he couldn't be trusted, he was not an honorable man and, now, he was the enemy. Derek's heart, which he usually wore on his sleeve, was with New York.

I stood uncomfortably nearby listening to that. I admired Sinden and had represented him once in contract matters of his own. He felt a fondness for Derek that had remained intact, no matter what Derek said or how he behaved. He thinks he understood this unorthodox young man as well as any human could. We had gone through so many of his problems together.

Four years before, in fact, Harry had said to me one day, "I've been in hockey most of my life, and I've met all kinds, but I just want to tell you, there's only one guy that I ever loved, and that's Derek Sanderson. Take good care of him, Bob."

Now Harry called me aside, as the press conference broke up, and said quietly, "Do you think I could speak to him for a couple of minutes? I'd just like to wish the boy well."

I brought Derek over and they stood facing each other, for a few awkward moments, until Harry spoke. "I want you to know there are no hard feelings," he said. "I wish you luck in New York and success. I know you have been saying some harsh things about me, Derek, but I know you don't mean them."

Derek nodded and said, "Oh, I mean them, all right." I winced. Even in that moment of pure sentimentality, he was true to character.

In New York, the media blitz started all over again. As much as any athlete of my time, Derek Sanderson has been through the cycle: the early scrapping, the arrival, the days of glory, the nights of discontent, then the fall from cowboy heaven. And, for some, the comeback.

Would Derek be one of the rare ones who retrieve lost promise? Emile Francis and I had our fingers crossed when the 1974–75 season opened in October. A transformation seemed to have taken place. Derek had kidded Emile about his square ways, telling him he ought to grow a mustache and wear high platform heels. But, while saying that, Derek went out and trimmed his hair, moved to Canada for a month to prepare himself for the season and even began to get to bed early.

He applied himself. He was saying the right things. Doing the right things. At a press conference in New York, the photographers wanted him to pose with some tasty young ladies draped all over him. For the first time in my memory, Derek said no. He didn't want that image. He knew that, this time, he had to prove himself all over again to the whole hockey world. For two years he had done nothing. He had been written off by a number of people whose opinions counted and he was labeled a troublemaker.

Out of fairness to Emile and the Rangers, and Derek, we had negotiated a one-year contract. I felt, and Derek agreed, we didn't want them stuck with a long-term contract if he wasn't producing. Even so, it was a fair bet. The Rangers were paying him well—$20,000 more than the Bruins—and if he did the job, then I could come in and bargain hard for the next one.

When the '74 season began, Derek was only twenty-eight. He knew what was at stake and knew he had to produce. For all his machismo, the publicity, the put-ons, in my heart I still believed he had superior talent. More important, impartial hockey people felt the same way.

I went to the Rangers' opening game in New York, at Madison Square Garden, in October. The crowd gave Derek a standing ovation when he appeared on the ice. I got goose bumps. The Rangers won, 6–3, and to me he looked like the lean, hungry Sanderson of his rookie days. It was as though someone had flashed it on the Times Square Message Board: DEREK IS BACK.

The same fans who had once despised him in a Boston uniform now came unglued over him. The press purred when he gave them lines like: "We want to win the Stanley Cup. That's our goal. Of course, you might want to make it with Raquel Welch, too. That doesn't mean she'll let you."

The Rangers were not expected to win the Stanley Cup. And they didn't. They battled most of the year for second place in their division, and Derek was in the thick of it. Derek was great and reestablished himself completely. It was a splendid comeback and I was proud of him. But the fortunes of sports are unpredictable. On October 30, 1975 Derek practiced with the Rangers in the morning, learned he was traded to the St. Louis Blues at noon, and as irony would have it played for that team against his original teammates, the Bruins in Boston that night. In true Derek fashion on his first shot he scored St. Louis's first goal and of course it was a short-handed one. That awarded him a standing ovation from the still affectionate Boston fans.

Derek knows I always believed in him, even in those weary moments when I just could not make him understand the *seriousness* of the situation. Once, only once, was I able to turn the tables on him.

One day I received a call from Derek, who was on the verge of apoplexy. "Goddamit, Bob," he hollered, "goddamit, we'll get those sonsabitches. We'll get 'em!"

"Take it easy," I said. "Calm down. What's this all about?"

"Now, you know me." He forced himself to lower his voice, before building to a crescendo. "I usually don't mind what the guys write about me. They can write anything they want and I don't beef."

"Derek, what are you talking about?"

"This story, Bob. This story I got right in front of me about last night's game." He was screaming again. "I'm looking at it, AND I STILL CAN'T BELIEVE MY EYES. Bob, I can't believe it. But here it is right in the paper. Right in the Toronto paper!"

He then read the offending passage to me: "Missing from the

Bruins lineup last night were superstar Bobby Orr, workhorse Johnny Bucyk, and *asshole* Derek Sanderson."

So help me, and Derek, that is exactly how it appeared in print. "Asshole Derek Sanderson." In a prestigious family newspaper. I have no idea how it happened, but I suspect that some hockey fan in the composing room thought he would have a little fun, and someone down the line would catch his "humor." Somehow, it must have just slipped by.

But there was no point in trying to explain that to Derek. Besides, it was all I could do to keep from rolling around the floor of my office in laughter.

"This isn't funny. You know that, Bob. This isn't funny at all."

Wiping the tears away from my eyes, I tried to agree with him. "I understand, Derek. This is no laughing matter."

"I can take anything, Bob, but not this. I'm going to sue. And before I'm finished, I'm going to own that paper and run that bastard out of town."

Trying to regain my poise, but not working very hard at it, I said, "I don't think we can do it."

"Why not?" he fumed. "We'll get that son of a bitch for libel. He can't do that to me."

"Well," I said, my voice now serious, "in my professional opinion, we could never win the case. All he would have to do is go out and get your best friends for character witnesses, and they'd have to admit it was true. The truth is a defense."

I don't believe Derek appreciated my legal opinion.

But it was just one more zany incident in the eight years we had shared. As I say, he's two people, a true Gemini, Dirty Derek and the other Derek Sanderson, the one whose popularity in Boston was once so strong, the hospitals reported a run on babies named Derek.

Recently, his mother received a letter from the publicity director of the Rhode Island Reds, against whom the Rangers had played an exhibition game. The most revealing paragraphs were these:

"... Mrs. Sanderson, you cannot imagine how terrific your son, Derek, made a little boy named after him—Derek King—feel on this night. First of all, little Derek King is a handicapped boy with only one leg and immobile arms. He is three years old and goes to the Meeting Street School for the handicapped here in Providence.

"Well, little Derek has had dreams of meeting Derek Sanderson because of his father naming him after Derek. Also the boy loves hockey and will never be able to skate, of course. . . .

"Derek presented little Derek with a stick, autographed by the entire Ranger team, and he skated the boy around the ice to meet the players and also made the youngster and his father his guest in front-row seats."

With the letter was a photograph, taken that night, showing Derek on the ice with the little boy, holding him gently, kissing his cheek.

So, I've seen all sides of him, and I know his warm qualities as well as his capricious ones. This isn't meant to be a valentine, but I like Derek Sanderson, I have affection for him, and on balance the fun of the past eight years has outweighed the aggravation. The final score was close, but Derek wins, as he so often does.

3

A Cool Penny a Paper

————

THE FIRST DAY of my new life came somewhere back in November of 1964, when I found this big, handsome athlete standing in front of my desk telling me that his car had been crumpled in an auto accident.

Earl Wilson, then the star righthanded pitcher with the Boston Red Sox, had lived in the neighborhood near my office in Allston, one of the districts of the city of Boston. I was a criminal attorney who was also engaged in a general practice of the law. It was a good practice, good enough to have eight lawyers working with me out of my office to bring in a healthy income.

But success can't dim the sweetness of that moment when an old jock (high school and college division) looks across a desk at a pro athlete and says, "I played a little ball once myself." We hit it off, Earl Wilson and I. He was a big, handsome specimen built on the order of Jim Brown, with a strong facial resemblance as well. He had a tall, regal walk. His friends called him "The Duke."

We quickly became friends and Earl, that year, was a frequent guest in my home. Late into the night we talked about the problems of being black in white America, and of the prejudices that still ran deep in the 1950s, when he was scratching his way up from the Louisiana delta. Much of this was new to me. To look at Earl Wilson, 6-4 and 220 and unbowed, you would think there was no way this man could be hurt. But he had been, many times, and it had become part of his defense mechanism to make light of it.

"Mississippi," he said once, laughing, describing the long drive south at the end of a baseball season. "When I'd get to Mississippi, I'd stop at the border, load up on hamburgers, coffee and gas, lock all the windows and keep going until I was out of the state."

I don't know how other people measure such things, but some indignities last a lifetime because they go to the heart of how people value themselves. And I came to understand, through Earl, how a man can keep that anger buried inside him and finally become afraid to face it.

"Bob," he told me one night, "the longest walk in life isn't when you get knocked out of a game and have to carry that sense of defeat to the dressing room. You can accept that because, at least, you had some control over it. The longest walk is the one you take out of a restaurant, or a hotel, or a night club, after you've been told, 'Sorry, we can't serve you here.' "

At seventeen, Earl had left the town of Ponchatoula to play Class D ball. He was to spend most of the next ten years in the minors, often living in black rooming houses, three and four men to a room. From Bisbee, in 1953, he moved to San Jose and El Paso and Montgomery, towns where he couldn't sit at a lunch counter with his white teammates or stay at the same hotel. Meanwhile, Jackie Robinson had made history and Willie Mays was becoming a national idol.

Wilson was up twice briefly with the Red Sox, before sticking in 1962 and finishing with twelve wins and eight losses. That was to be his only winning season in Boston. He had the big fast ball then, and a live arm, but he never seemed to fulfill his promise.

I hadn't represented athletes in my law practice at that point, but soon I found myself handling his taxes and arranging his personal appearances. In baseball, up to that time, no lawyer was welcome to negotiate a contract for a player.

In those years the club-player relationship can only be described as feudal and paternal, sometimes warm, often degrading. The player dealt directly with the club, went to management when he needed an advance, called when he needed to get out of jail. It isn't done that way anymore. Some of the charm may have been lost along the road but the new way, I think, is better because the players' interests are better protected.

In the view of management it would have been an act of naked disloyalty for a player to refer his contract to a lawyer. The battle of wits at contract time was part of the lore of the game, but the players were clearly outgunned.

That was the background in June of 1966, in the middle of the season, when the Red Sox traded Earl Wilson to the Detroit Tigers, having written him off as a .500 pitcher, or worse. The pride of the big righthander was stung, and fortunately it was just what he needed. He finished that season with eighteen wins, thirteen of them in Detroit, with the most innings, the most strikeouts and the lowest earned-run average of his career.

That winter, with all the years of struggle so close to paying off, Wilson made a bold and symbolic decision. He asked me to *negotiate* his contract. Aware of the unofficial taboos of baseball, we did so in a fashion I can only classify as discreet.

I flew to Detroit with Earl and together we worked out his position—what to look for and how to ask for it. The hitch was that I stayed behind at Earl's apartment, while he sat in the office of the Detroit general manager, negotiating with Jim Campbell. Whenever a problem arose, or a question we hadn't covered, Earl would excuse himself, go to an outside phone and call me back at his apartment for more advice. Eventually, an agreement was signed.

Certainly, I would have preferred to be with Earl in the flesh, but at that time it would have been impossible. Even so, I was happy that the matter worked out well, without making waves, and I was aware we had broken new ground. Jim Campbell has often told people the Tigers were still using, years later, the deferred-compensation agreement we designed in 1966 for Earl Wilson.

Of course, our dealings were made more acceptable by the fact that Wilson went on to win twenty-two games in 1967, and become a contender for the Cy Young Award. The Tigers were to lose the pennant on the last day of the season in one of the American League's wildest scrambles as, bitter fruit, Earl's old club, the Red Sox, slipped under the wire.

Today the attitude toward lawyers has changed so radically that it now is a condition of the collective-bargaining agreement in baseball that every player is entitled to be represented by counsel. This, of course, takes the pressure off the player. I had worried right along with Earl that the Tigers would brand him as a wise guy, or a troublemaker, if he showed up with an attorney. It's unimaginable today what a closed door sports management once maintained. Not only didn't they want the players consulting lawyers, they didn't want them talking to their own families. Years ago, when the late Tony Morabito owned the San Francisco 49ers, he made an offer to a young halfback who asked, nervously, if he could discuss it with his wife.

"If you do," the owner countered, "I'll have to call *my* wife and ask if it's okay to offer that much."

That was the odd mentality in sports then: it was disloyal of a player to bring in outside help at contract time, but not disloyal for the club to trade a player—such as Earl Wilson—whenever it felt the club would benefit. That was strictly business.

And so it began for me, not with a splash, but by dipping a tentative toe into a cold pool. Earl Wilson, who had soul before it was popular, whose dignity I will always admire, opened the door to sports and to the fundamental changes I would confront over the next decade. Within five years I had over 300 clients in all sports, from superstars to supernuts, with grand dreams and zany schemes.

My law associate, Lenny Shapiro, wound up with ulcers sorting out the screwballs from the sincere, while running interference for me as I developed the first bona fide practice as a sports attorney in this country.

Many times I was to wonder whether I shouldn't have studied medicine. It had been my father's profession, and my brothers and sisters, all older, had followed him into it. But for a reason that seemed as valid then as it does now—I can't stand the sight of blood—I didn't want to be a doctor.

But business and negotiation was something else. Home was Portland, Maine, and as long as I can remember, doing a little business was as natural as drawing breath. At four or five I was filling up a large pitcher with ice water and going out into the streets to sell it, a penny a glass, to construction men working near our home.

At eight I had my first regular job, delivering newspapers twice a day. Early in the morning and late in the afternoon, I pitched the Portland papers onto the doorsteps of my customers. I made a cool dollar a day. One penny a paper for 100 customers. Whatever I earned was turned over to my mother, who channeled it to whichever brother or sister was then being supported through school.

It goes without saying that life was simpler then, at a time when many people scraped to get by. I was part of a generation before television that grew up *outside*, who worked and played and lived in the yard, on the sidewalk, in the street.

Somewhere along Congress or Commercial Street, on those cold days with the wind buffeting me and my bundle of newspapers as I walked along, swaying under the load, I learned the fundamentals of good business. Treat the customer fairly and try to do the right thing. Be efficient. Be reliable. Don't leave the paper lying in the snow. Deliver it on time, even though it was raining. I must have stumbled onto a decent formula, because I started with a dozen customers and soon had close to a hundred.

My parents were a fine blend of contrasting qualities, and a great deal of both of them found a ready vessel in their youngest son. Joseph Woolf was stern, cautious, penurious and stayed within himself. My mother, Anna, was warm, open, giving and outgoing. She loved people and even today, past eighty, those with problems are drawn to her for strength. Many years passed before I knew that the kind of love that was always around me didn't exist in every family.

My father was the Last Angry Man. I have never known anyone with his feeling of fair play, and his compassion for the underdog and the unfortunate. He was an idealist, a humanist, but with absolutely no business sense. Once he actually paid for a newspaper ad volunteering to give free medical attention to anyone who was sick or infirm. He hated any kind of injustice.

He smiled infrequently and we used to call him "Smiling Joe," a family joke. His economic philosophy could be described as Early American, summed up in his automatic response whenever I asked, as a little child, for a nickel for an ice cream cone. "Go to work," he would grunt. And I did.

My mother was heroic. She had drive and business instinct, and kept us going financially. She became one of the first Jewish women schoolteachers in Maine. Shortly after she married Dad, she resigned as a teacher and went into real estate, with astonishing success. I learned from her that the key to success is faith in your own ability, a conviction she never lost. She was the eternal optimist. "Somehow," she would assure us, in cheerless moments, "everything will turn out all right." It usually did.

We lived very well when I was quite young, in a beautiful, stately home with more rooms than I can remember. Then the stock market and real estate crash wiped us out, along with most of America, and we soon found ourselves—all of us—

living in a one-room apartment over a cafeteria. At night, I could tell from the aroma drifting upstairs what the special of the day was on the stoves below.

It was a tribute to my mother's will that I only knew years later how our conditions had changed. There were no outward signs from Anna or the rest of the family that we were in any kind of distress. I was too young, of course, to know what luxuries were missing, or what hard times those were. But Mother handled the new circumstances with grace and courage and, in many ways, we carried on as a family just as if we were back living in the big house of better days. Instead of feeling sorry for herself, she set an example for the rest of us, always working as if each task had a deadline, and the results would be inspected later.

After our father passed away in 1953, my brothers, Harold, Irving and Milton, my sister Esther and I drew even closer to our mother, and tried to return to her the love, affection and security she had lavished on us. I had learned the value of this kind of security as a kid growing up free-spirited in Portland. This is the kind of small, dry, unhurried town so basic to the heritage of Maine, the kind that is so ripe for jokes. But I loved it, and still do, and go back as often as I can, maybe six or seven times a year. It helps cleanse my mind of the latest crisis or legal tangle involving one of my athletes. There is something encouraging about a place that never changes, where the air and the streams are still pure and no one forces himself on you. It was in fact in Portland that I married, in 1963, the lovely Anne Joy Passman, and her parents as well as my brother Harold still live there.

There is, always will be, a lot of Portland in me, even though I became a big-city kid at fifteen, when the family moved to Boston to begin its financial comeback. I enrolled at Boston Latin High School, one of the top secondary schools in the country. I would come to owe a great deal to a gifted coach who befriended me there.

Our financial needs at home were such that I had to keep working. Yet, I loved sports, particularly basketball, which I considered my best game. Football was out because you had to practice every day after school and, by then, I'd be working.

At sixteen, in 1944, just about the time I was old enough to qualify for a driver's license, I founded my own company—the Woolf Supply Company—making myself the middleman between factory and store for various household items. When I think back on it, I have to laugh at my gall. Had I been the owner of a variety or drug store approached by sixteen-year-old Bob Woolf, I would have thrown myself out the door in two minutes.

"Sir, allow me to introduce myself," I'd swing into my sales pitch, "I'm Mr. Woolf, of the Woolf Supply Company of New England. I represent the company in the Boston area and we want you to know that we carry nothing but the best brands at the lowest prices. We also promise you prompt delivery. You won't have to go into town to pick up your order. We'll bring it directly to your door. You will be surprised how quickly you'll receive your merchandise."

The looks I would get ranged from quizzical to the pained expression of someone who has just heard a street kid offer to watch his car tires for a dollar. While the store owner was still trying to decide if I was real, I'd hit him with a rapid-fire, alphabetical recital of every possible household item from aspirin, Anacin, Arrid, Alka Seltzer, absorbent cotton, Aspergum, band-aids, bulbs, Bromo Seltzer, birthday candles—all the way to zinc ointment.

If they agreed to purchase one or two items—to get rid of me, or out of curiosity, or to see if I could deliver—I had them. Instantly, I made my big move. I'd march directly out of the store to the "company supply vehicle," parked at the curb.

It was a gorgeous, fourth-hand, twelve-year-old heap crammed with boxes and crates of supplies. I had so many things piled inside that I had to tie the doors shut with a rope. The Teamsters wouldn't have awarded it any prizes for looks or efficiency, but it worked. In a matter of minutes I'd be whirling through the door with the order, and pretty soon I'd have my little book out, writing a larger order for $100 or more.

Of course, there really wasn't any Woolf Supply Company of New England. It just occurred to me that customers might not be comforted to think they were relying on a sixteen-year-old kid, who was trying to figure out how he could hold a job and play basketball at the same time. But I doubt that anyone confused Woolf Supply with Sears, Roebuck.

Luckily, a very understanding man named Steve Pattin coached the Latin basketball team. I walked into his office one day and explained that I had to work, but wanted to try out for the team. "Son, if you're good enough to make the squad," he said, "and your teammates don't object, we'll let you skip practices and just play in the games."

Those years were the endless story of "only-in-America" for me. By my senior year, even though I couldn't practice with the team, I was the captain and high scorer. I repaid Coach Pattin for his kindness by allowing him to purchase his Christmas toys for his children from me—at only a 10 percent markup. Business was still business.

Happy times were back. Mom was building a reputation in real estate. Dad had set up his medical practice in Boston. And young Robert won a basketball scholarship to Boston College. I was to treasure the days I spent there, a young Jewish lad at a Jesuit institution. I have only fond memories and gratitude for the fine education I received. While there I met one of the most colorful characters in sports—General Al McLellan.

I have no idea how the General got his rank, although he might have fancied a kinship to George B. McClellan, relieved by Lincoln as commander of the Union forces during the Civil War. General Al was our coach, and worked on the side as a part-time bouncer at one of the local watering spots. He was a master of the malaprop and, among other minor failings, had a fearful time remembering names. He had a habit of introducing someone as "my close friend"—and then standing blankly, until the fellow identified himself.

"This is a tough game we've got coming up with Dartmouth,"

I heard him say one night on a radio interview. "But we've beaten them five out of four times and that isn't easy to do."

Another time he was the key speaker at a tenth-anniversary banquet, honoring the Boston College football team that played in the Sugar Bowl under Frank Leahy in 1941. "I want all you men to know," said the General, with a sweep of his hand indicating all the returning heroes, "that we're very proud of you men—you men who are *monstrosities* both of mind and body."

Our first practices at Boston College were right out of Dogpatch. They were held in an open field, without baskets or backboards. There was no gym on the campus at the time. All we did was run through plays against imaginary opponents.

The General also had an arrangement where the team ate its pregame meals in the club where he worked on the side. The General was always looking to save a few dollars against the budget, so instead of taking cabs we walked to the Garden together, as a team, from the restaurant. He carried a whistle with him and whenever we came to an intersection he directed traffic. A long, shrill blast followed by the brisk command: "Okay, boys, let's cross now, all together."

We had fun playing for the General. It was the innocent life, marred only by our arch rivals, Holy Cross, one of the best basketball teams in the country. A slight, nimble guard named Bob Cousy, who handled a basketball as though it were a musical instrument, was making headlines. I covered him on a night he scored twenty-three points, the equivalent in today's game to scoring sixty points.

In my sophomore year, we thought we had the answer to Cooz and the Cross. Boston College had imported a "seven-foot giant" from Amarillo, Texas, named Elmore Morganthaler. Elmore actually measured about 6 feet 9 inches, but he still towered over most of the fellows then playing the pivot. The George Mikans and Bob Kurlands, the giants who could play, were still rare.

Elmore was awkward, but he had a nice little touch and

enough muscle to dominate people. The trouble with Elmore was the classroom. He had read a book once and didn't enjoy it. Whenever he took an exam he wrote across the top, in bold letters, "See the General." At the end of one semester, he was on the road back to Texas.

That year, without him, we trailed Holy Cross by only 32–28 midway through the second half. So the General ordered us into a stall. He wanted to hold down the score, considering a four-point loss to be a moral victory. So we stalled, and one of our players actually sat on the ball, as the Holy Cross players just stood there, disbelieving.

Another time we traveled across to Tufts University for a game that got exceptionally rough. The crowd began to roar. "Those dirty Micks," someone hollered, and others picked it up. "Those dirty Irishmen!" In the Boston College lineup at the time were Bobby Fitzgerald and four Jewish boys, Dan Bricker, Gerry Levinson, Mort Stagoff and Bob Woolf. It was just as well the crowd didn't know that.

Basketball was a popular sport then with young Jewish kids in the east.

My crowd had rather structured goals: we hustled for school and spending money, played basketball and thought about becoming doctors. Except I decided early that I lacked the constitution for it. My sister, the doctor, invited me to watch an operation one day and that ended whatever medical ambitions I might have sheltered. Instead, in my junior year I joined my mother in her real-estate firm. By the time I graduated from Boston College I had a half dozen people working directly under me.

My affinity for law, I think, developed when I saw, in my real estate dealings, how important a lawyer was to big business. I went on to the Boston University Law School, became president of my senior class and, at the start of that year, petitioned the Supreme Court to allow me to take the bar exam before graduation. I expected to enter the Armed Forces momentarily. My request was granted. I passed the bar before completing law school.

After a two-year hitch in the Army, I returned to Boston to open my first office, a one-room, Norman Rockwell piece of Americana: the diploma framed on the wall, the file cabinet with lunch spread on the top of it, a clean desk waiting for a client. By this time I had divested myself of my holdings in the "Woolf Supply Company," and withdrawn from my mother's real-estate office.

Some of my classmates told me I was crazy to open my own practice fresh out of school and the service. The normal routine was to work for an established firm for years and then, when you had enough contacts, strike out on your own. But I never gave a thought to working for someone else. I had been going it on my own power since I was eight years old. It simply never entered my mind that I might fail.

In one of my very first cases, I won an acquittal for a client in district court on a criminal charge. My elation at this victory was dampened slightly when I asked for my fee, $100, and was told: "Why the hell should I pay you anything? All you told the judge is what I told you in the first place!" And he walked out, slamming the door to my office. From then on I collected in front, a policy, unfortunately, I didn't always follow with some of my athletic clients.

I had another early case where my own office was robbed, and a few days later the police called me down to the local precinct to identify some of the items taken. When I walked into the station I heard a yell: "Here he comes! Here's my lawyer now. He'll straighten this whole thing out."

The man was a recent client of mine, and when the police sergeant asked if I really knew him, I said, yes, of course.

"Well, he's the guy we picked up for robbing your office the other night."

I stared at the prisoner for a long minute, dumfounded. "Well," he demanded, "you're still going to represent me, aren't you?"

I said, "I will if you give me my stuff back."

He shrugged. "I can't. Already sold it."

In the late 1950s I found myself in court almost every day on a different criminal matter. I defended so many unsavory clients that when I walked into the courthouse one day the local district attorney hit me with, "Here comes Bob Woolf, defender of the guilty."

"That's okay," I shot back. "I'd rather be known that way than be like you, Mr. District Attorney, prosecutor of the innocent."

Maybe I acquired a reputation, and a successful record, because I so much hated to lose. It wasn't any inner fire that compelled me. I just couldn't look a client in the eye if I didn't keep him out of jail, no matter how damaging the evidence against him.

There are cases that can propel a young lawyer to fame or wealth, and others that are the stuff of good theater. I remember the odd ones, such as the client who made the mistake of stealing from absolutely the worst victim—such as the President of the United States.

President Dwight Eisenhower had donated a very expensive coffee pot to Boston, to be used in some type of promotion with the March of Dimes. It was gold and silver, encrusted with diamonds and valued at $50,000. The urn was flown to Boston, met at the airport by my client and diverted to an associate in Florida. This move disturbed some very interested parties, such as the Secret Service and the FBI.

I was as curious as anyone as to why someone would steal a property belonging to the President. "I didn't really mean to," my client told me. "It's just that I'm a souvenir nut. And when I saw this thing with the presidential seal just sitting there, I couldn't help myself."

Under the law, my client had what is known as an "irresistible impulse." Legally, this is a state where a man, for whatever reason, has no control over his actions. Fortunately, he didn't have to do any time for that caper. Just a little probation.

As we were walking down the courthouse steps following the

trial, he was so thrilled he kept assuring me I would always be his lawyer. "Listen," I said, "don't do me any favors. And if you feel you're ever going to get any more 'irresistible impulses,' do it with a candy bar at the supermarket. Not the President's coffee pot."

So perhaps you can understand why, when Earl Wilson happened along in 1964, I was open to new directions. The idea of mingling with pro athletes appealed to me. Food for the living ex-child and might-have-been star in us all.

Earl referred to me such clients as Reggie Smith, George Scott, Joe Foy, Lenny Green, Bill Monboquette, and others on the Red Sox. In 1967, when the Sox won the pennant, I was representing about fifteen of the players. Although most people first heard my name during the Ken Harrelson episode, I had already represented some seventy athletes by then. It simply snowballed. When those players were traded or retired, they recommended others to me from around the league.

It evolved the same way in other sports. Sam Jones was my first basketball client, and before long he sent over Don Nelson, John Havlicek, Larry Siegfried, Bailey Howell, Wayne Embry and just about every other great Boston Celtic of that time, except Bill Russell. At one point, nine Celtics were among my clients.

In hockey it started with Glen Slather, who referred Derek Sanderson, who in turn, sent over Ted Green, Gerry Cheevers, Wayne Cashman and others. When Glen was traded to New York, he urged Vic Hadfield and Bruce McGregor to seek me out.

My associations with football players followed the same pattern. I started with the Boston area players on the Patriots—Jim Hunt, Gino Cappelletti, Larry Eisenhauer, Houston Antwine, Jon Morris. From that group, I was to represent more than forty Patriots at one time or another, over a period of eight years.

My home base was of course Boston, but soon my practice spread into almost every major league city in the four major team sports. All of this may sound simple, but it has made my life incredibly complicated. It was not planned, but was more accident and good fortune than anything else.

So here I was, suddenly dealing with innumerable well-known athletes, and all of them had come to me solely on the word of others. I take that for the compliment it is. Lawyers receive no other applause, except money, and that doesn't feed your soul.

My first obligation is to my client *within the ethics of the law*. I have lost some, and dropped others, who had a more pliable idea of what was right and wrong. The opportunities for compromising one's integrity are endless in sport, and growing worse.

There is no longer a spirit of leaving a little on the table. Today everyone wants to get it *all*. In my early tentative years in this field, I'd return with a contract to find a surprised and grateful athlete. "Bob," they'd say, "I didn't think you'd ever be able to get this without causing hard feelings with the club. I didn't want to make waves, no matter what."

When they discovered this could happen—that a lawyer could go to management, win for them what they felt they deserved on their contract and not create any new problems—attorneys like Bob Woolf became a way of life with athletes.

Soon, my practice extended beyond the big leagues. I started to hear from a flock of clients from the so-called minor, or off-Broadway, sports. In a few short years my law experience had swung from arson, assault, bank robbery and embezzlement to soccer, squash, street hockey, swimming, softball, boxing, badminton, bowling, baton twirling, backgammon, bridge, auto racing, demolition derbies, stock cars, speed skating, ice boating, channel swimming, blind golf, pool, billiards, water polo, water skiing, polo, team parachute jumping, sky diving, horse racing, volley ball, jai-alai, judo, karate, wrestling, paddleball, platform tennis, archery, motorcycling and gymnastics.

The truth is I found sports to be more fun than the general run of crime matters, and a little less cruel. The really appealing

fact of sports is that if you lose, you can always come back another day and win. In criminal court, when the decision goes
the other way, your client may not get another turn at bat.
What bothered me was that I dwelled upon the losses. They
stayed with me for a very long time.

I had several chances to become an assistant district attorney,
and declined them all, for the same reason: it would just have
bothered me to send someone to jail. Even if he deserved it.

Once, a client of mine was sentenced to six months in a case
I felt we deserved to win. I was visibly upset, so much so that I
found my client consoling *me*. "Bob," he said, "don't let it
bother you, man. I can do six months standing on my head.
I thought I was going away for at least ten *big* ones. Six months
will be like taking a vacation."

That may have been his idea of a vacation, but not mine.
I wanted out, not really from the law itself, but from the hurt
that never seemed to leave.

I thank you, Earl Wilson!

4

The Way of the Hawk

———

HE WAS BASEBALL's original flower child. He should have been an actor, or maybe the first centerfold in *Cosmopolitan*, instead of Burt Reynolds. He was the fellow who for two years made Boston light up like an electric circus. He was Kenny Harrelson, of Savannah, Georgia, and his name had all but disappeared from the sports pages.

Now there it was again, on a Saturday morning in mid-October, 1974. The headline said: *"Hawk May Forget Golf."* The story went on to say that Ken Harrelson had failed for the fourth time to qualify for the pro golf tour. He was broke and out of sponsors. Three years had passed, the story said, since he had quit baseball to follow the sun. He was thirty-three and washed up in two sports.

I sipped my first cup of breakfast coffee, the one that thaws your brain, and I thought about Ken Harrelson. The Hawk. Three years out of baseball, five out of Boston. Where had all the good times gone?

He had more pure magnetism than any athlete I had ever known. The clothes, the hair, the impulsive generosity, he strode through life in a neon glow. A complete stranger might admire his necktie. Zip. He'd hand it to them. Or, someone would say, "Hawk, that's a great looking watch," and the next thing you knew his watch was on the admirer's wrist.

He had a nose that led him like the hood ornament on a Packard. The profile inspired the nickname, and his style made it come alive. His clothes did not just harmonize, they gave a *concert*. He fancied such accessories as medallions and purses and paisley scarves tied at the neck. And the hair. For a while it fell over his face like one of the hags in *Macbeth*. It was too shaggy for the late Gil Hodges, then his manager at Washington. So the Hawk had it trimmed by a teammate, who achieved the kind of effect people used to get with porridge bowls. Hodges traded him anyway to Kansas City.

Notoriety had come to him first in Kansas City, where he beat Charles O. Finley, and he beat the system. He became, after much confusion, of a kind not unknown to either Finley or Harrelson, the first athlete ever to sign for two bonuses. Finley fired him in midseason, August of 1967, after the Hawk had publicly zinged his boss for firing manager Alvin Dark.

That was the end of what had been a symbiotic relationship. Harrelson had ridden Finley's mule, won the club hand-wrestling title and averaged nearly a run batted in a game in the five weeks before Charley canned him. No player ever talked himself out of a job and into a sweeter deal than the Hawk.

Unbelievably, Finley's action had the effect of making him a free agent, open to all bids (this time through a flaw in Finley's temper, not his contract, as was to be the case years later in the famed liberation of Catfish Hunter). In a time when pitchers were dominating baseball, Harrelson was a bona fide power hitter.

After earning $13,000 a year with the A's, he signed for three times as much in bonus and salary with the Red Sox, then embroiled in what their fans had labeled "The Impossible Dream." Hundred-to-one shots to win the pennant in 1967, the Red Sox survived a four-team race to win it on the last day of the season, with the Hawk in right field and batting fourth.

Harrelson was at the peak of his sudden fame when I first met him midway through the 1968 season. He was on his way to becoming the Player of the Year in the American League, and RBI champion, as the right fielder and cleanup hitter for the Boston Red Sox.

The Hawk was proving himself as a talent, as he had already proved himself as a character, a throwback to that gaudier time when ballplayers were named Goose and Rabbit and Lefty, and in the winter spent every dime they had earned in the summer.

It had been a prudent investment by the Sox, who were desperate to replace their sidelined young outfield star, Tony Conigliaro. Sadly, an eye injury had ended the season—and, as it turned out, despite two courageous comebacks, the career —of Tony C. The Hawk won a couple of games for them with his bat, coming down the stretch.

The Boston heroes that year were Carl Yastrzemski, known as "Yaz," and the educated pitcher, Jim Lonborg. The Hawk was ineffective in the World Series, won by St. Louis, but his time was coming.

In 1968 he made it big, and on his own terms, fulfilling the prophecy of his rookie year. Like an actor who vows to defeat the city of concrete and steel, he had pointed his bat at the sky and said, "Someday I'm going to make $50,000 with this baby, because if there is one thing the Hawk can do it's hit a baseball."

And that year he could: thirty-five homers, 109 runs batted in and lots of game-winning hits. Suddenly, he had the town in the palm of his hand. Boston, this city that loved heroes, needed them, sought them and sometimes used them badly, had an improbable new one. He dabbed shoe polish under his eyes to cut the glare of the sun, taped his wrists to create a more menacing presence at bat, and flashed the peace sign to the crowd each time he ran to his position.

Nearly two million fans poured into Fenway Park that season.

The Hawk loved them all. He signed autographs endlessly, accepted every invitation and lavished praise on the Boston management. At the end of the season, the Red Sox tore up the second year of his contract and raised him to $50,000 (up from $35,000). He had arrived.

Although the Sox limped home in third place, it had been a storybook year for the Hawk, and over the winter everybody wanted a piece of him. For little or no money of his own, he had an interest in a clothing store, a golf course, a restaurant. He endorsed dune buggies. A record company was getting ready to release a 45 RPM, putting his deeds to song. Boston gourmets could now buy their submarine sandwiches at Hawk shops all over town. He was that rare article, a *hot property*, as hot as any athlete outside of New York had ever been. Ted Williams had never seen such deals.

He was constantly on the go, and traveling with the Hawk was always a production. Whenever we swept through an airport he hailed two cabs, not one. One was for us, the other for his luggage, trailing after us like a small storage van, loaded with a couple of trunks and a half dozen suitcases. There was no clothes bag slung over the shoulder for Ken Harrelson. He didn't arrive in a city, he invaded.

The Hawk lived high, and he lived best in front of an audience. Separated, and later divorced, he had leased a plush apartment in the fancy part of Brookline, a suburb just a mile or so from Fenway Park. He had a wardrobe of fifty slack suits and as many pairs of shoes (and above the pockets of his shirts and pants, there was inscribed his name, "Hawk"). It even appeared on his bathroom tiles. This was all kept in order by his houseboy, Wendell. That's right, his houseboy. Wendell was the Hawk's man, who fixed his meals and laid out his clothes and did the minor chores of a man whose time and place had outgrown him. Also, when you had a closet as full as the Hawk's, you needed help.

One day he called me and mentioned the name of an investment company, in which he had just been given a chunk of stock. "Bobby," he said, "I want to give Wendell 5,000 shares. He's a good fellow and things are so great with me that I'd like to share some of it." He was like that. He was a giver, and he agreed with everyone.

He had the tastes and the flair of the old movie stars of the '40s. He was hardly the prototype of the modern-day ball-player who, on the whole, was basically conservative. He wanted to live and he wanted it now.

He went through life making entrances. If we decided to see the Celtics play, for example, the Hawk would never enter the arena until the first quarter was nearly over. He'd say, "Let's wait. I've got to go in and get my standing 'O' [for ovation]." Then he'd stroll down the aisle and the whole place would rise and cheer the Hawk.

No one ever stretched one good year farther. But he had something else, a kind of machismo, that simply announced he was coming. The way he dressed, you could not have missed him any more than you could miss a brass band. He had charm, and he made every woman feel beautiful. He was courtly and gallant, in the old-fashioned sense.

The 1969 season was less than two weeks old when I ran into Larry Claflin, a columnist for the Boston *Herald*, in Gino Cappelletti's club, The Point After, in downtown Boston. Larry said, "Bob, I heard a rumor that the Hawk was going to be traded."

I laughed out loud. The idea was just absurd. I was still laughing when I left the next morning for Phoenix, where I had some missionary work to do for one of my basketball clients, Neal Walk. He was the player the Suns drafted when they lost the coin flip for a fellow named Lew Alcindor. On April 19, 1969, three days after I had laughed at Larry Claflin's rumor, I was in my room at the Caravan Motel, going over the contract, when the phone rang. I was expecting a call from the Suns.

It was the Hawk. And I could tell from the crack in his voice that something was haywire. "You're not going to believe this, Bobby," he said, his voice working up to a wail, *"but they have just traded my ass to Cleveland*. Can you believe that crap? *Cleveland! Can you believe it?"*

No, I couldn't. He was the most popular player on the club. He had performed for them. The town was practically married to him. For one of the few times in my life I was truly speechless. I didn't know what to tell him, he was so obviously hurt. So was I.

As he rambled on, giving me the details over the phone, I slumped down on my bed, cradled the phone against my shoulder and covered my eyes with both hands, like a little kid not wanting to look at something bad. My mind was racing on, pouring out resentment toward the Red Sox and the cruelty of professional sports.

That afternoon Dick O'Connell, the Boston general manager, had asked Kenny to drop by his office when he got to Fenway Park. The Hawk didn't suspect a thing as he eased himself into a chair, and waited for O'Connell to speak. But what he heard staggered him. He had been traded to Cleveland in a deal involving five other players—four of them pitchers. Boston sent with him Dick Ellsworth and Juan Pizzarro, in return for Sonny Siebert, Vicente Romo and catcher Joe Azcue.

Hawk stared at the man across the desk. O'Connell's lips were moving, he was reminding him that he would be reunited with his old manager, Alvin Dark, now running the show in Cleveland. But it was like trying to listen to someone over the roar of an airplane engine. His head began to clear as O'Connell led him to the door, patted his arm and assured him, "This should be a great break for you."

Harrelson left the park, drove directly to his apartment, tossed down a few healthy belts and had a good cry. Now he was on the phone to Arizona. "I'll tell you one thing," he was shouting, "there is no damned way I'm going to Cleveland. I'll quit before I ever do that. To hell with the contract. I'll never play this goddamn game again."

The conversation was getting slightly more emotional than

the third act of an Italian opera. When I found myself agree-
ing with him I knew it was time to hang up. "Ken," I said,
finally, "I'm coming home on the next plane and don't you do
a thing until I get there. You got that? Don't say anything,
don't do anything. I'll be home by the time you wake up
tomorrow morning."

That, in itself, was no small feat. They don't run shuttles
between Phoenix and Boston. I caught a flight to El Paso,
buckled my seat belt for six stops, and arrived at Logan Airport
to see the sun coming up. I sat all night like an owl, unable to
sleep with so many thoughts tumbling through my brain.

I blamed myself that it had happened, that the news landed
on the Hawk uncushioned. How could I have been so naive?
So unprepared? There was the rumor and, now that I thought
about it, one or two notes buried in sports columns in the
spring that might have been clues. The big sports attorney, with
his hands on all the strings. Where was his pull now?

But every day is a lesson in life. And I had learned mine that
day. No one is immune. When a team is determined to make a
move, performance matters little, sentiment not at all. The
Hawk was just another suitcase to be moved into the second
cab. I swore never again to take for granted the security of an
athlete.

Somewhere up there, over the heartland of America, a plan
began to form in my mind. And it crystallized over the next few
hours. We'll retire the Hawk. I was groping for an angle, a
gimmick, a miracle, anything that might gum up the trade
badly enough to return all the players involved to their teams,
meaning that the Hawk would remain in Boston and live
happily ever after. At the same time, he wouldn't have to put
the knock on Cleveland.

At that point I was a little schizoid. One part of my mind
told me yes, we could maneuver them into calling off the deal.
But deep down I knew that someday he might have to play for
the Indians, and it wouldn't help anyone if he kicked the tar
out of the town before he ever got there. Still, I was willing

to take a shot at the retirement angle.

I slid this idea into the talk at breakfast that morning, and the Hawk ate it up. No one had ever told baseball to shove it before. The thought appealed. The more we talked the better he liked it. He began to talk about it not as a retirement, but as an *abdication*. He'd show them. Charley Finley had bounced him just two years ago, and now the Red Sox were pulling the rug from under him again.

"Let's have a press conference," he said, banging his fist on the table, rattling my coffee cup, "and tell them I'm never playing this game again." He was still boiling.

My hardest job that morning was to keep his friends from pouring suggestions into the Hawk's ear, which, only partly hidden by his hair, made an irresistible target. It was early, but there was a considerable crowd in his apartment that Sunday.

"Listen, Hawk," one of his pals, a former big-leaguer named Lee Walls, was telling him, "let's call Alvin and tell him for another twenty-five grand you'll make the move. They'll give you the $25,000 and that will do it."

This had been going on all morning. Finally, I walked over and got him aside. "Are you going to listen to what I have to say, and go along with it, or is this some kind of public forum?"

"Bob," he said, "you're my guy. I don't care what anybody says. I'm with you."

He gave me his look of altar-boy innocence, but I knew he'd see it through. He was bitter. His two years in Boston had been a big love affair. Now he had been rejected, and he felt like a jilted lover. The Red Sox, he thought, had given him the business. Good. I wanted him to stay in that mood.

My office called a press conference for 12:30 that afternoon, an hour before the Sox were scheduled to play the Indians—a nice touch of irony—up the street in Fenway Park. I told the Hawk I just wanted to dash home to wash up, shave and change clothes, and I'd be back to take him to the office. When I returned his motor was running again.

"I've got to go over to the park," he said, "I've just got to see some of the guys."

There was no point in arguing with him. The next hour was a mob scene. We walked around the Red Sox clubhouse with confused smiles on our faces that implied whatever anybody wanted to make of it. No one knew what was going to happen. Siebert, Azcue, Romo, Ellsworth and Pizzaro didn't even know what uniform to wear. The trade was being held up, the players were in limbo. In just about every other trade in the previous fifty years of baseball, the people involved showed up the next day ready to work for their new employers. This time no one knew quite what to do. Dick O'Connell and Gabe Paul, the two general managers, were stymied.

As we drifted around the clubhouse, making loud, mindless talk like the crowds in the lobby before a play, the questions were all the same. "What's he gonna do?" Carl Yastrzemski asked me. Dick Williams, the manager, looked disbelieving: "Is he really going to quit?" The Red Sox and the Indians were two of the most confused teams ever to play a baseball game. Each roster was short three men, including two pitchers. The other five players in the trade weren't sure which locker room they were supposed to be in, and neither manager knew what to tell them.

"I gotta see Al Dark," Harrelson said, abruptly. In a flash he was out the door, heading for the visitors' clubhouse, me trailing behind. It occurred to me that the Hawk was moving now by reflex, but in a curious, unspoken way he seemed to be hoping that somewhere in this trip he would find it was all just a bad dream, and everything would revert back to what had been before.

Dark and Harrelson were fond of each other, joined in spirit, at least, as the targets of the Finley purge. Alvin hadn't forgotten how the Hawk had defended his handling of the team in Kansas City. Dark greeted the Hawk warmly. The trade had been his idea, he meant it as a compliment, and couldn't understand it when Kenny told him he intended to quit. Ken tried to explain about his outside interests. Al didn't understand that.

Finally, they shook hands and Dark said he wanted him, period, even if he was crazy, and the door would stay open. The Hawk was touched. After he had assured Alvin for the third time of his desire never to play for anyone else, I hustled him out of there and over to the press conference.

When we arrived at my office the sidewalk looked like the staging area of a rock-concert riot. Hundreds of fans were lined up, spilling into the street, waving signs of support for the Hawk. Inside, there were more writers and radio-TV people around my desk than in the press box at Fenway Park. Clearly, this was where the story was. They play all those games, day after day, year after year. How often did a guy *retire* at the peak of his career?

The timing was terrific, though accidental. Boston had been invaded by visiting press, there to cover the playoff games of both the Celtics and the Bruins, and the annual running of the Boston Marathon. So, unexpectedly, Hawk's retirement scene was to receive national coverage.

"This is the last time you'll ever see the Hawk in baseball," he said, softly, his voice filled with the kind of genuine emotion that athletes feel when talking about themselves. "The Hawk's not going to do it anymore. I can't hardly believe it myself."

Some of the writers were struggling with the idea, too. "What will you do for work, Hawk?" asked a somewhat skeptical Tim Horgan of the Boston *Herald*.

"I'll work in my sub shops," he said quickly, off the top of his head.

Sure enough, the next day's papers were loaded with the Ken Harrelson story, under a photo that showed the heartbroken fellow with an apron tied around his waist, concocting a submarine sandwich with peppers, onions and other high-voltage goodies for his fans. "I'll never play baseball again," he was quoted. "I'm just too hurt. That's all there is to it."

For the next several days I studied the press reaction with full interest. The Boston writers sided with the Red Sox, while most of the out-of-town newsmen treated the Hawk with some sympathy. That didn't surprise me. Over the years, I have found it to be a natural instinct for the local press to stick with management, at least on most trades. It's a form of self-protection. The player has been traded. He's gone. Management lives on, and the writer still has to deal with it on a daily basis.

But we had something priceless, national exposure. It had been the purest kind of luck when so many visiting scribes left their trenches to hear the Hawk. At this point, to be honest, Harrelson and Woolf still didn't know exactly what they were doing. We had an idea, but no master plan. The Hawk might even fantasize and think he was going to work in his sub shops forever, laying on the onions and peppers and pimentos, but with his style it would have been damned tough to get by on the pay.

On the other hand, I knew that I had my first major case in sports, one whose outcome would interest the fans of two cities and the entire baseball establishment. I was curious, myself, as to what the ending would be. For one of the rare times, the ball had been thrown back to management, and only a player of Harrelson's popularity could do it. A lesser name, a journeyman, would have been blackballed forever. But this was the player of the year. You just couldn't ignore him. Suddenly, the Hawk was holding the cards and asking for a new shuffle.

We didn't have long to wait. That same night, Sunday night, after the press conference had been on the evening news, we heard from both teams. Dick O'Connell called to make it clear that there was no way the Hawk could come back to the Red Sox. To consider even that, he indicated, would undermine all future trades and lead to anarchy and ruin.

Gabe Paul was cordial, sincere, confident that fair-minded people, reasoning together, could work out their problems. He invited Hawk and me to fly to New York for a *secret* meeting Monday night in the upstairs dining room at "21." That did not strike me as the ideal place for a secret meeting, but I agreed.

When I told Hawk about our rendezvous in New York, where the Indians were to open a series against the Yankees, he was skeptical. "Everyone in baseball," he informed me, "knows that Gabe is a tight son of a bitch."

Patiently, I said, "Look, let's see what they offer. We have to take the position that the moves from now on are theirs. But under *no* circumstances will we *ask* for more money. The first time we raise the subject, they'll say we're just trying to hold them up."

We flew to New York that night for our seance with Gabe Paul, telling absolutely no one except, of course, a photographer for *Life* magazine who had been assigned to follow the Hawk.

When we reached "21," there just happened to be a Cleveland sportswriter and photographer waiting inside the door. Gabe said he couldn't understand how they got there. I couldn't either, since I didn't think there were many newspaper fellows who ate at "21." But I wasn't in a very strong moral position to make an issue of it, having to introduce the photographer from *Life*. So much for secrecy.

The meeting produced nothing. Gabe was a gentleman, a refined, soft-spoken man with a cherubic face. But he never made an offer and neither did we. He was waiting for us to make a pitch. We didn't. We simply explained the Hawk's unique situation in Boston, and why he wasn't going to leave. Gabe was just trying to feel us out, and I think he was surprised when we didn't try to maneuver him into some kind of contract.

On the way back to Boston that night, I concluded that it was time to get back to reality, to talk dollars with Hawk for the first time. I said, "I know all this really upset you, but baseball is your game. You can't make the kind of living you want right now doing anything else. How much will it take to get you to go to Cleveland?"

Hawk looked at me carefully. He, too, knew that we were no longer playing let's-pretend. "I don't know, Bob," he said. "The money is more in your department. What do *you* think?"

"Six figures," I said, instantly, surprising myself even as I said it. "I'm going to get you six figures."

The Hawk was shocked. For the first time in a week he came alive. "Do you really think so? Do you really think they'd give me a hundred thousand?" He threw back his head. "Oh, wow, the Hawk a hundred-thousand-dollar ballplayer."

That did seem like quite a leap. He was now earning $50,000, in itself a dramatic improvement over the $13,000 he was drawing with the A's in 1967. Now, in just two years, was he really going to upgrade himself by $87,000?

"How are we going to do it?" the Hawk asked, incredulous.

"We're going to wait for them to make an offer. And just know this—the minute they do—whether it's $5,000 or $10,000 or whatever—we're all the way home. They'll be opening the door and not us."

It wasn't that easy, of course. For one thing, there was the matter of keeping the Hawk from going off in all directions. He was getting pressure from every side. He had a multitude of friends and now each of them had become a drugstore lawyer. In the midst of all this I received a call from his mother, a vibrant woman, whose instincts were timeless: "Take care of my baby," she said. "Don't let him be hurt. Take care of my baby." I gave her my word that whatever we did, it would be the right way.

On my way home early Tuesday morning it suddenly dawned on me why I felt exhausted, drained. I hadn't had a night's sleep since the previous Friday night in Phoenix. And it seemed as if I had just closed my eyes when the phone in my bedroom rang. It was Bowie Kuhn, the commissioner of baseball, asking me to bring the Hawk back to New York for a meeting that day with him, Joe Cronin, president of the American League, O'Connell and Gabe Paul.

I was awake now, excited, the adrenalin flowing. I could feel it was about to break wide open. They were coming to us. I called the Hawk to give him the news and he told me, matter-of-factly, "Bob, I'm not going. Forget it. That's all there is to it." I could picture him smothering a yawn.

Don't ask me why he didn't want to go. I didn't take the time to find out, either. I just said, "Get your clothes on, Hawk. I'll be at your apartment in twenty minutes and you're going, like it or not. We've come this far and we're not going to blow it now."

I hung up the phone, dressed quickly and drove over to his pad, as he called it. When I got there he was still sitting in his underwear, discussing household matters with Wendell, and repeating over and over, "The hell with it. I won't go. The whole thing is shit. To hell with it."

His entourage was there, reinforcing him. I looked around the apartment. The bar would do justice to an intimate lounge. The wall-to-wall carpeting was thick enough to hide in. The bed was oval, with a leopardskin spread. He had a closed-circuit television system to entertain his chums. I knew I had to get him out of there.

I worked on him until he finally, reluctantly, gave in. He went to his closet, picked through his wardrobe, consulted with Wendell and emerged half an hour later in the wildest outfit I had yet seen him wear. I thought to myself, "Is he going to see the commissioner of baseball in that getup?"

No, it wasn't an audience with the pope, but lawyers by conditioning always feel that in matters of legal import a low profile is desirable, unless you can arrange for no profile at all. So here was the Hawk, a multicolored silk scarf at the throat, held by a ring set with an ebony stone; a white turtleneck, under a deep blue, V-necked pullover sweater that almost glowed, bouffant sleeves and flared trousers. I don't think you would have mistaken him for a banker.

The next thing, we were in New York, getting off the elevator to meet the commissioner, and we walked into a swarming hive of reporters and television cameras. Howard Cosell was there, and so were Kyle Rote and Frank Gifford. I also recognized Dick Young and Jimmy Cannon, those masters of American sports journalism.

Through it all Hawk moved with supreme confidence, as he

always did, even when it wasn't well founded.

A smiling Bowie Kuhn came out to meet us. He was a large man, balding, a wisp of gray hair on the top and fluffy sideburns, scholarly looking but with an impression of power, as though he had been a boxer in the Ivy League. Kuhn had been in office only a few months, and they were turbulent ones. There had been a screwy trade between Houston and Montreal, in which he interceded, and an investigation involving certain owners who held stock in a company that had an interest, it developed, in Las Vegas casinos. And now Harrelson.

"Gawdamm, Commissioner," the Hawk greeted him warmly, offering his hand, "they sure are making you earn your money."

As we moved through the crowd, Howard Cosell, as only he can, nailed me:

"Bob," he demanded, holding a microphone under my chin, "have you researched the reserve clause?"

"Howard, I haven't researched anything. We're not here for a fight. We're not bringing any suits against baseball."

We ducked into the commissioner's office and our reception was cordial. Kuhn sat behind his desk and the rest of us settled into chairs around the room. The commissioner began by saying that he was sorry the impasse had happened, but that if it took until three in the morning he was going to stay there—and by implication, us—until the situation was resolved.

I spoke first and gave the Hawk's position, pointing out what I thought were the unique circumstances surrounding the case. When I finished Joe Cronin was indignant. A hall-of-famer, Cronin had spanned the Ty Cobb and Ted Williams eras in baseball. It pained him, it really did, to think that a fellow would let his outside income interfere with baseball. In his day, he said, they would have played for nothing. "I don't understand," he said, shaking his head, sadly, "I just don't understand."

I was sure he didn't. Kuhn simply acted as the mediator. O'Connell was very quiet. And Gabe sat there, uncomfortably, wondering how much it was going to cost him.

After two hours, Kuhn asked if Hawk and I would mind waiting in another room while they met privately. We came back thirty minutes later and Dick O'Connell cleared his throat and offered Harrelson a raise to $75,000 if he would sign a two-year contract.

I told him no, ignoring the pleading look in Hawk's eyes. I said at that figure my client would still be losing money. This time they stepped into the other room. In a few minutes they were back with another offer: $75,000 for this year, and $100,000 for the second.

Looking quickly at my watch, I asked to speak alone with Hawk for a moment. As soon as I closed the door he was hissing, "Take it, take it, Bob." I said no. "It's five o'clock," I said. "They've got a whole hallway full of reporters out there and Bowie Kuhn is not going to let them spoil it for another lousy $25,000. If they've come this far, they'll go all the way."

So I told them no again. That prompted another conference. The Hawk and I went back to the adjoining office and slumped into chairs. He looked at me like a client whose lawyer had just demanded either an acquittal or the gas chamber, and the jury has gone to deliberate. "They're not going to do it," he said, darkly. "They're not. They're not going to do it."

Those were the last words I heard until the door opened twenty minutes later. I had fallen asleep. Suddenly, the Hawk looked over and discovered that he had been talking to someone who was not conscious. My head was on the desk and I was sleeping as innocently as a newborn babe, if not more so. The Hawk was beside himself.

The Committee to Save Ken Harrelson was ready with another offer. The Hawk had been into the Red Sox for a loan of about $19,000 and O'Connell said they would cancel it —as part of the deal—if he accepted the last proposal: two years, at seventy-five and one hundred thousand respectively.

Adding the $19,000 to his salary for the first year brought the figure to $94,000, and that was close enough. Sold. I then tried to ease the bite somewhat by suggesting to Gabe that he could defer $50,000 of the money, both years, so that it would be paid to Hawk at a later date.

I always suspected that the Red Sox, and not Cleveland, put up whatever extra money was needed to complete the deal, which would have made it even more unusual. In big-league sports, with rare exceptions, when a player is traded his former team is immediately relieved of all the obligations of his contract. Any new deal was supposed to come from his new employer. But Cleveland wasn't as solvent as Boston, nor as generous historically. Although I couldn't care less from which source the money came, my hunch was that the Red Sox had bought their way out of trouble.

We made an agreement not to discuss the contract with the press. Kuhn made a thoughtful gesture when he invited me to join the others in the picture-taking ceremonies. To my knowledge, it was the first time a lawyer had been embraced within baseball, or any sport for that matter, at such a level of negotiation. It was, at that time, as much a turning point for me as for the Hawk.

He, meanwhile, was flying. "I'm going to Cleveland," he trumpeted to anyone who would listen, "and we're gonna win the pennant."

Gabe Paul startled me a moment later when he told the press, "Well, we have signed Harrelson to a new two-year contract at a *substantial* increase." He wanted the folks back home to know that he was spending money, while in almost the same breath he suggested to the Hawk: "Well, you wouldn't mind paying your own way to Cleveland now, would you, Hawk?" And he meant it.

Two things happened in the aftermath of the meeting which I thought were noteworthy. One pertained to the prejudices of some of the sports media, the other to the insecurity of pro athletes, who rank with night-club comics as people who need the most reassurance.

As we emerged from Kuhn's offices, Jimmy Cannon, then the reigning curmudgeon of New York syndicated sports columnists, left no doubt that he felt we—Woolf and Harrel-son—had pulled a heist. He was the last of the old Broadway writers from the Damon Runyon era, who came to newspapering from the streets, who were not establishment men at all but had a strong moral streak that resented easy scores. His line of questioning was slanted exactly that way, and in his column the next day Cannon pictured us a couple of hustlers who grabbed their $25,000 and ran.

Jimmy, of course, only missed by $70,000 or so and, in the process of relating his inside knowledge of the negotiations, failed to note that the Hawk in 1970 would become the first $100,000 player in Cleveland history, placing him ahead of the likes of Bob Feller and Lou Boudreau.

Meanwhile, Woolf's client was as skittish as ever. On the way back to Boston, his mood changed completely in the midst of a rough flight through heavy turbulence. With each bounce of the plane, he clutched the armrests tighter, and the color drained from his face. "We're gonna crash, Bobby, I know it. I always knew it would end like this. I came this far, I get me six figures, and now this. We're going down, Bobby, I can tell it."

He wasn't kidding. I was beginning to hang onto the seat a little myself, not relishing the idea of the Hawk taking me with him. He didn't stop sweating until we were on the ground in Boston.

Within twenty-four hours he was bound for Cleveland, where the town was preparing to turn out for a "Welcome Hawk" day. Vernon Stouffer, the owner of the Indians, was determined to show us that the Hawk could have as much going for him there as he had in Boston. The Hawk was willing to be convinced, and he loved the attention.

He rented a penthouse suite in a building that overlooked Lake Erie. This became his next toy. Even though the ballpark was only a few blocks away, he had a helicopter fly him there for the games. He also rented a suite of rooms at a nearby motel to entertain his friends. Wendell was on his way from

Boston and a young hockey player named Derek Sanderson, then a new client of mine, was going to move in and look after the pad in Brookline for the summer.

So it was all beautiful again for the Hawk, except for one thing. He couldn't hit the side of an aircraft carrier with a shovel. He wasn't hitting a lick. Each day I was afraid to look at the Cleveland box score. After the first month he was batting something like .161.

About that time it occurred to me I might do some business with the Indians, and I wrote a cheerful letter to Gabe Paul asking if he would be interested in putting on sale, in the Cleveland ballpark, the 3,000 "Don't Walk the Hawk" records we had left over in Boston.

A week later I received a brief note from Gabe, saying that at the pace the Hawk was then going, the Indians "would gladly take a walk anytime." I took that to mean that he wasn't interested.

In less than two years Harrelson would be out of baseball. During spring training, the next season, he shattered his leg sliding into a base. He lost speed he could not afford to lose, and would never be the same again. He tried to come back in the summer of 1970, couldn't hit and couldn't run, finished the year with one homer in thirty-nine times at bat.

The next season he batted .199 in fifty-two games and the Indians gave him his release. At twenty-nine, he was finished.

At the winter baseball meetings in 1969, the owners and general managers had passed what one Boston writer dubbed the "Woolf Rule," which said that players involved in a trade would report immediately to their new teams, even if one of the principals in the trade—like Harrelson—refused to report.

In looking back, they felt that Harrelson's strength in negotiating stemmed from the fact that five other ballplayers were sitting around idle, and baseball—not confronted with this situation before—was helpless to react.

Yet, as the years went by, and Kenny was forced out of the game by injury in what should have been his prime, I felt that we had taken a stand that was correct, a stand that won a little more consideration for those involved in trades. Today a ten-year man can't be traded without his approval.

When the Hawk left Boston he lost all the fringe deals he had going there, and when he left Cleveland he lost the rest of it. All he had to fall back on was his dream of making it as a pro golfer, and that lasted three frustrating years.

Of all the stories in sports, maybe the saddest is the fellow who loses his talent in the high noon of his career. The transition couldn't have been easy for the Hawk, who had heard cheers few men ever hear. I didn't see or talk to him often once he turned to golf, but I thought about him, and I had an idea of what he might be going through.

Then, only a few weeks after I had read of his failure on the tour, he passed through Boston, and we got together. He had adjusted to adversity with surprising ease. He had remarried, settled down. He was dressed conservatively, his hair trimmed to a modest length. Did my eyes deceive me? Was this the Hawk?

"Bob," he said, quietly, with a maturity I hadn't seen before, "when you're doing it, when you're hitting home runs, you can get away with anything. But when you're not delivering, it won't work. *They won't buy your act.*"

He was by far the most colorful athlete I had ever worked with; there was a pure joy, an innocence, an original chemistry about him that can't be manufactured by the press, or contrived by players who simply want to rebel.

And there was an irrepressible quality about him, too, and I wondered how long he would be down. Not long, as it turned out. By the end of 1974 he had a new job. Ken Harrelson had moved into the Red Sox TV booth, as a color analyst.

The Hawk had returned to baseball and back to Boston. He did a fabulous job in his rookie TV season, as I knew he would. They don't make stories any more with happy endings. This one, I figured, was close enough.

5

More Than Money

————

THE TEMPER of Arnold (Red) Auerbach is among the
most famous in sports, as pure as a living flame. In his coaching
heyday, in the '60s, it was said that the National Basketball
Association office paid its monthly phone bill out of the fines
collected from Auerbach.

I have had my clashes with Red, the man who built the
Boston Celtics' tradition, and I enjoy thinking back on them.
That, incidentally, is the only way to enjoy them. I must admit
that our relationship today is strained, as relationships with Red
often are if money is involved.

He is tough, explosive, at times rude, and in rare private
moments a disarming and appealing man. Once, he admired
a letter opener in my Boston office, shaped like a small pistol.
Red owns what is probably the world's most exotic collection
of letter openers, all sizes and styles, from every corner of the
globe. When you pulled the trigger on mine, a blade came
out, and Red was intrigued by it. I handed it to him. "Red,"
I said, "I'd love you to have it."

It used to please me immensely to walk into the office of the
Celtics' general manager, and see it sitting there on his desk.

It was a token of our friendship, our mutual respect. Then came our long negotiation in 1969 over the new contract of John Havlicek, who was being pursued at the time by the young American Basketball Association. I walked into Red's office after John finally signed—the highest salary ever paid a Celtic —and the letter opener was gone. I never saw it again.

It isn't really that Auerbach begrudged John a dime of the money, or felt it was beyond his worth, given the salary demands that were rampant in basketball. It was simply that he hated to lose, whatever the contest—hoops or dollars or pitching pennies at a crack. Red wasn't mad at John Havlicek. He was mad at Bob Woolf. He felt that I had gone back on my word; the way Red negotiates, he offers a figure and if you don't accept it he feels betrayed. Also, I had added the final insult, by obtaining for my client a figure far in excess of what Red had intended to pay.

You have to understand the complicated ties that exist between an athlete and his coach, or general manager who decides what the player will earn. Often there is a feeling between them that is close to love. But at the contract table, the general manager assumes all the warmth of a mortgage banker dispossessing another widow. So the lawyer, or financial agent, steps in, absorbing the shocks so that when the player signs, his attitude, we hope, won't be poisoned. Or management's.

John Havlicek was a bridge between eras in Boston. He broke in with the great championship teams of the Bill Russell days, coming off the bench as Auerbach's sixth man. By 1969 he was the leader of the band, playing under an old teammate, Tommy Heinsohn. How differently his career might have developed without the Auerbach influence isn't clear. But they made good chemistry: Red, intense, moody, emotional; John, quiet, gentle, unflappable. John moved like a cool stream. Red goes through life like hot lava.

But both have a quality called loyalty, and that is why, in this age of the grab-and-run athlete, John Havlicek could resist what was then the biggest package in pro sports to remain with the team of his salad days.

John is, to begin with, the kind of person who causes people to lose their critical faculties. Basketball is the most physically demanding, in terms of wind, legs and stamina, of all team sports. For a dozen years no player has driven himself harder than Havlicek, game after game, at both ends of the court. Physically, John's secret is that he has an unusually low heartbeat, around 40 beats per minute (72 is normal), which allows him to run constantly without tiring. In fact, heart specialists have frequently asked to examine John. People around the Celtics insist they have never seen him sweat. John told me once that the only time he really perspires is when he wears street clothes, and then only slightly underneath his arms.

This rare physical trait, along with a solid 6–5 frame and total dedication, make Havlicek, in my estimation, the best athlete of his time. He has it all: the speed, the stamina, the strength, the grace. He is the kind of fellow who can let you name your game, and he will beat you at it.

He comes from the soil of middle America, from a small town in Ohio called Martin's Ferry, the son of a close and conservative family. He confided once that everything he did as a youngster, he did on the run. If his mother sent him to the store on an errand, he ran. If he went to the schoolyard to play ball, he ran both ways. At lunchtime he would run home, eat, then run back to school to be the first in line at whatever they were playing.

An all-around athlete in high school, John was so exciting a football prospect that Ohio State—meaning Woody Hayes— kept a locker with his name on it in the varsity dressing room. John never went out for football, or baseball, and had been all-state in both in high school.

He enrolled at Ohio State on a basketball scholarship, and he stayed true to the sport, but his peripheral feats became the stuff of campus legend. Part of the basketball preseason training at Columbus was running. Although he had never competed at that distance before, John ran the mile under five minutes in his first try, a record for Ohio State players. No one before him had ever come close to the standards set by John.

When he graduated in 1962, the Cleveland Browns drafted him for football—even though he hadn't suited up in four years. That spring he reported for an informal tryout with several Cleveland veterans, under the penetrating eye of Paul Brown, one of the profession's recognized geniuses.

John had been a schoolboy quarterback who could heave a football seventy yards. But with his hands and reach, the Browns were taken with the idea of trying him as a pass receiver. They timed him in the forty-yard dash and couldn't believe their stop watches—4.5 seconds. Paul Brown timed him again to make sure. Again it was 4.5. Only two Browns in history—the legendary Jim Brown and halfback Bobby Mitchell —ever ran it as fast.

The training camps of Paul Brown were elaborately systematic. Paul had someone chart and record every ball thrown and caught and, at the end of three weeks, Havlicek had the best record in camp, dropping only two passes. He was the last man cut by the Browns that year. NFL teams then weren't allowed to carry as many players as they are now; they had drafted Gary Collins, who became another great receiver in the Browns' tradition, and with their own veterans, including Ray Renfro, the team had no room on the roster. John wasn't heartbroken. He had been drafted by the Celtics and he knew he had a basketball job waiting in Boston.

At one time it was rumored that the Celtics drafted John because he was white. The story went that Red Auerbach wanted Chet Walker, but owner Walter Brown felt the Celtics had their "quota" of blacks—Bill Russell, Tom Sanders and the two Joneses, Sam and K.C. I have never believed it. Walt Brown was a super human being and Red Auerbach has always been color blind. The Celtics were the first team in pro sports in this country to start an all-black lineup—the four players mentioned above plus Willie Naulls, with Havlicek the first man off the bench.

In the crudely honest locker-room humor of the day, the Celtic starters referred to John as "the white hope." For a fact, he fit into the team's mold and carried on its traditions. It was this sense of "being a Celtic" that brought about one of the most unusual negotiations I've ever conducted.

In the summer of 1969 the struggling American Basketball Association was battling to make an impression on the sports scene. They needed talent and they needed to make news. During this time I received a telephone call from Jim Gardner, then commissioner of the ABA. Gardner said that he and the owners were eager to get a player of the caliber and character of Havlicek. They had learned, through the pipeline that exists in every sport, that John was negotiating a new contract with the Celtics. They wanted the opportunity to bid for his services. Up to that point—the ABA was only a year old—the league had picked off some NBA stars, but none of the magnitude of Havlicek.

I called John at his home in Columbus, where he was working for the summer, and told him of the possible offer. He had little to say, but I told him I felt that he ought to listen to the ABA's offer, since this new league was willing to pay some extravagant sums of money.

When I phoned Gardner back he was thrilled. It occurred to me then that the ABA people never really thought Havlicek would listen to them. Gardner was quite nice about it. In order to protect John's privacy, he said he would send his own jet to fly us to Rocky Mount, North Carolina, Gardner's operating base. He assured us that everything would be done with the utmost secrecy.

A few days later the private jet landed at Boston's Logan Airport, where I boarded, then headed to Columbus, where we picked up John and his wife, Beth. The three of us were cheerful as we flew toward the Carolinas. The whole episode had the air of a James Bond spy movie, particularly when we were met quickly and quietly at the Rocky Mount airport and whisked off to a motel, where our names never showed on the register.

We stayed in Rocky Mount all the next day meeting with Gardner and the ABA people. Gardner made the presentation on behalf of the league—and it was staggering.

At the time, the ABA was pushing a financial program named the Dolgoff plan, after a former New York tax accountant who developed it. This plan was intended to be used for corporate executives but was expected to work equally as well for professional athletes. The plan purported to assure equity growth if a certain amount of money were placed in mutual funds and other investments. The Dolgoff plan was the backbone of all the fabulous contracts signed by athletes in the boom years of the 1960s. This was the era when sports fans in America first heard of million-dollar contracts, and figures higher than a man could count. In truth, a million dollars, hard cash, was never really involved.

For example, let's say a 7-foot center from UCLA is coming into the bidding war between the two leagues, looking for a million-dollar contract. The proposal would be as follows. We'll give you the million. We'll give you $250,000 in cash: You'll receive $50,000 now, as a bonus, and $50,000 a year for the next four years as salary. Plus . . . we will take another $100,000 of *our* cash and invest it for you in the Dolgoff plan. At the end of twenty years that money will have grown to $750,000 through investments, and it will be there waiting for you when your playing days are over.

Such a plan, of course, makes little allowance for the vagaries of our economy, or for those times when the stock market is down and you can't talk to your broker because the cord won't reach the window ledge. But on paper, at least, the prospect could tell himself that he really did get a million—$250,000 now and $750,000 in twenty years. In reality, the team had a cash investment of $350,000. The player's ego would be massaged, and the team could tell its established stars, "We didn't

give that kid a million. He only got $350,000 for four years."
In fairness to Ralph Dolgoff, I should add that he preferred not
to state amounts as if they were *guaranteed* to be paid; but
management, in their efforts to present the most attractive
looking package, often chose to ignore this.

Almost all the prospects coming out of college in that era
were paid this way, so the million-dollar deals you read about
were honest in one respect, and artificial in another. But the
time was surely right for this type of deal. The stock market was
booming in the mid-'60s. When the market plunged in 1969
and '70, many of these young men were burned, the money
invested for them lost. There wouldn't be any $750,000
bonanza waiting for them in twenty years. This is why several
of them went to court looking to get out of their contracts,
arguing that they would never see what they had been promised.

When we finally got into serious discussion with Jim Gardner
and his associates, that day in North Carolina, I was asked what
I thought would be a fair price for Havlicek. My first impulse
was to give them an absurd figure. "Two million dollars," I said.

They didn't bat an eye. They simply put their heads together
for a few minutes, and then came back with an impressive
Dolgoff plan. "We'll give John Havlicek $50,000 for the next
forty years," Gardner informed us, "for the two million."

Obviously, there was a catch. It wasn't going to be cash.
It would be part cash, the rest investments. I figured their
actual cash outlay would be $400,000. So we declined. I
countered that we would consider $2 million, *cash*, to be paid
the way we wanted it paid.

They looked at me as though I had just discovered the force
of gravity. The room was crowded and several people spoke
up at once. Even Dolgoff was there. Finally, Jim Gardner said
they needed time to come up with a counter offer, and we de-
parted as secretively as we had arrived.

On the first leg of our flight to Columbus to drop off John
and Beth, I realized I had a problem. Not with the ABA.
Certainly not with John. How was I going to break this news

to Red Auerbach? When disturbed, Red tends to scream. He is, of course, an original, a character, and I admire him for that and for what he has meant to pro basketball, and Boston.

He wanted to bring in John at his figure, and I couldn't blame him for that. He had a payroll to keep in line. In our last meeting, he had offered a salary of $105,000. We had asked for one and a quarter and we were close. But now the ABA had entered the picture. They had made a serious offer and were prepared to go higher, and the whole situation had changed.

I dialed Red's number with an unsteady hand. He was furious. "We had a deal," he roared. We didn't, of course, except in Red's mind. He had told us what the Celtics would pay John and, as far as *he* was concerned, that constituted an agreement. I'm sure he still feels that I went back on my word.

Auerbach has a sense of fairness. But it's his *own* sense of fairness, and may not correspond to how the rest of the world defines it. I strongly suspect that it was this approach that cost him the services of the highly talented Don Chaney, who jumped to the ABA.

Now began a series of daily phone calls from the ABA offices. Their next offer was a three-year contract for between $500,000 and $550,000, all cash. Yet I didn't seriously consider it. I wasn't going to let John Havlicek jump the Celtics unless he would be set for life, and this offer was only competitive with Boston's.

Auerbach had calmed down, and now this curious ritual began. Every morning at 8, Jim Gardner would phone and increase the ABA's latest offer by $150,000. An hour later, Auerbach would call and say, "Bob, do you think another $250 would do it?" Let me spell that out so you won't misunderstand. *Two hundred and fifty dollars.* Red has a reputation for throwing around half dollars as though they were manhole covers.

I kept saying, "Red, I don't think you understand the seriousness of the situation." We had a communications problem. But Red didn't understand. He doesn't, to this day.

In a matter of a few weeks the ABA produced what was, at the time, the greatest sports contract ever offered. The league proposed to pay John Havlicek $1,200,000 over three years to play basketball. He would receive $400,000 in cash, each year, to represent the new, red-white-and blue league.

In order to insure this contract, the ABA agreed to a number of steps not then common in sports, such as: if the team or the league folded, or John was disabled, he still got the money in full; a certain amount would be placed in escrow; a surety performance bond would guarantee payment; the ABA owners, with a combined net worth of multimillions, would sign as individual guarantors.

It was, if I may say so, a model job of its kind. A few years later, when I negotiated Derek Sanderson's contract, I borrowed freely from the ideas of the proposal drafted for John and the ABA. I tried to insure that no matter what happened there would be no risk for him, even to the extent that he would be allowed to pick the team with which he would play. Nor could he be traded without his consent.

The Celtics responded to the greatest bid ever offered an athlete by submitting one for $600,000 less; even though it would be the biggest Celtic proposal ever, more than Bill Russell or Bob Cousy ever made at the crest of their careers. It was flattering, but still not in the park with the ABA package.

It was getting close to decision time. All the while, John had been on his usual even keel. But I was the one in torment. The irony of it was that I wanted John to stay in Boston. I had been brought up in the Celtics' tradition: You subordinate yourself to the team. To win you *must* be a family. That was the concept Auerbach taught, year after year. If you spent your life in Boston, as I had, this was your religion. So I fought with myself. I liked and admired Red. And I knew John Havlicek had higher priorities in life than money. On the other hand, it was my job to get the very best offers for him I could, from each side.

I was consumed with the idea that I might have to negotiate

a contract that would remove from the city the most popular athlete Boston had ever known. Ted Williams had dominated the town, but he wasn't universally liked, as John was. Bill Russell had been a giant, but he wouldn't sign autographs and many found him aloof.

The ABA was pressing for an answer, but I insisted that John had to give the Celtics the last offer. A meeting was arranged in Auerbach's office and I asked John to bring Beth. There were two reasons for this. Her presence would be a reminder to Red that it was a family decision, and a serious one. Second, I knew John would want her there. This was a close, sweet couple, unspoiled by the pressures of modern big-time sports. I knew this because our families had often celebrated New Year's Eve together, quiet nights in the best of company. Our wives were inseparable, capable of talking for hours at a time on the telephone. Only threats just short of a court order could get Anne off the phone. I'm sure John was raising Cain at the other end. A few years ago, on the television game show, "To Tell the Truth," Anne Woolf appeared as one of the unreal Beth Havliceks. She was convincing enough in her answers to win the vote of two panelists.

When John left on one of those marathon NBA road trips, for two or three weeks, Beth would sometimes stay with us. On games televised back to Boston, she wouldn't leave the set for fear of missing their private signal: at the foul line, as he prepared to shoot a free throw, John would brush the hair back over his right eye. He was saying *hello* to his wife.

Having Beth in the room when we met with Auerbach proved to be a good move. He was always charming to women and, out of deference to them, kept his temper under control, often with great effort. For the past several weeks, it had been clear that Red felt I was using the ABA offer for leverage, as strategy to squeeze an unreasonable ransom out of the Celtics. At the same time I was representing two of his other players, Larry Siegfried and Jim (Bad News) Barnes, and the tension was rising. Red was giving me a hard time with Siegfried, a crafty guard and another Auerbach student who went into coaching. Red kept going behind my back, telling Larry, "You don't need Woolf. I'll take care of you."

Meanwhile, Barnes kept coming up with a series of nutty demands. One day he walked in and told Red he wanted $50,000 a year and two Cadillacs. As Red hustled him out the door, Bad News called back over his shoulder, "How about $40,000 and one Cadillac?"

There was the usual, reading-of-the-will uneasiness as we settled into the chairs in front of Red's desk. It was impossible to sit in that room and not be imbued with a sense of the Celtic pride and the Celtic tradition. There was a montage of photographs on one wall, trophies and plaques all around, the tokens of eleven NBA championships in thirteen years.

This had been one of the true dynasties in sport, and Arnold Auerbach had started it, created it, shaped it. He drove referees nuts with his bitter, biting cracks from the bench, and he infuriated opposing coaches by his habit of lighting up a cigar in the closing minutes of what he had concluded would be another Celtic victory.

I used to bounce a banquet line off that. I'd say the only thing I found disconcerting about dealing with the Celtics, was that near the end of each negotiation Red would light up a cigar.

Only one who has been a diehard Celtics' fan can understand the mixed emotions I felt as I looked across the desk of Red Auerbach. "Red," I said, "you have to understand. I'm through negotiating with the ABA. I know what we have there, and a decision will be made here, this afternoon, and I want all parties to be aware of it. That's why Beth is here. The ABA has offered John over a million dollars. I'm not suggesting the Celtics pay that. I just want you to have all the facts."

He nodded. He was unsmiling, but polite and decent. We talked back and forth for over an hour, until Red stood and said, evenly, "Okay, this is as far as I can go. Take a few minutes to think it over." With that he left the room.

I turned to John. "This is your decision," I said. "It's your life. All I know is that right now there isn't anyone who can say a harsh word about John Havlicek. But just understand this. If you should jump, there is a small segment of the population that will think unkindly of you." I couldn't help grinning at him. "Of course," I added, "I don't know how much money it takes *not to care* what a small segment of the population thinks of you. . . ."

At that moment, I suspect I felt more pressure than John. Just by talking to the ABA, I was going against my own basic loyalty to Boston and the Celtics. I would be helping, maybe, to blemish slightly the reputation of a fellow I considered the perfect athlete.

John and Beth talked softly, heads together, for about ten minutes. Then John put a hand on my shoulder. "Look, Bob," he said. "I've worked all my life. I've always tried to do what was right. I never—believe me—never thought I would earn more than $25,000 a year in anything I did. I just can't believe these sums of money we're talking about here.

"But to tell you the truth, I love Boston. I love Red Auerbach and everything the Celtics stand for. I value my reputation. I value what I think is right. So my answer is this. Even if they offered me another two and a half million, I would stay with the Boston Celtics."

John's answer really didn't surprise me. But I was relieved that he did what I always thought he would. I guess I was brought up to believe in the good guy, the Jack Armstrong, All-American boy types. That's Havlicek: so rugged and straight-arrow and quiet-spoken, he seems to represent what we have come to think of as the great, corny old American values. As a matter of fact his voice actually sounds just like John Wayne's, which may explain his nickname, Hondo, the title of one of Wayne's best-known movies.

I've only seen Havlicek angry, really exercised, once, when a crude fan at Boston Gardens worked him over one night, heckling him with the kind of courage that comes from a six-pack of beer. After the game, John asked if I had heard the fan riding him. I had. John nodded. "I really got him good," he said.

I was fascinated. "Really? I didn't see it. What did you do?"

"I walked over to the box seats and I looked up at that guy . . . and I gave him a *dirty* look." He demonstrated by squinching his face. I had to cough back a laugh. That was Havlicek's idea of getting back at somebody.

There wasn't a happier fellow in Boston than Bob Woolf when John made his decision to stay. Red had acted with great courtesy throughout the meeting, and invited me to be at the press conference where John's signing would be announced. Red even introduced me. I was pleased when John stood and said that he always wanted his negotiations to be handled with dignity, and he thought these were. I glanced at Auerbach, but there was no expression on his pink, Teutonic face.

I remembered negotiating a contract once with Red, and calling to remind him about a clause we had agreed to include. "Dammit," he roared, "what do you want from me? My blood?" After three days my ears stopped ringing.

You can't dislike a man who is as consistent as Red Auerbach. In forty years as a player, coach and general manager, he has been one of the enduring legends of pro basketball. He is a genius, whose gruffness became part of his method. He operated on the theory that to get a pearl, you had to irritate the oyster. While he was a coach, his players seldom finished among the league's top ten scorers. Sam Jones once told me that if one of the Celtics was having too hot a night, Red would send in a sub and "rest" him. No one was bigger than the team.

It is never necessary to guess where you stand with Red. "What are you doing," he complained one day to Havlicek, "hanging around with a guy like Woolf?"

In his mild, civil way, John responded: "I want to pick my own friends, Red."

The passage of time will never mellow Auerbach. He just isn't a forgiving fellow. But I like Red, and he has been great for basketball. And so, by example, has John Havlicek, whose secret is simple. He always plays at a level close to his ability, and there is no conceit, no arrogance, in him. The fans sense this and they react to him, warmly. He has the open look of a man you can trust.

As a practical matter, lawyers should never get too close to their clients—especially athletes. The rule is that you take them to advise, not to raise. Yet I have never been able to remain uninvolved, which is partly the price one pays for being a sports freak. I count the friendship of John Havlicek as one of the fringe benefits of the business.

Every summer John invites us to vacation with them at his fishing cabin in Canada. He tries to tempt me with his description of the pastoral life: "It's all wilderness, Bob. No phones, no television, no noise. No one can bother you for a week." I always laugh. John Havlicek can survive that. He'd love it. I'd go nuts. I always tell him I'd never make it without a phone. I even have one in my car. My whole practice could go down the drain in a week.

It may seem strange, but wherever I go I find that Havlicek is the idol of many other star athletes. I'm constantly asked if he's all that he's cracked up to be. Maybe they can't believe that a man can perform at the pace John does, and live the way he does, and still be real. He's real. He only plays like he's superhuman!

6

Trial by Julie

———

IT HAS BEEN my experience that money, more even than sudden fame, or beautiful women, can spin a man's sense of values completely out of orbit. Protecting a client from that pitfall is often part of my job. The problem is that many athletes are not that eager to be protected.

They say that life is a lesson a day, and an important lesson for me began one day in the late spring of 1971, with a phone call from the basketball coach at the University of Massachusetts, a nice fellow, Jack Leaman. Jack was upset. He had just found out that the pros—that is, the ABA—were tampering with his most gifted player.

Julius Erving had just completed his junior year, and would not be eligible for the regular pro draft for another season. Jack Leaman had built not only his team around him, but his dream of transforming Massachusetts into a national power. Julius was the kind of talent coaches wait for all their lives.

"Bob, you've got to help me and Julius," pleaded Jack. "He has been contacted by the pros and he wants to listen. If you would, I want you to be his advisor. He doesn't want to sign, but he just wants to get an idea of what they have to offer."

I agreed to help, and I did so for reasons that went beyond my sympathy for a coach and a player he wanted so earnestly to keep. I just couldn't understand how the pros *could* flirt with Julius, even though some juniors—just a couple—had set a precedent before this by jumping. These were listed as "hardship cases," and involved conditions of poverty, so that in theory the player and his family would benefit from an early signing.

Julius Erving was not a hardship case. Jack Leaman assured me he came from a family that had always provided well for him, and Julius was such a nice young man that Leaman almost considered him a son.

The next day, the nice young man and I met for the first time at the Hartford, Connecticut, airport, a short drive from the UMass campus in Amherst. We flew together to Philadelphia and, on the flight, Julius began to fill me in.

He had been approached, he said, by an agent named Steve Arnold, very mod, very New York, who would become identified a few years later as one of the godfathers of the new World Football League. Arnold had gotten right to the point. "Would you be interested," he asked, "in playing pro basketball, *right away*, if I can line up a team to take you? I'll do it for ten percent of your contract."

Julius said he was interested. He was just "playing along."

Arnold had instantly made contact with the Virginia Squires and arranged for their owner, Earl Foreman, to meet secretly with Julius in Philadelphia—neutral turf halfway between Norfolk and Amherst. That night, Julius and I roomed together at a motel near the Philadelphia airport. We talked into the early hours, mostly about Julius and his family and the things he valued in life. I got the impression that this was a young man of strong character and warmth, just as his coach had pictured him.

Forgotten was a question Julius had asked me casually on the flight. He had read an article once, in which I was quoted as saying that a first-round draft choice should receive at least $100,000 a year. He asked if it was true. I said, yes, in the existing market, it was. He nodded, and gazed out the window, lost in thought.

The next morning we met with the Virginia people—Foreman, his general manager, Red Kerr, and the coach, Al Bianchi. Steve Arnold was also there. Their line was not untypical: "Listen, Julius, you had better take the money and run. There's going to be a merger of the leagues within three days and after that the money won't be there. If you go back to school and play as a senior, you'll lose out on the big dough. The merger is here, it's just around the corner, and that's going to knock out all the big bonuses and contracts."

This was pure con, and I told Julius so. But the Squires pressed on. For openers, they offered him $200,000 for three years, or roughly $67,000 per year. Julius seemed unimpressed. After an hour of negotiations, they increased their offer to $100,000 per year.

Well . . . you had to be there to believe it. It was as though Julius had been hypnotized. His eyes got as big as saucers. Once they said the magic words—"one hundred thousand a year"—Julius couldn't hear anything else, or see anything else. He was gone. Instead of just listening, as he had sworn he would, he was reaching for a pen. He wanted to sign right that moment.

I became panicky. My forehead felt damp. At that time it was scandalous to be involved in any deal in which a young player jumped from his college team to the pros. I could feel it getting out of hand. If he signed, how could I explain it to Jack Leaman? I was there to chaperone Julius on what had amounted to a coffee date. Now he was about to elope.

I asked for a recess and brought Julius into the room next door, where I had what now began to loom as my ace in the hole. Leaman, anticipating that Julius might need some additional moral support, had sent along his black assistant coach, Ray Wilson, and Julie's old high school coach. They were waiting for us.

"Julius," I said, locking the door behind me, "let me fill you in on a few things. First, there isn't going to be a merger.

That's baloney. Second, you'll get more money, a lot more, when you come out of school next year because the war will still be going on. You'll have both leagues chasing you."

I looked to the two coaches. They were in a state of shock themselves. They had never heard of such sums. They were torn by their loyalty—to sports, to their schools, to their jobs—and by their fear of advising Julius, unfairly, to turn down riches. "Would *you* turn it down, if it was you?" Julius kept asking.

"Man, I don't know," they kept saying, shaking their heads. There was a whole lot of shaking going on.

"Wait a minute," I said. I could feel a stampede coming on. I had to find a way to slow it down. His mother. That was it. "Julius," I said, "think of your mother. She wants you to finish school. She'll be crushed if you do this without consulting her. We ought to call your mother." I handed him the phone and he placed a call to New York.

A few minutes later, my ears strained, I waited for Mrs. Erving to react as her son repeated the terms of the contract. She paused. "Julius," she said, "you do whatever you think is best."

I put the phone down. I had one stroke left. "Look," I said, "let me get Walter Kennedy [commissioner of the NBA] on the phone right now. I'll prove to you there won't be a merger. You can ask him yourself."

I called Kennedy and quickly reviewed for him the events of the past twenty-four hours. I knew he would see it as more than just a case of one talented prospect who might go to the other league. It could have been the opening of another Pandora's box, the wholesale raiding of lower classmen and, in time, youngsters right out of high school. Where would it end?

Walter was alarmed enough to get on the phone with Julius. "There won't be any merger right away," Kennedy told him. "I'll guarantee that when you come out of school next year you'll be worth much more, with both leagues after you."

But Julius wasn't buying it—not me or the NBA commissioner or the old school ties. "Why don't we go back and talk it over with your coach?" I repeated for the dozenth time. "You promised him you would."

In his own mind he had already rationalized it. "Bob," he said, "I don't have anything left to accomplish at Massachusetts. I'm tired of playing against teams like Vermont and New Hampshire. I know I'm ready for the pros."

There was nothing else to say. I turned, and walked back into the room where the Virginia Squires waited to make Julius Erving a rich young man. We negotiated a little longer and, in the end, I was able to get him an even bigger offer—$125,000 a year for four years, a half-million-dollar package. This was cash. No Dolgoff plan. Even the fellows like Spencer Haywood and Ralph Simpson, who had been the first of the undergraduate jumpers, didn't get hard cash like this. I thought to myself, "I know superstars who aren't doing as well as this."

Although he had gone to Philadelphia insisting he wouldn't sign, that he wouldn't make a move until he had discussed it with his coach, Julius signed before we left the city. Up to the last instant, I tried to talk him out of it. "If you sign," I said, "you will have lost a little bit of character with everyone who knows you."

Julius looked at me as though I had spoken in some strange, alien tongue. Nothing could change his mind. He signed, and rose, and shook hands all around, a bright, smiling, loose-limbed, engaging young man. Not a care in the world. I was glad that I had insisted on one unusual clause in the contract. From experience, I knew that once a young athlete came into big money, he tended to develop amnesia where finishing college was concerned. To make that diploma look more inviting to Julius, I had the Squires agree to a $10,000 bonus clause, payable the day he graduated.

But in that static atmosphere that passes through a room when tension has been relieved, a bizarre thing happened. No sooner had Julius signed than Earl Foreman said to me: "I hope this kid is a helluva player. He is, isn't he, Bob?"

I shrugged. "I don't know, Earl. I've never seen him play."

"Geez, I've never seen him play either," Foreman continued. "How about you, Red? Is this kid that good?"

"Got me," said Kerr. "I haven't seen him. How about you, Al?" asked Red, passing the buck to his friend, Bianchi. "Never saw him . . . don't know anything about him," said Bianchi, as eyeballs began to swivel nervously.

However, I had reassured them at several points during the negotiation, by quoting a splendid source. "Bob Cousy," I kept telling them, "said Julius will be the best college basketball player in America next year."

A few months later, at the wedding of Terry Driscoll, who played for Cousy at Boston College, I went up to Cooz and told him I owed him some thanks.

"For what?" he asked.

"For saying that Julius Erving was the best college basketball player in the country. It made him a lot of money."

Cousy looked at me blankly. "I never said anything like that in my life," he snapped, and walked away.

I was dumfounded. I was certain I had read that quotation in the newspapers. Then the absurdity of it all struck me and I nearly laughed out loud. The Virginia Squires had paid a half million dollars to a player they had never seen, based in part on a quote that never existed. What more fascinating commentary on the current condition of professional sports could there be?

I'm not sure when it dawned on me that Julius Erving was no debutante. He had known what he was doing all along. It was a cute move, almost as flashy as the ones he would make so routinely on the court.

I have watched the times change in sports, and the players, and the morality. Now in the mid-'70s it is no longer socially disgraceful for an athlete to quit his school, and his team, and opt for the money, but only several years ago it was shocking.

The night we flew back to Amherst, I had mixed emotions, but I was on Erving's team. Even in a position not entirely to your taste, it is easy for a lawyer to get caught up in the spirit of a contract negotiation. It excites him, the way closing a big deal excites a salesman. Julius and I had brought off a big one, and there was no point now in lecturing him. We talked about his future. I was no longer uneasy about facing Jack Leaman. I had called from Philadelphia, had broken the news, and was on my way now to spend the night in his home. Jack understood. He didn't blame anyone. But as we sat in his living room, his wife and a few close friends around us, it was as though someone had died. Jack Leaman had lost his basketball team.

I continued to represent Julius. I went to Norfolk with him for his press debut with the Squires. His mother and sister were there. I remember feeling secure about his future. Julius Erving was in control. They were going to love him in Virginia, this handsome black man with the oddly elegant name.

He called two or three times a week to ask my advice on the little problems that come with new money: What kind of car to buy? How big an apartment? Can he get a deal somewhere on clothes? On the court he was an immediate sensation. And he kept getting better. The writers were running out of extravagant things to say about him. It looked as though they would have to invent a new league.

Then, by the middle of his rookie season, I heard a rumor that he was dissatisfied with his contract. I was surprised. All the times we talked, he had never indicated the slightest discontent. Finally, I asked him about it.

"That's right," he said, airily. "I'm unhappy with the deal. I'm a superstar now. I should be getting more money. I met a friend who told me he could renegotiate the contract [with Virginia] and get me much more money. He says I'm being cheated. Would you talk to them about a new contract?"

I was stunned and I told Julius so. "There isn't any way that Virginia is going to renegotiate," I said, loudly, "and there is no way I'm going to ask them to do it. They made the deal in good faith. They've done everything they said they would. You get your check every week. What if you had gone down there and were terrible? Would you tell them to take $10,000 from your salary because you weren't as good as they thought? Remember, they didn't even know who the hell you were when they signed you."

Julius responded by telling me that Earl Foreman was worth $40 million. He had just gotten this news bulletin, which was absurd, from his new friend, who turned out to be Irwin Weiner, a New York agent who represented a number of NBA players, including Walt Frazier. Weiner had convinced him he could pull it off.

I learned long ago that, in matters relating to money, most athletes will believe anything. At such times, trying to get them to recognize the truth is like trying to untangle a hopelessly tangled fishing line.

"But, Bob," Julius was assuring me, "I still want you to handle my money and my personal affairs for me."

I gave up. "Okay," I said, "if this agent says he can get you a new contract, let him try. I won't. And I don't think he can. But, for God's sake, don't let him try to negotiate with the NBA for you. You'll just be getting into deeper trouble."

He gave me his word that this was strictly with Virginia. Naturally, the Squires never rewrote a sentence of their original contract. Meanwhile, Julius continued to use me as his attorney and, in a way curious to sport, even among those who disagree, we remained loyal to each other. For a bit longer. Julius visited my beach home in Florida with a ladyfriend. They used my car, had the run of the place.

Unbeknownst to me, while Julius was being entertained by my family, his new agent was in Atlanta working out a deal with the Hawks to have Erving jump to the NBA. Atlanta signed him to a five-year contract for more money. But there was one minor item. They didn't own the rights to him. Milwaukee owned the NBA rights to the player they were now calling the Fabulous Dr. J.

All of which plunged Julius into one of the great legal muddles of recent sports history, with three different court suits involved. All these fancy moves would send him shuttling between the basketball court and the Federal Court of Arbitration. And he got himself a distinguished attorney—Louis Nizer —to get him out of it.

Nizer's reputation had been made in fields somewhat more formidable than sports. He had tried landmark libel cases, represented some famous movie names in Hollywood's gaudiest era, and written several best-selling books.

The hearing was held in New York City in the summer of 1973, before the esteemed Robert Morgenthau. Originally, the arbitrator was to have been a gentleman named Archibald Cox, but other pressing matters arose in Washington during that time to occupy his attention. It developed that Messrs. Erving and Nizer were trying to build their case around the contention that Julius was really hoodwinked when he signed his original contract with Virginia.

Erving's claim was that Robert G. Woolf had not actually represented him, which was quite a revelation to me. His story was that Steve Arnold, the agent, had negotiated his contract for him, which was improper, inasmuch as Arnold worked for the American Basketball Association and didn't have Erving's best interests at heart. I doubt that Arnold ever claimed he did. But the business about his negotiating the contract was outright nonsense.

Two things surprised me about the hearing. First, on the basis of Erving's contentions, I *had* to be the key witness. Yet, I wasn't called until nearly the last. Second, Nizer neglected to talk to me beforehand, to hear my side of the story. He just accepted, as true, what Erving had told him.

Louis Nizer is a dapper man, short, rugged, wavy gray hair, a cultured voice. Flanked by one of his assistants, he sat across from me, idly sketching my likeness on a notepad even as I answered his questions. I was impressed with his talent as an artist. But I had begun to suspect that the drama of the case did not exactly overwhelm him.

Still, he was a young lawyer's hero, and the idea of being

questioned by Louis Nizer pleased me. A copy of his best-known book, *My Life in Court,* was on one of the shelves in my office.

"Now, Mr. Woolf," he said, his head bent over his sketch, "isn't it true that Steve Arnold did, in fact, negotiate this contract? And didn't Julius rely primarily on his, Mr. Arnold's advice, and were you not there to lend moral support to Mr. Erving?"

"No, Mr. Nizer," I said, evenly, "it is not true."

I went on to testify as to what actually had happened, just as I have explained it here. I cannot find the words to describe his reaction. His face froze. His eyes were startled, briefly. But being the skilled attorney he is, he just went coolly along in his cross-examination, continuing to sketch my picture on the pad in front of him, as he often does with witnesses in court.

What I had found offensive about the whole proceeding was the fact that Erving, and his agent, had set out to find a loophole. They seemed to have no respect for a legally drawn contract. I was a little surprised to find that Nizer's office would be involved.

When the hearing ended that day we walked out of the building together. "Bob," Nizer said, politely, "I find your testimony very disturbing." I replied that what I had testified was what *did* happen.

We stood at the curb, in the clear sunlight, trying to signal one of the cabs hurtling down Fifth Avenue. "Well," Nizer sniffed, "I didn't expect you to go out of your way to hurt my case."

A cab swung to a stop in front of us and Nizer opened the door. For a moment I thought he might invite me to share a ride. He didn't. He handed me the sketch, said, "See you later," and I stood there, watching the cab disappear in traffic. I glanced at the sketch. He had autographed it.

It came as no surprise to me when the case was settled out of court the next day. Virginia traded Erving to the New York Nets who, in turn, paid off Virginia, plus Atlanta, to make it all work.

The Nets clearly felt he was worth the price. Julius grew up practically around the corner from their arena. He was a cinch to captivate the fans and press of New York, just as surely as he was destined to become one of basketball's dominant figures.

The reality of sport—and life—is that we continually make allowances for those who have extraordinary talent. Julius really wanted two things, in this order: money and to play in the NBA. By waiting one more year, and doing the right thing, he could have had both. The ABA's big pitch had been merger. Four years later it still hadn't come.

The following season the money offered top draft choices had doubled, and he could have obtained a contract easily the equal of Atlanta's, without demeaning himself. The gag around New York at the time of the trial went like this: "Did you hear about the new Julius Erving doll? Wind it up and it signs another contract."

I don't believe I would want to go through life with an imaginary key in my back.

Sad to say, the owners are as guilty as the Julius Ervings. If they didn't go along with such moves, the contract jumpers would in time run out of places to land. These deals breed mistrust, even among teams in the same league. I found this was so with Julius when I later talked with Lou Carnesecca, who had coached the Nets.

"Before he ever went to the Squires," Lou told me, "Julius asked if I could get him to New York. I told him no. I wasn't touching any underclassmen. It was against the rules of the league. Next thing I know, Virginia has him.

"That's why, when Jim Chones [of Marquette] came along the next year, we grabbed him. We didn't wait. If that's the way the other guys were going to play it, we were going to have to operate the same way." Walter Kennedy's fears came true when, in 1974, the Utah team of the ABA signed a phenomenon named Moses Malone out of high school.

You trace the path of Julius Erving, and you find that he has rearranged the philosophies of most of those who came in contact with him. I wish him well, but I have no regrets that he is no longer a client of mine.

The irony of it is that, up to this point, Julius is ahead of the game. Whatever moral judgments one might make, the cold fact is that Julius Erving hasn't suffered for his actions. I follow his career and I look for growth. You can't dislike him.

I saw Julius in Providence in the fall of 1974, at a preseason ABA exhibition game. He had recently married Turquoise Brown, and he had a son, Julius Winfield Erving III. He was polite and friendly and we chatted about our families. In the stands around him were his former coaches, Jack Leaman and Ray Wilson, and a dozen players from that year's Massachusetts team. They were proud of Julius and they gloried in his success.

As expected, he became a superstar in New York and the darling of the fans. Time is in his favor. He has matured, visibly, and there is hope for his generation of young athletes, many who have been so easily swayed, so quick to forsake whatever values they have, or profess to have.

I bear him no grudge. And if Julius reads this, it would be a nice gesture on his part if he finally mailed me a check for the fee he agreed to pay me three years ago.

7

A Team for Big John

———

JOHN MATUSZAK IS ONE of those born athletes who, in an earlier time, might have modeled for Greek sculptors. A mountain of a man at 6–8 and 290, he has a bouquet of wiry brown hair—a kind of caucasian Afro—a 53-inch chest, 34-inch waist and palms like catcher's mitts. He is an awesome human being.

John has a colorful personality to go with this incredible torso and when he shakes your hand you tend to lose all the feeling on the right side of your body. It may not be stretching the truth to say that Matuszak—pronounced ma-TOO-zak—was the most interesting negotiation the Houston Oilers ever had. In fact, he may have been their two most interesting negotiations!

To set the scene for the saga of Big John, and my own involvement, I have to go back to the birth of the American Football League. That's really where it all began, the boom in pro sports, the era of quick riches, the need for player representatives to negotiate contracts for players like John Matuszak.

When one looks back, it isn't necessary to wonder how it all came about. You only need to wonder what would have happened if the National Football League had said "yes" to a modest Texan—a contradiction in terms—named Lamar Hunt.

In 1958, Hunt was a young man of twenty-eight who had an incurable yen to own a pro football team. He had the money to buy a team, or a whole league; his father, H. L. Hunt, was one of the richest men in the world. But when the NFL, by now conservative and clubby, said, "Don't call us, we'll call you," Lamar wouldn't be put off. He started his own league, the American Football League, and touched off a revolution that would change the geography as well as the complexion of professional sports.

In time, the AFL begat the American Basketball Association, which begat the World Hockey Association. Along came the World Football League and not one but two American pro soccer leagues.

Those new leagues, the expansion that followed and the television treasure hunt they inspired turned sports in this country upside down. In 1960, no player in pro basketball earned as much as $50,000 a year. By 1975, a total of ninety made $100,000 or more and the average salary in the NBA was a staggering $92,000 a year.

In 1960, the highest paid player in the NFL didn't make $30,000. In 1968, Joe Kapp, hardly the most talented player in the league, signed a contract with the Boston Patriots for $200,000 a year.

So how did it all happen, and why? The answer is simple and complex: a chain reaction coupled with an inordinate amount of television exposure.

The AFL threatened the entrenched position of a major sports league for the first time in modern history, and triggered salary wars—which would inflate prices in every area of sports in the years following. To gain parity, the AFL had to start grabbing its share of the top college talent. It did so with dollars. To retaliate, the NFL had to come up with more dollars of its own.

For years the two leagues fought a bitter financial war until they had to call a halt, or bankrupt the sport. Thus, the pro football merger of 1966.

But the doors were opened. In due course the ABA would come along to drive basketball salaries out of sight. And, in 1972, it was the World Hockey Association doing the same in that sport. Concurrently, baseball was pulled into the act because the stars in that game saw what was happening to salaries elsewhere.

Meanwhile, television was gambling multimillions that the national appetite for sports couldn't be sated. By 1974, each pro-football team was guaranteed $1.7 million by television networks. A year later, major league baseball signed a four-year package worth $93 million.

So now the athletes were demanding a fairer share of what they saw as the rich new markets for their skill and muscle. And expansion, with the stocking of new teams, made high living available to more athletes than ever before.

A ballplayer making low wages didn't need an attorney, business manager or agent. When he started making $100,000 per year, he realized that it was time to seek professional advice. Little had been done in sports in this area when I started, and I actually coined the phrase "sports attorney" to describe my work. The sports representative has had a tremendous influence on sports in this country over the past decade.

I, and others like me, got involved because there was a need —a need created by the times. The necessary ingredients—the perfect blend of new leagues, expansion of old leagues and television saturation—combined to spawn the six-figure player contract. The tax ramifications alone of these types of contracts would certainly warrant obtaining professional help. Also, the athlete of today is far more sophisticated and concerned with his future than his predecessors were.

Just as it is in any professional endeavor, experience is invaluable to a sports representative. His basic charge is to establish a fair market value for his client, and the only way to know for sure what he's worth is by comparison to others like him.

At the beginning of my career, I developed a reputation around sports as an expert on tax laws. It was undeserved. I certainly wasn't the expert—just someone smart enough to consult those who were, and learn everything I could about taxes and how they affected athletes. But, because of this reputation, I found myself barraged with phone calls from athletes all over the country, whom I didn't know and didn't represent, seeking my advice. In going over their individual situations, I gained a virtually complete picture of the salary structure of every team in every sport.

Once armed with this information, I was ready for the inevitable battles that would ensue. I have found that I am sometimes able to avoid battles by not becoming actively engaged in the negotiations but by advising the athlete before-hand what he should be receiving in his contract. I advise this method when I am aware of a particularly close relationship between the player and his management. The final result of the contract is far more important than my becoming directly involved. Often management doesn't even realize that I *am* involved. Ninety percent of the contracts I negotiate are done routinely, with no problem. But the ones that spring a leak, that develop into hassles, are the ones that stir the blood and make the news.

Which brings us back to the case of John Matuszak versus Sid Gillman (and the Houston Oilers), which is really two stories.

The first began to unfold with a letter from Sid Gillman that arrived on my desk in the spring of 1973. He was then the general manager of the Oilers, later to become their coach, relieving a stumbling Bill Peterson at midseason. A few words about Sid Gillman, one of the geniuses of football, an absolutely tireless worker who practically invented the passing game still in vogue in the 1970s. He has full cheeks and a jutting jaw and there is a leonine quality about him. You get the feeling that Sid could be charming if he had the time, but he never had the time, not in Los Angeles or San Diego or Houston, because he was too busy trying to win football games.

Whenever he coached, his players complained that Sid didn't understand them. What he didn't understand was losing. He had no use for it, or for phony sentiment. Once, against the New York Jets, Sid made a pitch for the sportsmanship award by going for a two-point conversion, late in a game the Chargers won, 53–7. "In Sid Gillman," the owner of the Jets, Sonny Werblin, grumbled later, "the milk of human kindness has turned to yogurt."

When it came to negotiating a contract, Sid relied on fundamentals in his attack—the old power play. No tricks or gimmicks. Just your basic bread and butter wedge. He tipped his game plan in that direct first letter. The Oilers were offering a package worth a little better than half of what I had determined was Matuszak's true market value. Gillman also informed me, in the letter, that this was his *first, best* and *final* offer. For a top draft pick, they weren't exactly offering the riches of Persia.

Gillman had earned the reputation of a tough negotiator at San Diego, where money was tight and he had to balance the jobs of coach and general manager. That's always a risky act, on the one hand needing the loyalty of your players and on the other trying to hold the salary line.

Gillman's letter did not surprise me. Gillman's reputation in such matters was legendary. Having anticipated Gillman's move, I was prepared to shift into my basic defense. I would try to disarm him by going to my files for the contracts that were pertinent to the negotiation that would follow, packing them in my attaché case, and then making a personal presentation. I had found, while handling some 700 contracts over the preceding five years, that approach rarely failed. It worked simply because what most general managers want is a fair break. Just as I don't want any athlete I represent to wind up on the short end, they don't want their client—the owner—to get stuck, either. But sometimes a sports representative, by virtue of his exposure and research, has a better idea of the market than the men who are paying the wages. I've had to educate more than one general manager as to the wage scale in his own league. There is less communication between sports executives than one might think, partly owing to caution about the antitrust laws. These laws restrict monopolistic practices such as price fixing and conspiracy.

So I looked on my assignment primarily as the task of exposing Sid Gillman to the facts. The year before I had worked out Walt Patulski's contract with the Buffalo Bills. A Notre Dame product, Walt was the first pick in the nation, and also a defensive lineman, exactly the same position Matuszak was in now. Walt had signed for a third more than the Oilers had described as their "final offer." I was disinclined to let Matuszak sign for less.

A contract negotiation is part mood and part ritual. All you hope for at the first go-round is a fair hearing and some mutual trust. Once in a while you get a nice surprise. One such instance occurred when I met with Weeb Ewbank, then doubling as coach and general manager of the New York Jets, on behalf of Burgess Owens, a safety out of Miami, the Jets' first choice in the 1973 draft. I was apprehensive. The Jets were famous for putting their first-round picks through marathon sessions.

However, after two or three chats and then four hours with Weeb, we had it all wrapped. An owlish figure on the sidelines, flapping his arms at an official who had wronged him, Weeb in private had a kind of Edmund Gwenn gentleness. All he wanted was a contract that was fair—not enough to make Owens complacent, but enough to make him eager to report and become part of the team. Weeb was a realist. We settled for $35,000 more than his original offer.

I don't know that I have ever had a higher compliment than he paid me at the press conference later. Weeb told the New York writers that it had been a smooth negotiation, because

Owens "had a professional" on his side. He was making a point. Weeb was still burning because, the year before, the Jets' first draft pick, Jerome Barkum, the tight end, had cost himself a starting position when he held out and missed vital time in training camp. Weeb felt Barkum had been badly served by his advisors.

Not only does a holdout damage his chances of winning a regular job, but animosity is created on both sides. Management is disenchanted because he missed work. The player is unhappy because he thinks he is getting a raw deal.

A player holds out because of bad information or a lack of it. Nine times out of ten, he is represented by an agent who doesn't know his client's fair value. Thus, when he can't deliver what he has promised in order to persuade the athlete to sign with him in the first place, the agent throws the blame on the team.

"They're cheap," is his usual response. "They're cheating you." So even when the player does sign, and he hasn't received what his agent said he would, he feels he has been robbed—which is a poor way to start out with any new employer.

Such an attitude precipitated the Duane Thomas affair in Dallas and similarly almost happened with Raymond Chester in Oakland. Both were first-round draft choices who signed for less than they should have. I'm not faulting either the Dallas or Oakland management, because if they can sign their talent for less than it's worth, good luck to them. Football is a business, and from his viewpoint the general manager is doing the best job he can for his employer.

Thomas went on to have a super year with the Cowboys, but the bitterness festered in him when he came up to his second season, earning just $20,000, up $2,000 from his rookie year. The mistake he made was to pop off in the newspapers about it and portray the Cowboys as skinflints and racists. The relationship between player and team was poisoned—a great career apparently ruined.

Ray Chester was the rookie of the year that same season, and had signed for the same type of deal with Oakland. When he arrived with the team in Boston that next season to play against the Patriots in the opener, he phoned and asked for my advice.

I listened to his story and told him: "Raymond, don't try to renegotiate the contract. You signed it in good faith. You agreed to the terms. Don't go back on your word. When the time comes for a new contract, the Raiders will have to make it up to you. I will suggest, though, that in a very nice and light way, you talk to Al Davis about your feelings and maybe he'll do something immediately."

Davis has been through all the jumps. One of the shrewdest men in sports, he went from unemployed assistant coach—fired at USC in a recruiting flap—to commissioner of the American Football League in something like seven years. He had returned to Oakland as the team's managing general partner. Davis always has a look about him that suggests he has slipped an egg into your pocket, but he has a sense of fairness.

Chester handled it as the gentleman he is. He went to Davis without threats or anger, and Al told him: "We can straighten this thing out right now."

Sometimes it happens that way. Sometimes logic prevails. But I understood right away that with Sid Gillman, I was going to need more than a smile and a nice philosophy. It wasn't just that Gillman bargained hard. He was a moralist. He believed that easy money was bad for discipline. In some ways— for one who was criticized so often as insensitive—his manners were almost courtly. He once booted Ernie Ladd, the brute of a tackle, from his San Diego training camp, for insulting a waitress.

As a follow-up to his letter, I phoned Houston to arrange a meeting. "Sid," I said, brightly, "I got your letter and I'd like to come down and talk about it."

"What's there to talk about?"

I laughed, an uncertain laugh. "Well, Sid, I have great respect for you and your background, but I'd just like to bring you up to date on some of the things I've done with the other fellows in the draft this year."

"I don't talk on the phone."

"Well, Sid, what should I do?"

"Just bring the young man down and we'll sign him."

"Sid, I couldn't recommend that."

We hung up, as awkwardly as though it had been a wrong number, which in a way it had been. Gillman's position was certainly a switch. With all the other top draft choices I had represented over the years, the team had always been in a rush to get them signed. Now Sid acted as if he didn't give a damn.

Two months went by and nothing happened. Then I received a letter telling me that I was to be honored, along with such notables as Red Auerbach, Nat Holman, Dolph Schayes and, yes, Sidney Gillman, by the State of Israel at a dinner in Boston. Perfect, I thought. I'd meet with Sid in a convivial atmosphere and get this contest settled. I called his office and left word with his secretary that I would be happy to pick him up at the airport. The word came back: "Don't bother."

At the banquet, I sat beside Gillman and told him at one point: "I'm sure that if we just got together for a couple of hours we could accomplish a lot on Matuszak."

I almost fell off my chair when Sid said, "I haven't got the time."

I knew he had a creative mind but this type of offense had me blitzed. So I sat tight, because, quite simply, I didn't know what to do. In the end, this proved to be my best counterattack. Good breaks often reward patience.

So about six weeks later I found myself in Canada, completing a contract for Mickey Redmond of the Detroit Red Wings. The annual National Hockey League meetings were going on at the same time. At a press conference for Redmond, one of the writers asked me how I was making out with Matuszak. I told him, frankly, that nothing had been done and we were experiencing some problems.

One hour later I received an "emergency" phone call, which pulled me out of a meeting. It was John Bassett, then the owner of the Toronto Team in the Canadian Football League, whose son was later to become affiliated with the WFL. Quickly he got to the point: "Would your fellow be interested in playing up here? We have the rights to him in Canada and we'd love to get him."

I told Bassett I thought Matuszak would listen to any legitimate offer. The next morning I reached John in Tampa, and within twenty-four hours he was flying to Toronto. His arrival was treated as a major event by the newspapers, and photographs of the two of us strolling the downtown streets of Toronto moved through the wire services. The picture was carried throughout the country and appeared prominently in Houston newspapers the next day.

By the time I returned to my office in Boston, Sid Gillman was on the phone. The sudden warmth in his voice was like sunshine flooding a window. "Bobby," he said, "this is Sid. Why haven't we heard from you? We've got to get together. Why don't you come on down as soon as it's convenient, and we'll get this business settled?"

Now, this was the same man who had been ball controlling me for months without any sign of cracking. But, like any experienced coach, Sid knows—when its fourth and eight, punt. Once I reached Houston we needed less than a day to come to terms. When it was over, as I was packing my briefcase, I said, "Sid, may I ask you something? Why did you put me through all of that?"

He grinned. "I send out fifty contracts every year," he said. "It works eight or nine times. I thought it was worth the shot."

Gillman fascinated me because he represented a type. Auerbach, Lombardi, Paul Brown, Bear Bryant, Woody Hayes, Gene Mauch and John Wooden, like Gillman, belong to a category of coaches who had almost no life off the field or court or diamond. Winning was their obsession, and obsessions had defined them as men and coaches.

A member of his staff once told me how Gillman spent six weeks, while his coaches were scouting the colleges one spring, editing 200 hours of game footage into training films. He had broken it down into categories—techniques of blocking, deep pass coverage, short pass coverage, the kicking game—all to help his assistants teach the areas in which they worked.

He edited, separated, labeled and organized the films in boxes, the kind that sets of dishes are packed in. The night before his coaches were due to return, he moved the boxes into the hallway, to make room for the staff meeting he would hold in his office the next morning.

And overnight, the janitor picked up the boxes, hauled them off, and *burned* each and every one. When the assistants checked in, they were greeted by a raging Sid Gillman. But he wasn't mad at the bungling janitor, who had done this idiot thing, but at the fact that the film couldn't be *replaced*. There was no doubt in the minds of his coaches that if Sid could have located the same 200 hours of game footage, he would have sat down and started the whole process all over again.

As a teacher of the technical arts, there was no one more respected in all of professional football.

Matuszak had a so-so rookie season although he was a starter. By the time the 1974 season was approaching, it became obvious that he would not be happy playing for Gillman again. Houston had become the cellar of the NFL, with two wins in thirty games. As the '74 training camps opened, the veterans were outside the fence, on the picket lines, striking for what they called freedom issues. Gillman was in a hurry to get the Oiler mess cleaned up, and he considered the player strike a conspiracy to keep him from it. Ed Garvey, the head of the players' union, had presented the owners with sixty-seven demands. Gillman was livid.

John Matuszak, a young man who wears his heart on his sleeve, is quick to choose sides. When the strike was being considered, John lobbied for it among his fellow players in Houston. One night he invited his teammate and friend, Steve Kiner, over to his apartment for dinner. I knew Kiner as a former client and free spirit.

John had prepared the table, served his guest a dinner of veal scallopine with spaghetti. As he settled into his own chair, John looked up and continued a conversation that had been in progress from the moment Kiner entered the room. "Steve," he said, earnestly, "we've got to do it. We've got to strike. You're with us, aren't you, man? You're going to stay out, right?"

Kiner's fork was in mid-air. Without looking up he said, "No, John, I'm not. I'm going in. I think that's best for me."

Without another word, Matuszak rose, reached across the table, picked up Kiner's plate and carried it to the sink. Steve finished what was on his fork, dabbed his chin with his napkin, pushed back his chair and left. The dinner was over.

It isn't hard to see how the momentum develops in such disputes. Suddenly, personal issues become general ones. Language becomes more emotional: rules become not only unreasonable, but an affront to human dignity; teammates aren't cut or released, they are *purged*; the coach becomes a tyrant, a despot.

Big John felt patronized and stifled, victimized by rules from which he had no appeal.

And then along came the World Football League, in a single breath making sympathetic statements about the players' struggle for dignity and mentioning colossal sums of money.

The '74 preseason schedule had just gotten underway, the veterans having trooped cheerlessly back into camp, when Matuszak telephoned me at my office. It was the last week in August. It was, I thought, a kind of courtesy call. I asked how things were going in camp. "Swell." Any problems with Sid? "No."

Near the end of the conversation, John asked me to forward to him whatever funds we had banked and invested for him. It amounted to around $30,000. He said he thought it was time he learned to manage his own money. That struck me as a fine ambition, and within a few days his check was in the mail.

The next thing I knew, John had left the Oilers for the crosstown Houston Texans in the WFL. It was a full week before

I heard from him directly. I was getting it all secondhand, how John had worked out on a Monday with the Oilers, slipped off with his helmet and shoulder pads, had his helmet repainted the next day in Texan colors—they had no headgear to fit him —and appeared on the field at the Astrodome Wednesday night with his new team. After one series of downs, he was banished to the bench by a court order. The Texans' defense, none too strong to begin with, had no plan for stopping process servers.

Big John accepted the court order on the sideline, a bemused expression on his face, like the recipient of a gag gift at a stag party. The crowd, what there was of it, maybe 8,000, hooted at this historic ceremony.

Nothing like it had ever happened in the modern history of sports. No athlete had ever jumped leagues and, two days apart, played for two different teams in the same town. Pro football had become one big fruitcake.

I began to understand it a little better when I heard that John had acquired a new agent; Bob Woolf was still his lawyer, he assured everyone, but he had an agent now to advise him on certain enterprises.

The fellow was named Gary Caposta, a twenty-four-year-old commodities broker who lived in the same apartment complex as John, lifted weights with him, and who had made characteristic promises to make him rich, enticing him with offers to help him win the heavyweight boxing title.

His new employer, Steve Arnold, the founder of the franchise and a longtime player agent himself, and the WFL office kept issuing statements that John did not have a valid contract with the Oilers. They indicated that through their own legal wizardry, they had found a loophole that would allow John to escape.

I was astonished, perplexed and angry. There was nothing irregular about his contract and the Oilers had fulfilled every obligation. Instinctively, I felt bad for John, as though he were a nice neighbor kid who had dropped out of school and run off with the circus. They were going to make a test case of him, with little concern for the risk to his career. They were telling him, "We'll fight it to the end, John," when in truth he was the only one who could lose.

It was a desperate step by people who knew their boat was about to capsize. You could almost feel sorry for Steve Arnold. While the other WFL promoters were bailing out, Arnold got stuck with the Houston franchise. He couldn't unload it. Now he was promising, at least publicizing, a contract reportedly worth one million dollars to Matuszak. It was their last gamble to excite the fans, and, more importantly, stir up new investors.

John wasn't so naive. He knew he was being used but, for reasons of his own, he really didn't mind. He had convinced himself that he had been treated callously by Gillman and the Oilers; he rather enjoyed the attention and, maybe, the Texans might actually deliver.

It was later revealed in court that he had signed a contract with the Texans for five years at $50,000 a year. He was to be paid his Oiler salary of $40,000, in full, if court action prevented him from playing during the 1974 season. The Texans also waved a kind of Dolgoff plan at him that was supposed to return hundreds of thousands of dollars to him in his retirement.

Meanwhile, John was making pompous public utterances. After a preliminary court hearing, he faced the television cameras and announced, "I have faith in our judicial system."

And, sure enough, the Texans had found no loophole in his contract. They were attacking the standard NFL contract as unfair and one-sided, since Big John, at the time he signed it, had no other choice of employment except to play in Canada.

At the pretrial hearing, the attorneys for the Texans led Matuszak through his testimony. Why, they asked, had he finally signed with the NFL? "I love my country," he said, adding in a touching afterthought, "The home of the free and the land of the brave." That was designed to remove any doubt as to which country he meant.

I remembered our quick visit to Toronto and almost choked. Still, I felt vindicated when the Texans built their case not on the contract but on general grounds, a possibility Steve Arnold had vigorously denied.

But I was taking none of this lightly. The case still had to be heard by a state court, with a ruling favorable to the WFL still possible. The ramifications for all of professional sports were frightening. If the NFL's standard contract was ruled invalid, it could have led to every athlete in every sport becoming a free agent. The panic in sports would have been like the U.S. departure from Saigon.

To argue the case, the WFL had retained a prestigious Houston law firm, Fulbright, Crooker, in which Leon Jaworski had been a partner (and would be again). A lawyer in their office, Tom McDade, who was preparing the case, told me flatly he thought they would win. McDade was no rookie. He had won an earlier case for the WFL against the Dallas Cowboys, who wished to restrain the WFL from signing their players. He had also been involved in suits in hockey and basketball.

The circumstances of Matuszak's leap had made the whole episode seem like a farce, and not many people were taking the legal action seriously. But it worried me. In October I saw Pete Rozelle in Miami. I said, "Pete, I think you know I had nothing to do with Matuszak jumping. I'm going to do whatever I can, whatever is right, to get him back into football, and back in the NFL."

Not long after that I was with Upton Bell, son of the late NFL commissioner, who had recently been assigned the WFL's Charlotte franchise. He braced me on Matuszak. "What the hell is this guy doing?" Bell demanded. "Is he nuts? He could wreck the whole sport." And this was an executive with the World Football League.

Meanwhile Matuszak, restless to be back in a uniform, saw the WFL beginning to flounder and knew he had to make his peace with the Oilers or the NFL. He finally summoned enough courage to ask me to get him back. He still thought the lawyers for the WFL might win his case. Moreover, he saw himself as a figure of history and, even better, possibly a free agent who might make a new and better deal.

John had not yet seen one cent of the Texans' money, nor, I was convinced, would he. I was also convinced that his career was about to go down the drain and he was unaware of it.

Now the NFL trading deadline was coming up, on a Tuesday, and Sid Gillman predictably had gone on record as saying he wouldn't have Matuszak on his team. If he wasn't traded by Tuesday—less than a week—he was through. And I couldn't blame Gillman.

The lines were clearly drawn, so I went back on the phone with half a dozen teams, always checking back with Gillman between calls. I was maneuvering to find a team for John, a team that wanted a 6–8 defensive tackle with potential and hadn't been turned off by his instincts toward martyrdom. Some of the teams wanted to know what was going on. Others asked if he needed psychiatric help. All of them wanted assurance he would play.

Since the Oilers had written him off, and Sid had consented, more or less, to letting me help find a deal, none of this could be construed as tampering. Of course, teams do tamper. It's illegal, but so is adultery, which is why it's so unpopular.

Kansas City and coach Hank Stram emerged as the team with the strongest interest, but they wavered. The Chiefs were afraid of the litigation still pending. I tried to be honest with John, to let him wait for his court ruling even though I didn't want him to win it. But now time had run out. The trading deadline was on us and I told him if he wanted to play in 1974, he had to make his move now.

As it happened, I was lucky. He had tried that week to collect some of his money from the Texans, hadn't been able to get it, and had run out of illusions. "To hell with it," he said, "I'll go to Kansas City."

Now a strange thing happened. With the trade set, Bud Adams, the owner of the Oilers, suddenly decided that it wouldn't go through until Matuszak agreed to pay the Oilers

$10,000 for legal fees and mental anguish. Adams felt he was entitled to recover what John had cost him, but it wasn't merely cheapness. It was partly revenge for all the grief John had caused.

Sid Gillman, who was instructed by Adams to negotiate this point, had a fit. The Oilers had a chance to swap a nonplaying headache for Curley Culp, one of the league's most respected tackles (who had signed a future contract with the WFL), and a first-round draft pick in '75. And Adams was willing to sink it for $10,000, which doesn't even cover the cost of aspirin in sports today.

Somehow, Gillman talked him out of it and the deal was made. It turned the Oilers around. Culp made their three-man front click, and they went on to a 7–7 season, including a win over the Super Bowl champion Pittsburgh Steelers. Sid Gillman was the American Football Conference's coach of the year.

Five days after the trade, a district court in Texas ruled against the WFL, the Texans and Matuszak by a vote of 2 to 1.

The Chiefs paid John a full salary for a half season's work. It was a losing and bitter season for the Chiefs, resulting in the firing of Hank Stram, the only coach they had ever known.

But in Houston, after the season, all was not well. Sid Gillman and Bud Adams parted company by "mutual agreement," after Adams had accused his general manager of overspending and ignoring the budget, which you certainly couldn't prove by *my* negotiations with him. Adams also said that Gillman wouldn't talk to him, and there was no communication, except when one of Bud's well-meaning friends dropped by to say that Sid had called Adams "a fat Indian." It's an unlikely story. Gillman has never been one to deliver insults through third parties.

I later heard that their first clash over money came when Gillman spent $25,000 on a fence to enclose the team's practice field. Sid said he was tired of hearing the wail of the sirens as the trucks pulled out of the fire station across the street, and having the five o'clock traffic circle the block, with people leaning out of their car windows and shouting, "Screw the Oilers."

When I closed the files on the Matuszak case, I found that Gillman was gone, Stram was gone, the Houston Texans had left town and the World Football League was bleeding from many wounds. The only survivor was, in fact, John Matuszak, who had broken a contract, jumped his team and come out a winner. I keep thinking there must be a message in that, somewhere. But I hope not.

8

Caught in the Draft

———

I PULLED into the driveway late one summer evening in 1973, near midnight, having taken the family to a movie, and discovered a *body* on my doorstep.

Closer examination revealed that the body was Calvin Murphy, curled up in the fetal position, sound asleep.

But I'm getting ahead of myself. For the moment, let us leave aside the question of what he was doing there, unconscious, outside my door. One way or another, Calvin Murphy, the world's smallest living professional basketball player and reformed baton twirler, captured your attention.

He was a senior at Niagara College when we first met. I had been hearing about him for weeks from John Havlicek, who had hired Murphy as an instructor at his basketball camp outside of Boston, the summer of 1969. As a sophomore and junior, he had finished second to Pete Maravich of LSU among the nation's scorers. "Bob," said Hondo, "you ought to drive out and meet this kid. You won't believe him."

What I saw was a warm, animated young man whose voice, in moments of excitement, would rise into a squeak. I also recognized the competitive instincts of one who had spent a young lifetime proving his worth. Little did I realize he would provide my first experience with the deceptions of the pro draft system. He was 5 feet 9 inches tall. I tried to imagine such a raisinette in a world populated by Chamberlains and Bill Russells.

I stood at courtside watching Havlicek, Murphy and the great Sam Jones put their campers through the paces. I was amused when, during a break, the little guy cavalierly challenged the rest of the faculty to a race. Havlicek and Jones were two of the swiftest men ever to play for the Celtics.

Calvin's challenge was unique. "I bet I can beat both you guys," he said, laughing, "dribbling from one end of the court to the other." He did it three straight times. What made the feat all the more remarkable was that Calvin, a college senior, outdid the two pro stars dribbling two basketballs, one with *each* hand, while his opponents had to control only one each.

It didn't take a genius to figure out that this youngster had talent that went far beyond his inches. He had been a national baton-twirling champion, testimony to his great hands, and had performed at halftime of the Buffalo Bills' football games. I was to watch him score more than 100 points on successive nights in a semipro league around his hometown of Norwalk, Conn. He was simply a superb athlete, with the build of a gymnast. Even at 5-9 he could dunk the ball. His hands, his feet, his eyes, his temper, everything about him was quick.

At the end of his senior season, in 1970, a week before the pros were to draft, Walter Kennedy, the commissioner of the NBA, called and invited me to New York. He wanted to discuss Calvin. The draft was only three days away when I walked into Kennedy's office.

Walter lived in Connecticut—had been mayor of Stamford, in fact—and had followed Murphy since grade school. "The NBA wants Calvin badly," he told me. "We feel he's a great talent and we want him in our league." This, of course, was at the height of the war between the NBA and the ABA for college talent. The maneuvering, the infighting before the actual selection was a challenge to the human spirit.

"We're very interested in playing in the NBA," I assured Kennedy. "But in fairness to Calvin I have to listen not only to the ABA, but Marquis Haynes as well. They've both shown great interest." Haynes was doing nicely with a barnstorming group spun off from the original Harlem Globetrotters.

Walter leaned across his desk. "Bob, we want him. What kind of money will it take?"

"Over $100,000 a year and a good bonus," I said, "*unless* he's drafted by the Knicks. If the Knicks take him, I'd let him sign for $50,000 less than I would anywhere else."

I was baiting a hook. My rationale was obvious. Calvin was so dynamic, and so nearly unique, that he could earn a fortune in fringe money from endorsements if he were based in New York.

"We can't fix it for the Knicks to draft him," he said, in a tone that was almost apologetic. "They don't pick until 17th [and last, having won the championship]. Calvin will be gone before then. In fact, we have the man right here who is going to draft Calvin well before that."

On that cue, Carl Scheer, who had left Kennedy's staff to become president of the new Buffalo franchise, stepped through the door. I wasn't at all displeased. Calvin had played his college basketball just outside the city limits, at Niagara, so the move seemed a natural.

"We're going to build our franchise around him," Scheer vowed. "We know it's going to take a lot of money, but we'll pay it to get him."

I left New York that day in a buoyant mood. I knew what it would mean to Calvin to be selected in the first round. It was a distinction he wanted with a passion. He had worked hard all his life to master a game designed for giants. And now he was going to get his reward.

The draft was to start at mid-morning on Monday, in New York. At breakfast I took a phone call from Jerry Colangelo, the general manager of the Phoenix Suns. "Bob," he said, "we're going to take Calvin Murphy on the first round. Do you think he would have any objection to playing in Phoenix?"

"Jerry, I'm sure he would have no objection. But you're not going to get the chance. Carl Scheer told me that Buffalo [which picked seventh, in front of Phoenix] was going to take him."

"Well, if for some reason they don't, we're going to grab him. The kid would be great with our team. I just wanted to check it out if we get the chance."

Three hours later, Calvin Murphy was on the line: "Mr. Woolf, I've just been drafted by the San Diego Rockets."

I was startled, but happy. San Diego had the second choice of the entire draft, which meant that Calvin had been the second most wanted player in the nation. "Great, Calvin," I said, heartily. "Who was the guy that went in front of you?"

"A bunch of guys," he said. "They didn't take me until the second round."

I was dumfounded and I won't forget the wound in Calvin's voice. Didn't Walter Kennedy, the commissioner himself, assure me that there was no way he could last late enough in the first round for the Knicks to select him? Here not only New York, but *everybody*, had passed him by. Hadn't Carl Scheer told me, positively, that Buffalo would take him on the seventh pick? And wasn't Colangelo on the phone, just three hours before, telling me Phoenix wanted him if he was still around?

What had happened? How did it go wrong?

The answer, I learned, was all too simple and it taught me an important lesson. No one, but no one—commissioner, owner or gypsy mystic—knows what will happen when teams draft their future, whether it's basketball, football, baseball or ice hockey. The draft, which really is the spinal cord of our professional sports system, may also be the biggest con game going. Everybody cons everybody. As a result, at times, almost total confusion reigns.

I don't mean to suggest that those involved in sports are

incompetent when it comes to judging talent. To the contrary, they seldom overlook one who can play. But at the time of the draft the pressure is on, for real, and some unaccountable decisions are made. I learned never to take anything for granted in the draft, or the recruitment that takes place before and after that process, a large subject worth exploring.

Of all the young men I have represented, the case of Calvin Murphy seemed to best illustrate the uncertainty of the system. Aside from the practical considerations—what city, which team, how much—there is a huge emotional drain. In some instances it is the most traumatic experience of a young lifetime, as it was for Calvin.

"What does it mean, Mr. Woolf?" Calvin asked at the time, confused and hurt by being shunted to the second round. Suddenly, he had been knocked off the pedestal, his dream of being a Number 1 pick—in his mind, the stamp of quality— now just a dull ache.

"Don't worry," I said. "Maybe you didn't get taken on the first round, but you're going to get paid like one. And what's really important now is your future." I was still a little uptight when I called Bob Breitbard, owner of the Rockets, to congratulate him on selecting Calvin.

"Of course, Mr. Breitbard," I said, lightly, "you *know* this is going to cost you," and I quoted a figure close to the one we had mentioned in Kennedy's office.

I waited a moment for the San Diego owner to stop sputtering. "But he wasn't picked on the first round," he protested.

"In this case that doesn't count," I said. "The commissioner told me in his office three days ago that Calvin would be paid at that level if he was picked in the NBA, and I expect the league to live up to its promise, regardless of what round he was selected or which team picked him."

He reacted as a gentleman. He would check with Kennedy, he said, and if what I said was true then the Rockets would honor that agreement. Which they did.

Pittsburgh, a club in financial trouble at the time, had drafted

Calvin in the ABA, and was never considered as a serious option. But Marquis Haynes, one of the grand old men of commercial basketball, made it a tough decision in the end. We met with Marquis, owner and star of the touring Harlem Magicians, at 2 A.M., on April 2, 1970, in a hotel in Hartford, after one of Calvin's 100-plus nights against a local semipro team.

Haynes greeted him warmly. You could sense an empathy between them. "Calvin," said the tough old showman, "for years I've had the reputation of being the greatest dribbler in the world. But I've seen you play, and I know that isn't true anymore. You're the best. That's why I want you for my team."

Calvin melted. Haynes, because he *was* such a wizard at handling the ball, had been one of his boyhood heroes. I think Marquis looked on Calvin as his successor. He surely gave that impression when he offered him six figures a year, plus a percentage in the ownership of the team.

Murphy might have picked the Magicians right then and there except for his bride of a few weeks, Vernetta, a lovely and softspoken young lady. "Calvin," she said, firmly, "I don't think it would be right, your traveling all over the country, playing every night away from home." That was one of the two arguments that sent us off to San Diego, where Calvin signed his contract.

The other involved his pride and competitive spirit. There was no question that Calvin would have been a brilliant attraction with the Marquis Haynes troupe. No doubt they would even have figured a way to get his baton twirling into the act. But that was show business, not basketball, and Murphy had a point to prove. It was very nearly an obsession, so deeply did he believe that he could play with the best and the biggest.

Calvin once told me, *"The worst prejudice in sports isn't skin color, it is size.* The little man has to keep proving himself every season, often game by game, over and over."

Frustration and impatience are the curses of those athletes who are undersized, and Calvin was plagued with an inordinate capacity for self-criticism. Even after he had established himself in the NBA, he cried one night in the locker room after missing a shot that would have won the game.

From the moment he signed with the NBA, Calvin was a novelty, the only sub-six footer in the league, and he tried to handle it with good humor. He told interviewers no, he did not feel inferior, standing in the shadow of Abdul Jabbar or Thurmond or Chamberlain. "I'll only be a basketball player a few years," he explained. "I have to be a human being for a long time."

He agreed with the worldly-wise observation of Fred Patek, who at 5-4 was the Kansas City shortstop. Asked how it felt to be the shortest player in the majors, Patek replied: "A heck of a lot better than being the shortest player in the minors."

As for his talent, once, on a jump ball, he outtipped 6-11 Nate Thurmond. His first pro coach, Alex Hannum, said admiringly, "His only weakness is that he jumps so high it takes him too long to come down."

It was clear to me later that Calvin's size alone caused the NBA teams to back away at the last moment, in the first round of the draft. Suddenly, a 5-9 guard seemed a gamble not worth their Number 1 pick. As matters developed, there was a story behind San Diego's decision to take him at all. They did so on the recommendation of a scout named Frank Hamblen, a young fellow who had played at Syracuse two years before, and had guarded Murphy, holding him to "only" fifty points.

Hamblen learned from his friends, that the next year Syracuse came up to the Niagara game swearing not to be so embarrassed again by Calvin. All week they practiced a defense designed to stop Murphy. A quick little fellow was assigned to impersonate Calvin, and given the advantage of not having to dribble—he simply could *run* with the ball, in order to approximate Murphy's speed. The fellow was a third stringer, but as Calvin he was sensational. Everything he threw up fell through the net. By the end of the week, the Syracuse varsity were convinced that it had the proper defense, forcing him to go to his left, never letting him go to his right, etc.

All the real Calvin did was score *sixty-eight* points.

In keeping with the uncertainties of life in professional sports, by the time Calvin had gained some security in San Diego, where the fans had quickly come to love him, the franchise was uprooted only a few weeks before the 1971 season, and moved to Houston, Texas.

There, Calvin had established himself as the starting guard and one of the most exciting players in the NBA. Calvin, of course, was winning his fight. Not all athletes who go through the trauma of the pro draft are as fortunate. A case that comes to mind was that of Gary Wichard, a really decent young man who played quarterback for C. W. Post College, just outside of New York City.

I had agreed to represent Gary, who attracted national attention, unusual for a small-college quarterback, in his senior year. In 1972 his statistics were impressive, but what really launched him was a rave appraisal from Y. A. Tittle, one of pro football's all-time great quarterbacks. "This kid," said Tittle, after watching him in action, "is a fine quarterback with the best arm in the country." Of course, that quote made headlines in the New York papers the next day and, in time, the national news magazines included Tittle's observation in their roundup of pro prospects. Wichard couldn't miss.

In January of that year, his reputation won him an invitation to the Senior Bowl in Mobile, *the showcase* of college football talent each year for the professionals. Every season, the best sixty or so prospects are invited to appear in the Senior Bowl, and the coaches, scouts and brass of the National Football League attend en masse. The timing is perfect for the pros, because it pits the top talent against one another all week in practice, and provides a final, dress rehearsal before the draft.

I was in Mobile with Gary Wichard, and before the week was out I felt as though I had watched a nice young man drown. He was awful. He could do nothing right. He was playing so poorly in practice that they sent for his college coach in hopes of calming him down.

Meanwhile, his chances of going high in the draft—which were considerable before he got to Mobile—were now being ruined. Without fail, everyone I talked to in pro football, scouts or coaches, said they couldn't believe how inept he was. He was unimpressive, no question. But I also believe that the pros, led to expect something extraordinary, were overreacting.

And as embarrassed as anyone was Y. A. Tittle. "I don't know how I got quoted like that," Tittle told me. "When they asked me at the time about the kid I said he was the best passer in the *county*, not the country."

Gary Wichard, encouraged by a father whose pride was unrelenting, thought for certain he would be drafted in the first two rounds. I knew he wouldn't and I tried to convey the message as gently as I could. The day of the draft arrived and, to my surprise, Gary showed up at the headquarters in New York. Usually, only the Heisman Trophy winner or the player certain to go as the Number 1 pick is brought in for the actual draft. I told him I thought he would be better off at home.

Several rounds passed, the embarrassment deepening with each one, as Gary waited without hearing his name. By the time the Baltimore Colts picked him on the 16th round—the next to last round on the *second* day—he was nowhere in sight. He had been the 414th selection out of 442 players. It was a sad thing to live through, knowing how badly the boy wanted to be a pro, how inflated his hopes were. He was cut by the Colts and, the last I heard, was playing minor league football.

Two years in a row I represented the Number 1 football player in the country, both linemen, Walt Patulski of Notre Dame and John Matuszak of Tampa. The Buffalo Bills called me two days before the 1972 draft, when Patulski was coming out of school, and informed me that they intended to make him the first choice in the country. Would I bring him to Buffalo? I would indeed. We met with the Bills' management, but with the Calvin Murphy experience, I did not take Walt's top spot as fact until the morning of the draft, when Pete Rozelle casually strolled over to me at the headquarters, as the teams were adjusting their staff tables, and asked: "What is the correct way to pronounce Patulski's name?" Traditionally, the commissioner announces the Number 1 selection.

The next year I had been retained by Matuszak, and I had a notion he might go first, even though he had played for a small college. He was a defensive tackle, and that position was the first priority of Houston, which had won the Number 1 pick by losing thirteen games the past season. From the opening of the draft at 10 A.M. New York time, the Oilers had fifteen minutes in which to exercise their option.

Normally, the first pick is instantaneous. But for reasons unknown, the clock was running without word from Houston. Fourteen minutes had passed when I turned to Jim Kensil, the Number 2 man at the NFL, whose assignment was to handle the phone and relay the information to Rozelle, at the podium. "Jim," I whispered, "when you answer the call from Houston, wink at me if it's Matuszak."

Moments later the phone rang. As he passed me, Kensil said, "Bob Woolf, you got your wink."

The odd thing here was that Houston—even though just about every other team picking high did—never approached me or Matuszak in advance of the draft. After having gone through the experience of Gary Wichard, you had to wonder if this was another small-college player who was going to get lost. But then you realize that publicity doesn't mean a damned thing, after all. With the computers and sophisticated scouting systems employed in all sports today, no one is going to get lost.

Matuszak was a perfect example. Here he had played with little or no fanfare out of Tampa, which doesn't exactly compete with the Big Ten, and he still emerged as the Number 1 pick in the land. So no young athlete really has to worry about going to a small school. If he has the goods, the pros will find him. They might not always get him in the right round, but he won't go begging.

Of course, you can't convince the players that publicity doesn't count. They are conditioned to believe that news clippings and contacts rank just slightly below their speed at forty yards.

In 1973 I thought I was going to represent a Notre Dame lineman named Greg Marx. The year before I had negotiated contracts for four of his teammates, including two first-round picks, Patulski and Mike Kadish, who went to Miami.

When Marx failed to go in the first round, I discovered that he held me responsible. "Bob Woolf," he told friends, "didn't take enough interest in me." I was flattered by Greg's sentiments. But I can assure him that when it comes to judging talent, having Bob Woolf as your representative means as much to the pros as your astrological sign.

It may mean something at the negotiating table, though. Any person who is respected by management is going to be treated better, and be better received, when it comes to negotiating a contract. The fly-by-nighters, the con men, the hustlers and leeches who come into sports every year, are not treated with respect, often not even with courtesy. Most general managers and owners have been through the negotiating game often enough so that they can tell the legitimate people from the fakes.

Actually, the best of the senior athletes probably ought to have an agent just to screen all the other agents, who come hovering around like so many fruit flies. They come at them with a laundry list of temptations, appealing to his avarice and greed. They give him money while he's still in school, show him a good time in the big cities, even provide female companionship, if that is his wish.

All of this is done to get the young man's name on the agent's contract, which will assure the agent of a ten percent cut of his contract, and fifteen to twenty-five percent of any endorsements they might obtain for him along the way. Some employ a variety of tricks to advance their work. In 1973, two brothers traveled the country displaying a phony telegram, supposedly authorizing them on behalf of the Los Angeles Rams to offer the prospect $50,000—if he first signed with them as his agents. It was, of course, a fraud. Another agent had a different technique. He'd forge a higher figure on his existing contracts—often doubling the actual amounts—and use them to seduce new prospects. In one year alone, he flew over 200 athletes from all parts of the country into his office.

At one time there were several hundred different individuals, or offices, competing to represent athletes in their financial negotiations. Each year about fifty or so go out of business. Each year about fifty new ones rise to take their place, looking to make a fast dollar. For the good of sports, I feel that representatives of professional athletes should be licensed and a federally authorized board appointed to supervise their actions.

The good ones, respectable lawyers such as Arthur Morse of Chicago, Jack Mills of Denver, Larry Fleischer of New York, and Alan Eagleson of Toronto, go on year after year, continuing to upgrade the level of this still relatively young field of sports attorney. You rarely see a player represented by the competent Donald Dell of Washington winding up as a holdout or in a serious dispute with his team.

Unfortunately, dozens of players get themselves tied up to the fast-acting, smooth-talking operators who pass as agents. When Jim Plunkett was coming out of Stanford he was hit with a hundred different approaches. Luckily, friends of the school had formed a committee to weed these characters out, and Wayne Hooper of Oakland, an attorney and a gentleman, was hired to work out his contract.

Others are not as lucky. Many times the young man has to make his own decisions and this is when the vultures swoop in again. They approach him right on the campus; meet with him in his room; take him to dinner; feed his ego; assure him he will get picked high in the draft because they have powerful *connections* in the league. They know all the famous writers in the nation and will make sure he gets the best publicity. Finally, they have a couple of big endorsements ready for him the moment he signs.

There is a particular approach related to endorsements, a vague but romantic area for the athlete, one that means both money *and* fame. The agent convinces him that the money he will make from endorsements alone will almost pay their fee.

A young fellow with no reliable guidance is easy prey for such sales talk. There is an agent in Texas who had eighteen suits filed against his office, at one time, from athletes who claimed he had swindled them out of their contract money.

This type of misrepresentation had become so blatant that the various Player Associations were finally getting involved, and bringing court actions against these unsavory types who had no right to be in the field. They had no background, no experience, no conscience. They had no idea what a player should be paid, outside of what they read in the newspapers.

These men were hungry and unscrupled and they put tremendous pressure on college seniors about to graduate.

I remember Dave Cowens, later to become a great player with the Celtics, phoning me from Florida State and asking me to fly to Tallahassee to discuss representing him. I explained to Cowens that I didn't wish to fly around to campuses so athletes could interview me. "If you're drafted and want me to represent you, I would be delighted to do so."

A few months later, just before the draft, I was vacationing at my winter home in Hollywood, Florida, when I received another call from Cowens. "Bob, the pressure is murder," he said. "I just don't know what to do. I'm getting hit with deals from all sides. Please, couldn't you come up and meet with me and my coach, Hugh Durham, at the Tully Gym tomorrow?"

Although I was reluctant, I agreed because Cowens seemed panicky. So the next morning I flew to Tallahassee, making three puddle-jump stops along the way, and grabbed a cab to the gymnasium. I went immediately to the coaches' office, arriving at the time we had set. No Cowens. I asked all around. Finally, one of the coaches told me: "Oh, he left for New York last night."

It was a puzzled, weary and irritable Bob Woolf who boarded the next plane out of Tallahassee. The next I heard of Dave Cowens he had been drafted by Boston. It was six months before we met, and I had a chance at last to ask what happened. "I'm very sorry, Bob," he said, and I know he meant it. "Things were happening so fast I didn't know what to do. I just caved in. This agent came down and flew me up to New York right away and signed me with the NBA."

The Cowens case was unusual in this respect. During that phase of the basketball war, the league would sign a player before the draft, and then the team that eventually selected the player—in Cowens' case, the Celtics—would have to honor that contract.

As Cowens is an example of how the pressure works on a player, Bob Lanier's father is an example of how the pressure affects a parent.

A phone call also started my dealings with Bob Lanier, the super center for St. Bonaventure and destined to be the first player chosen in the 1970 NBA draft. His dad phoned and said that Bill Russell had recommended me as a lawyer to negotiate for Bob. I was flattered. I had been friendly with Russell, but had never done any work for him, even though at one time I represented nine of his teammates.

This was still weeks before the college draft, so we made tentative plans to get together later and review matters. We did get together, briefly, at Calvin° Murphy's wedding and had a pleasant chat. We agreed to meet again before the draft.

Late in the season, while Bob was finishing his career with the Bonnies, his dad called and asked me to meet him after a game, at center court. Sure enough, when the game was over Mr. Lanier hurried out of the stands and met me on the floor. His first words were: "Why didn't you tell me I was supposed to get $25,000? Didn't you know as the father of this boy I'm supposed to get $25,000 and a piece of his endorsements? I'm the one who developed him. I'm the one who taught him."

I was stunned. "Mr. Lanier, is that why you brought me all the way up here? Is that what you wanted to talk to me about?"

"Yah," he answered.

Without another word I just turned around and walked away, in disgust.

I knew it was senseless to try and reason with him. Instead of the high-powered salesmen luring the players with sweet promises, they had played to the vulnerabilities of the *parent*. They had convinced Mr. Lanier that he was entitled to a share of his son's earnings.

He got it, too. While later working out Terry Driscoll's contract with Detroit, the team that had signed Lanier, I was told that his dad did collect $25,000. But his son had paid for it. The Pistons didn't care where the money went. They were committed to a certain figure for Bob Lanier, and any "bonus" for his father came out of that. Bob still had to pay taxes on it since it was part of his contract.

Where big money is involved, I have seen performances that would be absolutely comic if they were not so sad. Otto Stowe, the pass receiver, originally with Miami, signed with three different agents before I came along to complete his contract. Otto just simply went along on a joyride. When an agent showed up and wanted to wine and dine him, he seldom refused. And then to show his gratitude he would sign a little personal services contract at the end of a pleasant evening.

Dozens of youngsters do that every year. I've heard of players signing with as many as six separate agents, out of sheer confusion.

The fast-talking agent who has a binding agreement with a player may have made promises he can't keep. When he fails, he blames the team. The result is that the player starts his career resentful of his new employer.

Meanwhile, the agent (in most cases) is happy and relieved because he has taken his percent right off the top. That is, if he negotiated a package of, say, $200,000, the agent would exit quietly with his $20,000 right out of the young man's bonus money.

Please note that I said *in most cases*, because for every player who gets cheated, there are three agents getting shanghaied in return. That's why so many are out of the business in a year or two. They wine, dine and sign, and then the athlete, whose greed and lack of ethics they helped create, decides he won't pay the bill.

At the risk of shattering images, I must admit that many ball-players are not the most reliable people when it comes to paying their debts. In my own case I have been fortunate, despite the fact that I do not have a signed contract with any client. Our relationship consists of a handshake and, hopefully, mutual trust.

Which, in a long and roundabout way, brings us back to Calvin Murphy, curled on my doorstep. I have found in Calvin, and others like him, an innocence toward sports that can't be corrupted by big money. His emotions are genuine, he doesn't hide them, and that goes to the heart of what is important about the people we make into heroes.

The body stirred as I cut off the headlights and the kids piled out, banging the car doors. Calvin was awake instantly. "Oh, hi, Mr. Woolf," he said, bouncing to his feet. "I forgot to tell you I was coming to town."

Calvin spent the night in our guest room. The next morning, at breakfast, I asked him how he slept. "Okay," he quipped, "but to tell you the truth, I was more comfortable on your doorstep."

He has a quality of seriousness about him that seems to contradict his size and impish appearance. Calvin, like all athletes who have gone through the draft and the inevitable pursuit by the agents, voiced a fear which, had it not been so real, would be humorous. Following his signing in San Diego, he picked up a $50,000 bonus check and turned it over to me for safekeeping. My wife Anne and I had decided not to return directly to Boston. Calvin sat on the bed while we packed.

"A little holiday, huh?" he said, grinning.

I told him that we planned to stop off in Las Vegas, which was just a long fly ball from San Diego. Calvin practically froze. His eyes grew wide.

"What's wrong?" I asked.

"Oh, please, Mr. Woolf," he begged, "don't stop in Las Vegas. I don't want to be another Joe Louis!"

9

The Cost of Courage

IT WAS A STRANGE CONVERSATION, tense and clumsy, because we were talking about a man we both thought might be dying in another town.

"The club is going to honor the contract, aren't they?" I asked Charlie Mulcahy, the attorney for the Boston Bruins hockey team.

He spoke to the wall a few inches above my head. "Well, he didn't sign it, you know. He said there were a couple of things he wanted to check out, but he never did sign it."

"Maybe he didn't sign it," I said, my voice sounding oddly metallic in my own ear, "but you *know* he agreed to it verbally and had every intention of signing it." I was fighting back anger.

"He still didn't sign it," said Mulcahy.

At that moment, as I sat in the Bruins' office at Boston Gardens, Teddy Green lay motionless in an Ottawa hospital bed, the right side of his head caved in, his left arm limp, not yet able to talk. A few days before, doctors had removed splinters of skull from his brain. Within the week a second operation was needed to clear a blood clot.

His helplessness was the cruelest kind of irony for this man who had been the symbol of hockey's passions. Teddy Green was a rugged defenseman known for his swift justice. He was Boston's avenger, a villain to the rest of the National Hockey League.

In the most destructive stick battle ever fought by professionals, he had been cracked across the head by Wayne Maki, a young wing for the St. Louis Blues. Green had cuffed him once with a glove, then knocked him off balance with a rap to the shoulder. Then the referees skated in to stop it, and he relaxed and took his eyes off Maki. He never saw the blow, only knew that his world had gone spinning. "I took it really good on side of the head," he would recall it later, "and I went down and after that I was so much scrambled eggs."

The nearly fatal fight had erupted in the first few minutes of a meaningless exhibition game in Ottawa, the night of September 21, 1969. How it started, who was to blame, there would be time later to worry about those questions. But there was no doubt at all how the fight had ended. It ended with blood on the ice and Green unconscious.

From the time of the accident, nine days passed before I was allowed to see Ted. His wife, Patty, and his mother had remained at his bedside all during the crisis and a teammate, Ed Westfall, had been sent by the players. No other visitors had been permitted.

He was partly paralyzed, his mouth distorted and only the very center of his face visible, framed by the bandages that swathed his head. My heart ached for the two women who hovered near him, with the worn and hollow look that people get after days of vigil in a sick person's room. One of them leaned down and whispered, "Dear, Bob is here, Bob Woolf."

The head didn't move but, suddenly, tears welled up in Ted Green's eyes, a sight few would have thought possible, surely not his fans or those who had ever crossed him on the ice. Those tears, what did they mean? Gratitude, maybe, that a friend from Boston was there. And hurt, embarrassment, that

With my first client, Earl Wilson.

BELOW *Laughing all the way to the bank: (from left to right) The Celtics' Sam Jones; Olympic high jumper John Thomas; myself; Jon Morris, then with the Patriots; and the Celtics' John Havlicek.*

On August 3, 1972, Derek Sanderson signed his $2.65 million contract, to become the highest-paid athlete in the world.

FACING: ABOVE *On April 22, 1969, the Hawk unretires: (standing from left to right) Gabe Paul, then Cleveland president; Ken Harrelson with me American League president Joe Cronin; and Dick O'Connell, Boston vice president and general manager. Seated is Commissioner Bowie Kuhn.*
BELOW *All happy that in 1969 John Havlicek decided to stay in Boston Red Auerbach is seated.*

Wayne Maki (14) of the St. Louis Blues strikes Ted Green (6) on the head during an exhibition game in September, 1969. Among other things the ugly incident resulted in a fractured skull for Green, shown sprawled on the ice, his face contorted.

FACING: ABOVE *Calvin Murphy breaks us up at his signing. B*ᴄ *Breitbard, San Diego team owner is at left.* BELOW *Somb*ᴇ *moment: on May 15, 1970, Harry Sinden announces his retireme*ᴇ *as coach of the champion Bruins.*

ABOVE A short lived TV career: Mr. and Mrs. Bob Woolf with Banacek's *George Peppard* in 1973. Sanderson fared better.   BELOW My mother, *Anna Woolf, and my youngest daughter, Tiffany both born on May 7th, seventy-six years apart.*

John Matuszak, the NFL's top draft choice in Toronto. This wire-service photo on June 22, 1973, prompted fast action from the Oilers' Sid Gillman.

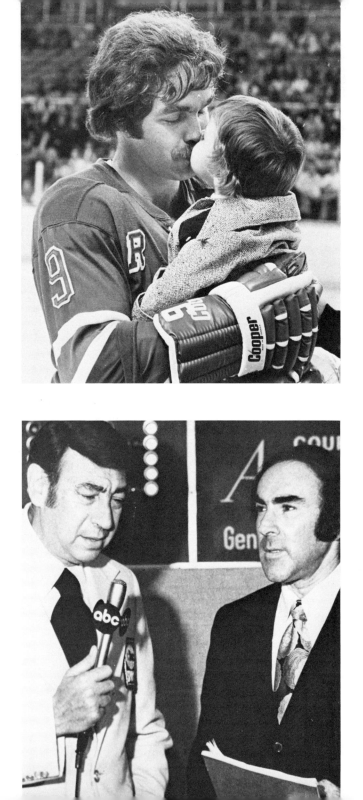

Family portrait in 1971 with Gary, Stacey, Anne, and Jim Plunkett, Randy Vataha, and long-time friend Ginny Campbell.

FACING: ABOVE *The other Derek (now a New York Ranger) with young handicapped Derek King in the fall of 1974.* BELOW *Telling it like it is to Howard Cosell during the 1974 NFL player draft.*

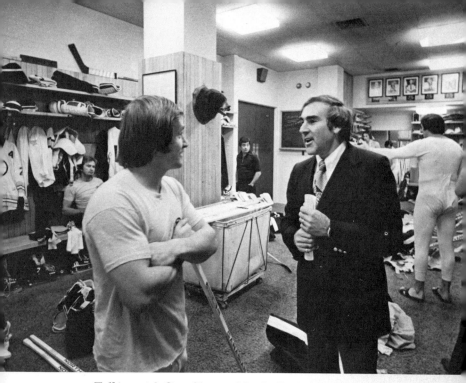

ABOVE   *Talking with Greg Sheppard in the Bruins' locker room during the winter of 1975.*   BELOW   *Marvin Barnes fortunately did not have to go to work in a factory. His mother Lula was on hand for the signing of a $2.1 million contract on September 17, 1974.*

*With Carl and Carol Yastrzemski in Japan—
and the ubiquitous Herman Matsui, escorting Anne.*

ABOVE *Don Shula and his* 1975 *first-round draft choice Darryl Carleton.* BELOW *Holding Stanley Cup with Johnny Bucyk of the Bruins after unexpected shower. Derek's father, Harold Sanderson, is third from left.*

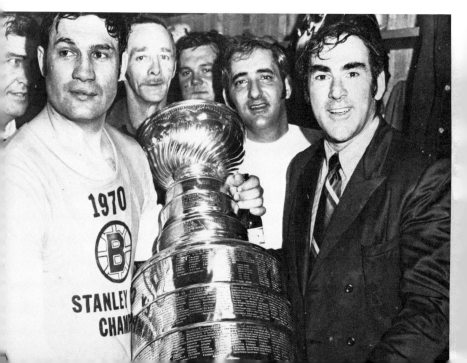

ABOVE   Pete Varney of the Chicago White Sox, first pick of the baseball draft, gets the press treatment at his signing in June, 1975.   BELOW With Luis Tiant and his father at Tiant Sr.'s seventieth birthday party, in 1975. Allowed to come from Cuba by Fidel Castro, the elder Tiant saw his son pitch for the first time in fifteen years.

A reflective stroll with Patriots' All-Rookie tight end Russ Francis (1975)

ABOVE *The opening of Bachelors Three, with partners Joe Namath and Derek Sanderson.* BELOW *Derek draws first and last blood on the Johnny Carson Show. With Allan King and Buddy Greco.*

Recreation time with Harpo Gladieux, Jim Plunkett, and a young neighbor, Danny Simons. Note Plunkett giving Gladieux the elbow.

he should be seen lying in such a state.

You'd have to be a statue not to have been moved. The feeling in the room was heavy with hand-wringing, of doom temporarily postponed. Hockey was the last thing on anyone's mind. They just wanted him to live, to get out of that hospital, to function again as a full person. A nurse turned his head so he could look at me.

With great effort, Ted tried to talk. His upper lip sagged and the left side of his face didn't move and his words were slurred. But the message was distinct. He said, "Maki, tell Maki not to worry about . . . this." There isn't much to add about that visit, because almost nothing else was said. Pain, mine or someone else's, it doesn't matter, has always made it difficult for me to talk.

When I returned to Boston, I issued a statement for Ted, saying that his accident happened in the heat of the game, and he bore no animosity, not to Wayne Maki or anyone.

Traditionally, *heat of the game* has always been a kind of moral defense in sports to excuse bad manners and irrational acts.

My own thoughts were a tangle. I found it difficult to accept that fatal or near-fatal injuries should be treated as a professional risk. I thought about Ted Green, the pride he felt in his own toughness. He had overcome many nagging injuries during his career to become an all-star, in the meanest part of the sport, the defense. He did so by sacrificing his body. He never avoided contact with an opponent or with the puck. He accepted the wrath of the crowd, which he often invited, and he did not resent, at least in the early, scrapping years, his reputation as a kind of bully.

Blocking shots was his forte. Backing up teammates in a fight, being the toughest cop in hockey, these were his badge of honor. Now he was on his back, staring at a hospital ceiling, lucky to be alive and no doubt convinced, if he thought about it at all, that he would never skate again.

I had promised his wife and mother—and Ted, too, if he was

listening—that his medical bills and other expenses, and his salary, would be taken care of by the Bruins. "Don't worry," I said, "I'll see to it."

Before I flew back to Boston, I stopped by the Ottawa police station. There was a rumor afloat that the police intended to bring some kind of criminal complaint against Green and Maki because of the fight. When I asked about it, a police captain assured me the rumor wasn't true. They had no plans to press any charges.

On my return to Boston I arranged a meeting with Weston Adams, Jr., the president of the Bruins, and the team counsel, Mulcahy. Charlie had negotiated most of the player contracts, and we had reached an agreement on Green's only a few days before the team flew to Ottawa for a preseason game.

The contract compared favorably with any written at that time in the NHL, and I was pleased with it. It was a three-year package which included—unusual for hockey then—an injury clause that said Green would be paid in full for the length of his contract, plus one year, if he were disabled and unable to play again. I certainly had no premonitions. But in contracts I had negotiated in other sports, injury clauses were becoming a part of the game. So I insisted on it as a matter of further protection for Teddy, who seemed to figure in more mayhem than the average player.

For nearly a decade it had been impossible to think of the excitement of the game and not think of Ted Green. But over the last three years a subtle change had taken place. Bobby Orr set an example for him, instructed him, and Ted had developed into a more polished and controlled player. His fights were less predictable and his sense of authority had found new, subtle expressions. Often, the *threat* of Ted Green accomplished what in the past had required hard action.

A look, a glare, could cause a player to veer off. When fights broke out, with Green on the bench, he could electrify the crowds and discourage the spread of the combat simply by swinging one leg over the boards.

He wasn't especially sensitive then. He didn't spend hours analyzing his responses and dwelling on the meaning of life. But as his friend, and attorney, I knew that Ted played the game the only way he knew how, and he had paid his dues and, at twenty-nine, deserved to collect some of the dividends.

Just days after we had settled on the terms, and the Bruins had agreed to the injury clause, Ted was struck down. Ironic hardly seems a strong enough word to describe it.

He was in training camp at the time, when the Bruins gave him the finished draft of the contract. Ted said he wanted to hold it for a couple days, just to look it over, for no special reason. It was during this "holding period" that the injury occurred, with its rippling waves of legal and moral confusion. The Bruins were not yet *bound* by the new contract because Green hadn't signed it. And, as Mulcahy's sparring had indicated, they were hesitant.

Attempting to be fair, I decided that the club was unsure of its obligation. Some of the players were less generous and suggested they were trying to weasel out of it. Derek Sanderson called from training camp. "What's the story with Teddy's contract?" he barked. "They're going to honor it, aren't they?"

I told him it just wasn't clear. Derek was a close friend of Ted and, in fact, was one of those who suggested to him that I negotiate his contract. "Well, if they don't," he threatened, "the whole damned team is going out on strike. We had a meeting on it last night. If they don't pay him, not one of us will play another game until they do."

The next day the Bruins called a news conference to announce that the full salary and expenses of Ted Green would be met by the team, and their concern now was only for his recovery. A player strike, caused by their refusal to pay the fallen Boston captain, would have been a devastating public relations blow. I'm sure they realized that. But I also was convinced that, in the end, they wanted to do what was right.

Slowly, Ted Green, who had heard his own last rites, began to mend. He left the hospital and returned to his home in a quiet little town called Transcona, east of Winnipeg, on the frozen prairie of Manitoba. The hair on his shaved head was beginning to grow out like whiskers. His face had a puffy, over-medicated look, but his spirits were good.

Green was built for power at 5-10 and 212, his normal playing weight. He had wavy dark hair and narrow eyes and a firm, square jaw. He looked like the pictures you saw of the typical young Canadian officer during the war.

His reflexes were still uncertain and he didn't move freely, but he showed no sign of depression as he sat out the season. He had felt the breath of the hairy unknown, and it had changed him. "I was a kind of helter-skelter guy before," he told his friends. "Well, I'm not that same person any more. I have a different set of values now. Off the ice and on the ice, I know I'll never be as carefree as I was before."

On the ice. I shook my head. There was a depression the size of a small cup on the right side of his skull. He did not yet have the full use of his left arm. But he was talking, at least thinking, about a comeback. There are certain athletes who, if they were sucked out of an airplane, on the way down would be thinking about a new technique they'd like to try, if they lived.

But for Teddy Green—and, in fact, for all of hockey—the matter wouldn't end within the family, with good deeds and pretty sentiments. The Ottawa police reversed themselves and filed a complaint of aggravated assault against both Green and Wayne Maki. Clarence Campbell, the president of the NHL, its leader since World War II, ordered a hearing of his own, a show trial for the sport itself.

Out of the hearing I reached one conclusion. For years I had seen observers shrug off the occasional violence of hockey, wonder why it was such an angry game and give it up as beyond human understanding. It was no longer a mystery to me. The players stay mad, they let their tempers fly as easily as they shed their gloves, and they fight because it has become *a condition of the job.* The warlords who run hockey like the fighting and believe it to be an essential part of the sport.

This became clear to me as I handled Ted Green's defense at the hearing, in the Ottawa offices of Ed Houston, the league counsel. Also present were Campbell, general manager Lynn Patrick, coach Scotty Bowman and Maki, all of the Blues; and from the Bruins, Wes Adams, Milt Schmidt, the general manager, coach Harry Sinden and of course Green.

I was given a free rein to cross-examine those involved, but it was soon apparent that no matter what I said or what points I developed, the judgment had been made. This was a closed shop. The case would be handled in the traditional hockey way —with a wink.

I have great respect for Clarence Campbell and what he has meant to hockey, but I disagreed with his view of what the game required in the 1970s. It startled him, and the others, when I said flatly that this kind of conduct, this promiscuous fighting with gusts of savagery, had to be stopped, not just discouraged. They asked what I would suggest as a way to stop it.

"Suspend them," I said. "You suspend players for life for gambling. Well, anyone swinging a stick at another player ought to be sat down." They agreed. An automatic, *three-day* suspension was the minimum penalty, at that time, for such violations. Sitting out three games is how a player is penalized for cracking open the head of another player with his stick! Can you accept that?

I can't and didn't. I argued that day, at the hearing, that more radical steps should be taken to limit the fighting, and the dangers of it, in any game. I proposed that protective helmets be made mandatory. They listened politely, nodding yes while their eyes told me no. I couldn't help but feel that if the old ice barons were really concerned about the safety and well-being of their players, the Board of Governors could enact the necessary rule changes in five minutes.

My thoughts turned to the several conversations I had enjoyed with Ted Green, over snacks, after the Bruin home games.

What hockey is, how it shapes the people who play, where it all begins, all this I began to see more clearly as he talked about his childhood in Canada, where the training starts early.

"We did everything for ourselves as kids," he said. "We flooded our rink and scraped it when it snowed. It was natural ice, outdoor ice, and we skated in weather when it was—well, I can tell you how cold it was. We had this one guy on one of our kid teams and he was dripping from the nose with a cold, and in no time at all he had an icicle hanging from his nose. We used to skate outside when it was 30, sometimes 40 degrees below zero. In those days everybody did that."

By his early teens, Ted recalled, it was clear that "aggressiveness"—a euphemism coaches gave to that instinct for brawling and bloodletting—was required for success. In his team picture, one year, every player had a bandage on his head. "Well, you know," said Ted, "as you grow up you wonder why these things happen on the ice. There were a lot of fights, and a lot of stick fights, I got into that I certainly didn't enjoy and I wish I had never gotten into them. But I was brought up this way through hockey and, in my early years in the league, they said the only way I would make it was by using my dukes, and that's the way I played. The fans, they cheered on the scraps, the papers talked about Terrible Ted and Tough Ted."

Well, what about legislating fights right out of the game, Ted? What about that? Even Ted Green hesitated, so deep, so close to the bone, does this tradition run. "Fighting," he said, "has been a part of hockey for one hell of a long time now."

The premium the National Hockey League puts on this aspect of the game was reestablished every time I talked with a team on behalf of a draft choice. Invariably, the interview would get around to how well my client could fight. Sometimes, the hockey general manager sounds more like a boxing promoter trying to size up some kid coming out of the amateurs.

Can he punch? Does he take a punch well? Has he got good leverage when he connects? Normally, I referred these questions back to my client, usually on the basis that I had never seen him fight. To my endless amazement, the clubs, if they got the impression the boy wasn't tough, frequently offered to enroll him in boxing classes.

What the hockey professionals have never been able to comprehend is the effect of this kind of mentality on the youngsters—the peewees, bantams, midgets and mites—who, by the thousands, are just starting to play the game. These little fellows see their heroes fighting and mauling one another, and accept it as the thing to do. For a fact, this was a by-product in Boston of the "Big Bad Bruins" image of the late 1960s.

Just as psychological studies have shown that violent crime on television badly influences the youth of the country, I believe strongly that fighting in hockey by the pros damages the young amateur. Boston is a hockey-fever town, surrounded by rinks that operate twenty-four hours a day. It was offensive to me, as I'm sure it was to their coaches and parents, to watch youngsters dropping their gloves and sticks to slug it out with one another. For a time, this became the stylish thing to do. The youngsters seemed to feel that getting in a fight was as important as scoring a goal.

Eventually, the brawling became so epidemic that coaches and arena managers became fed up, to the point of suspending one chronic offender for the season. Such actions curtailed the fighting. I have no doubt that tougher rules would have the same effect among the pros. But they resist, just as they avoid the issue of requiring players to wear a protective helmet.

A few more did, in the aftermath of the Ted Green mishap. But within weeks most of those, in response to the teasing of bench jockeys, one suspects, were bare-headed again. Some complain that they don't like the way they *look* in a helmet, or how it feels. They sure as hell would like the way it felt if they had one on while crashing headfirst into the boards, or taking a stick above the ear.

The warlords think they need fighting and the rugged, explosive image to sell hockey. I don't. Through the years, one of the least provocative teams in the league had been the Montreal Canadiens. Yet they seem to have won their share of Stanley Cups, and endured as the best gate attraction in the game.

The testimony at the hearing did little to clear up the murky confusion of what had happened that night in Ottawa. It began when Green intercepted the puck and Maki half stumbled, half charged into him. "I came off the boards and cuffed him with the back of my glove, and I hit him in the mouth and he fell down in front of me," said Green, with his accustomed candor.

Maki got up and, according to the Bruins, tried to spear Ted, jamming the blade of his stick between Green's legs. At this point the stories took sharply conflicting turns. Green said he rapped him on the shoulder with his stick, knocking him off balance again. Maki's teammates claimed that Ted caught him in the face, and his stick was still up when Wayne got to his feet and came at him. They said Maki's stick glanced off Green's before it hit.

"I wish it had," said Ted, "because it wouldn't have hit me so hard. But as far as I know it was a direct blow and felled me like a ton of potatoes. I went right down, and I knew I was in trouble."

Sequence photos of the fight seemed to bear out Green. They showed Maki blocking Ted's stick with his, catching it on the shoulder and losing his balance; then Maki coming straight overhead like a logger splitting a stump; and Green, dazed, one hand raised, sinking glassy-eyed to the ice.

Reviewing all this, I marveled at the scene that had taken place before the hearing began, moments after we walked into the law offices of Ed Houston. Green and Maki had not spoken to or seen each other since the fight. Teddy quickly eased what could have been a bitter, ugly afternoon by walking straight to Wayne, offering his hand and asking how things were for him.

Maki was a pleasant, average-looking fellow, a journeyman forward who had spent a frustrating career, hoping to join his brother, Chico, on the Chicago Black Hawks.

As expected, the penalties amounted to a slap on the wrist—a reprimand for both, a one-month suspension from league games for Ted Green when, and if, he ever again was pronounced fit to play. Wayne had already served his time.

Both were acquitted of the charges against them by the Ottawa police in a case that could have resulted in grave implications for all of sport. Injuries had always been dealt with, one way or another, within the game and had almost never been considered a matter for the courts. There were occasional civil actions: Jim Brewer, a pitcher whose jaw was broken by Billy Martin, sued and recovered damages.

John Roseboro, the Dodger catcher, did press charges against Juan Marichal, after the San Francisco pitcher took a bat to his head. The guardians of baseball leaned on Roseboro, and he settled out of court.

Even though they were acquitted, the Green-Maki trial was a warning to the head-hunters of sport, if only they knew how to read it. As time would prove, they didn't.

That season of 1969–70 moved like the arctic ice floe for Ted Green. He sat it out, getting his strength back by inches, as the Bruins went on to win the Stanley Cup, their first, by beating St. Louis in the last game, in overtime, on a pass from Sanderson to Orr. I sat in the Bruins' dressing room until the shouting was over and only a few people were left. Teddy was one of them. A wet suit, not sentiment, had kept me there. I had been pitched into the showers, at the height of the bedlam, by Ken Hodge and Wayne Cashman.

Teddy stood to one side, quietly, and then he sat beside me and looked for a long time at the floor. "Bob," he said, "I'll never play again. I'll never make it back." He was an island of sadness in a room filled with sunshine. I patted him on the shoulder and said what I knew he wanted to hear: "You'll be back, Teddy. Next year you'll be a part of all this." But, at bottom, neither of us believed it.

We were both wrong. He wasn't the same Ted Green on the ice—he wore a helmet and he used finesse instead of brute force—but he did make it back in 1971, and in the one great scorebook that's worth a lot of points. So in one of several ironies related to this story, Ted Green was still playing hockey five seasons later, first with New England and then Winnipeg of the World Hockey Association. He was aware that at any time, another serious blow to the head had the potential to cause permanent injury. I don't believe I have known an athlete with more courage.

He kidded about winning the sportsmanship trophy. "You know," he said, "I never thought of myself as a tough guy. There's a Jekyll-and-Hyde thing about a lot of hockey players. For me, my aggressiveness was only on the ice."

In a very clear echo of the past, in January of 1975, a grand jury in Minnesota indicted Dave Forbes, of the Boston Bruins, on a charge of aggravated assault against Henry Boucha, of the Minnesota North Stars. Boucha suffered head injuries when Forbes hit him with his stick. The league suspended Forbes for ten days. In that same summer, a hung jury was the result of the Forbes trial and the case against him was dropped. The failure to reach a decision, in my mind, left the way open for further such incidents.

So I summed up, in my own mind, what had transpired since that ordeal in Ottawa in the fall of 1969. Ted Green, who nearly died, was playing hockey again. The boys were still raising their sticks, and using them, and being sentenced to between three and ten days in the dock. And the courts were again showing an interest.

But the one most terrible irony of all came in the summer of 1974. Wayne Maki died, at thirty-two, of a brain tumor.

10

Never Throw Away the Key

———

AS A TYPE, coaches and managers are driven men, consumed by their jobs, restless, insecure and wound tight. They are also more than a little paranoid.

The job encourages that condition, whatever their qualities going in. The condition was best defined by Billy Martin, who said the secret was "to keep the five players who hate you away from the five who are undecided."

Through the athletes I represented, I had met all kinds of managers: tyrants, father figures, the quietly confident as well as the noisily nervous. And there were those who had a haunted look about them, as if they couldn't remember how they got there.

The pressures sometimes drive them to flights of strange behavior. They must please, or impress, or at least cope with everybody: his players, the fans, the owner for whom he works, and the press. Many of them are thinking about their next job. Only a few enjoy the luxury of free and honest expression, the blunt epigrams of a Woody Hayes or a Vince Lombardi, but it is a self-styled luxury which in no way minimizes the pressures of the job.

And no matter how successful they have been, each new season is a minefield. In 1957, the pressures swelled inside Buddy Parker until he quit as coach of the Detroit Lions, announcing his decision at a father-son banquet the night before his team's first preseason game. "I'm getting out," he told a stunned crowd. "This is the worst team I've ever seen. I like winning too much to go through a losing season." The truth was, Parker felt he had lost control. The Lions hastily promoted George Wilson to head coach, and the team won its division, then routed Cleveland in the championship game. Irony of ironies.

But the case of Buddy Parker wasn't an isolated one. In 1960, Eddie Sawyer suddenly resigned as manager of the Philadelphia Phillies, after his team had lost its *opening* game. Eddie had seen enough. "I'm forty years old," he said, simply, "and I want to live to be fifty."

I had not given much thought to the problems of coaches until a night in the spring of 1970, when I found myself staring at Harry Sinden, whose Boston Bruins were within one game of winning the Stanley Cup. I had just heard him make a statement that stunned me.

"Quit?" I responded, almost shouting. "You're kidding! You're on top of the world. What are you talking about—quit?"

Sinden didn't blink. For the second time he told me, "I don't give a damn what happens the rest of this series. Win or lose, I'm not coming back. They don't care about me."

Here was a man on the eve of what—to that point in his career—would be his sweetest moment. The Bruins, standing at three games to none over St. Louis, could wrap up the Stanley Cup the next afternoon, and Harry Sinden would reach the pinnacle for hockey coaches.

When Harry confided in me we were at the Colonial Hilton Motel outside of Boston. He had kept his team there in seclusion to shield them from the slap-happy fans ready to break loose over their first Stanley Cup in thirty years. We had been friendly in the past, working together on a summer hockey school, but at this point I was just a sympathetic ear—not his attorney.

I just couldn't believe that a man whose team was about to win the world championship would shun all the fringe benefits that go with it. Harry Sinden was just thirty-seven years old. He had never made any serious money in his life. Now he seemed on the verge, and he had decided to walk away from it.

"All my life," he said, grimly, "I promised myself I would never work for someone who didn't appreciate me. I've seen so many guys lose their pride just because they needed a job. I don't need one that bad."

Only a few people knew of Sinden's feelings at the time, not including the management of the Bruins. They must have suspected he was unhappy, that his pride was hurt. Early in the year the rumor had been afloat that the Bruins had to win, or Harry would be out. But if any fences needed mending, the Boston management didn't seem aware of it.

A few months before, Sinden had run across an old high school chum in the course of his hockey travels. The friend's name was David Stirling, and he was making a big name for himself in the modular home business. His company, Stirling-Homex, was one of the growing giants in the field.

Stirling had always liked Harry and told him before parting, "If you ever want a good job, give me a call." Sinden did. He discovered that he could go to work for Stirling-Homex at a salary considerably higher than what he was making with the Bruins, and also get an attractive stock option.

When he knew he had something to fall back on, he approached the Bruins and asked them to renegotiate his contract. It was Christmas week, the last year of a contract that paid him $22,500. He told Milt Schmidt, the general manager, he wanted a raise to $30,000. The Bruins countered with a hike of $2,500—to $25,000. It was then that Harry, in his own mind, decided that it couldn't have mattered to the Bruins who coached the team, as long as they were winning.

"They don't think a coach is important," he told me at the time. His voice was weary. "They think anyone can coach a team as long as you've got the talent to win. Half my time is spent acting as the traveling secretary."

Though it may seem odd, many owners do feel that way. A famous football owner was lolling on the sands of Miami Beach one winter, when a reporter located him with the news that his coach had just quit, after a championship season, to take another job. The owner sat up, took a sip from a tall drink with little pieces of fruit in it, and announced: "Coaches don't win championships. Players do. Players are eighty-five percent of a team." He paused, then added for the benefit of those who might be slow, "Coaches are fifteen percent."

As Harry Sinden watched his team sweep the St. Louis Blues with an overtime victory the next day, it wasn't possible to tell what ran through his mind. I suspected that there was at least a small ache in the region of his chest. His players had no idea he wasn't coming back. Privately, I thought he was just over-reacting, and would change his mind once he tasted that Stanley Cup champagne for the first time.

But he didn't. Two days later, he told me he intended to call a press conference and announce he was leaving to take an executive position with Stirling-Homex.

"Aren't you going to talk with the Bruins?" I asked. "You've got to tell them."

"No," he said. "Why should I? It won't make any difference."

"Sure it will," I argued. "I guarantee it, they'll come back at you with a great offer."

His nose curled. "No, they won't," he said. "I'll bet you anything you name, they won't care whether I stay or go."

I'm not a betting man and, in this case, I was just fighting for time because I felt Harry was making a critical mistake. The people at Stirling-Homex were putting pressure on him to quit without giving the Bruins a chance to counter their offer. They were perceptive enough to know that the story would cause a sensation on the sports pages around the land and bring their company a publicity bonanza at no great cost.

By the same token, I couldn't help but think that they didn't seem to have Harry's best interest at heart. I set up a meeting for the next day, the Thursday after the Cup clincher, for Harry to sit down with the Boston management to get the problem ironed out, I hoped.

My first inkling that it wouldn't be so simple came when I crossed the lobby of the North Station that morning and bumped into Charles Mulcahy, the legal counsel and vice-president of the Bruins. "Charley," I probed, "this is very serious. The guy is going to quit." I was looking for a reaction and I got one. "If that's the way he feels," said Mulcahy, "good luck to him." He kept on walking.

All along, I had felt the Bruins would work out a new deal to keep Harry happy. Now I wasn't so sure.

The meeting was between Harry and the Bruins alone while I was to wait outside. Sinden got right to the point. So did the Bruins. "Good luck to you, Harry," was the response.

There were no gestures. No responses such as, "What can we do to change your mind?" Not even, "We're sorry to lose you." Nothing was said that would indicate they wanted to keep Sinden, who was now more hurt than anything else. It dawned on me that the reason he didn't want the meeting in the first place was because he knew they would let him walk away.

When Harry joined me outside, we walked in near silence the few yards to the Madison Hotel, where the public relations man for Stirling-Homex had arranged a press conference. Finally I said, "I just can't believe it. Didn't they offer you any encouragement at all?"

"Nothing," said Sinden.

Harry was understandably resentful and would have displayed his feelings publicly had I not talked him out of it. "Listen," I said, "someday you might want to get back into hockey. You never know what can happen. So don't leave any hard feelings behind you. Just tell the press that you couldn't, at this point in your life, afford to pass up the Stirling-Homex offer.

That's the truth, as far as it goes."

I won't ever forget the expressions on the faces of the Boston sportswriters when the announcement was made. They were amazed. Every one of them expected to hear a routine statement that Sinden had been given a new contract by the Bruins, at a fat increase in pay, for winning the Cup.

The newsmen sat there in disbelief as Harry's words— "Gentlemen, I won't be back"—sank in. Then the shock dissolved and the excitement surfaced. There is a tangible feeling in a room when a big story breaks.

I remember thinking that the reaction was not unlike the night President Johnson appeared on television and told the world he would not run for another term. People had turned to each other and asked, "Did I hear him right?"

Consequently, Harry Sinden went away to build houses, and the Boston Bruins went on trying to win Stanley Cups. Neither fared too well. The next year the housing industry started to crumble. So did the Bruins, getting flattened by Montreal in the first playoff round.

Despite his self-imposed exile from hockey, Harry was growing in stature. Six different teams in the NHL were to make him an offer. Just as many teams in the new World Hockey Association had talked with him.

He could have parted company with Stirling at any time, because the company was on the verge of bankruptcy. But he remained out of loyalty until there wasn't any job left. Meanwhile, he learned how to negotiate.

One of the people in hockey who came after him was Charles O. Finley, the colorful and unpredictable insurance tycoon who dabbles in major league sports. One of Charley O.'s new interests was the California Golden Seals in the NHL. Finley had enjoyed an earlier success after grabbing another former Boston manager, Dick Williams, who led the Oakland A's into two World Series.

He made a characteristic pitch to Sinden.

"He wasn't trying to sell me on the team, or its players," said

Harry. "He was selling me Charley Finley and what he could do for me."

Sinden proved quite a salesman himself. He assured Finley it would take a super offer to entice him from the security of private industry, and the grand future he had with Stirling-Homex. He had a stock option, he reminded Finley, in a company that "was ready to go out of sight."

Which it soon did. In reality, both men were conning each other. But Harry did the better job, convincing Charley that he would be a fool to leave the deal he had. He was so convincing that Finley went out and bought $120,000 worth of Stirling-Homex stock, figuring he had the "inside" on the company's growth. A few months later he learned he had bought an Edsel, a ticket on the *Titanic* and a lifetime pass to night games at Wrigley Field, all in one package. If Finley holds a "Stirling-Homex" stock day at his ball park sometime, you'll know why.

So while Harry's future in Stirling-Homex was not a bright one, the doors of hockey were reopening. I had told him two years before, at the time of his "farewell" press conference, "Never close a door behind you; leave it at least a little ajar."

Now the strangest turn of all occurred. The Boston Bruins wanted him back. They were offering three times the money they refused even to consider giving him two short years ago. And they were going to give him what he wanted more than anything else—authority. He would become Managing Director Harry Sinden, a title that had a nice ring to it.

Twice in my career I have been mousetrapped by rumors. The first was when a sports columnist hinted that Ken Harrelson might be traded by the Red Sox, after his sensational year of 1968.

Now I was in Moscow, for that year's Team Canada–Russia hockey series, when Fran Rosa, a sportswriter with the Boston *Globe*, told me: "Bob, I just heard the weirdest rumor. Harry Sinden is going back to the Bruins."

My instincts were as reliable as always. I almost laughed out loud. No way, I thought to myself. We were back in the States less than a week when Harry was on top with the Bruins, and my old friend, Milt Schmidt, was nestling on the bottom.

How it happened was another instructive lesson on the workings of sport management. Milt *thought* he was the Boston general manager. At least, that's what it said on his office door. In recent years he had been relieved of certain duties. And now the Bruins, in the last months, had lost several stars to the WHA. Someone had to be the goat and Milt Schmidt, company man as player, coach and general manager for thirty-seven years, was getting moved aside.

As the rumors persisted he tried to clear the air. "What's this I keep hearing about Sinden coming back?" he asked Weston Adams, Jr., the president of the Bruins. "Nothing to it," said Adams, "you're our general manager."

That very same afternoon a press conference was hastily called to announce that Harry Sinden was the new managing director of the Bruins, a title, they made clear, that put him in command of the operation.

"I thought it wasn't supposed to be true," Schmidt confronted Adams.

"Sorry, but we couldn't risk any news leaks," said Adams, adding insult to injury. He was telling Schmidt, in effect, that he had to be considered a potential informer.

"Nothing in my life," he told me later, "ever hurt so much." When he asked the Bruins for a new contract, they responded by offering one year at a token raise.

Not long after that Milt was approached by the Philadelphia Blazers of the WHA. Suddenly, the Bruins had a new appreciation of his worth, and responded with another offer, a four-year package at a big increase, rather than let the NHL lose him to a league they looked on as little more than bandits.

Now Milt knew, as Harry Sinden had learned two years earlier, that he was just another carcass. But this is not meant as a commentary on how the Boston Bruins do business— most teams in all the sports operate pretty much the same way at the management level. Once the owner's favor is lost, you're gone. It doesn't much matter whether you have just won the championship, as Sinden had, or worked thirty-seven years for the same team as Schmidt had.

So it pleased me to work out a really handsome contract for Milt Schmidt with Abe Pollin, owner of the new Washington team in the NHL and one of the fairest men in sports. Milt was assured far more money than he ever earned with the Bruins, and new opportunities would be open to him. The thirty-seven-year investment wasn't in vain, after all. Milt just cashed it on another account.

It worked out well for both of them, and it taught me an invaluable lesson about the business. Through Sinden and Schmidt I began to understand one of the great inequities of sports. Those who coach teams, and those who administer them, have all the security of people who defuse bombs for a living. And except for pro football, where a few coaches— notably George Allen, Don Shula and Chuck Fairbanks—signed for big packages, such men are often woefully underpaid. In basketball and hockey, they must discipline athletes who may earn five times as much as they do.

Even in football, the owners who sign assistant coaches frequently take advantage of their eagerness to land the head job and pay them just enough money to get by on.

I sometimes wonder if there *is* enough money to compensate managers for what they suffer in a season that turns sour. What must Allie Sherman have felt in New York, when 60,000 fans chanted, "Good-bye, Allie"? Or Joe Kuharich in Philadelphia, when he read the signs that asked him to drop dead, and saw recruiting tables for the Joe-Must-Go club outside the stadium windows? And Dan Devine, whose family received phone threats, and whose lawn was littered with garbage by disenchanted Green Bay fans?

There is no remedy, of course, unless a law can be passed to change human nature. But they fire coaches with a good deal of cheerfulness. I don't judge them when one changes jobs or leagues. Their contracts protect them only so long as they win. An owner who pays off a coach deserves no credit for meeting a legal obligation he cannot evade.

Players get complacent, even owners, but never coaches. They are aware, when they take the job, that it once belonged to someone who was fired.

11

The Spirit Is Willing, But ...

OF ALL THE PROBLEMS besieging sports in my time—among them legal challenges, labor revolts, gambling rumors and salary wars—the most menacing was the drug threat.

I'm a fellow who can get high on Polish sausage. And the trend toward a casual use of drugs among professional athletes disturbed me for three basic reasons: it violates the law; it is destructive to the person who depends on them; and it goes to the very guts of the role sports has in our society—it undermines the way we look at the people we turn into heroes.

I have had one direct experience with the drug problem in sports and it was a classic lab case. Even now, a few years later, I write about it with some uneasiness and regret. At the time I never really thought I would someday be putting this down on paper, or revealing my side of that odd relationship in any public way. Some things are better left unsaid, and when Steve Kiner flew into and out of my life in just eighteen hectic months. I tried to put it all aside. His story, I felt, was one that would never come out of my files.

However, Steve Kiner has begun to make it back. He himself has gone public with some details of his long encounter with drugs. In his direct and disarming way, Steve made it seem not so much a fight as an educational experience from which he had finally graduated.

But it belonged now to the past, he said, and in 1974 he became one of the comeback stories in sport. Kiner was a starting linebacker for the Houston Oilers, up from the cellar to break even for the first time since 1967. Maybe that's when Steve began to get the message, after the Patriots gave up on him—for the second time—and dealt him to Houston, his fifth stop in four years.

When they ship you to a team that has won twice in thirty games, it must be a little like drowning. Steve Kiner's whole life must have flashed in front of his eyes. "It's the end of the hook," he said then. "It looks like they've made it pretty clear throughout the league what they think of me."

But the Steve Kiner who reported to Houston was a man transformed. He was short-haired, clean shaven, tanned as a life-guard. But still unpredictable: when the players struck he was the first veteran to cross the line and enter camp. While others groused and threatened mutiny, he said he *liked* Sid Gillman and the way he coached.

He was off drugs, about which he talked openly, and he had a fine year, I'm told. I hope it lasts. I found it impossible not to like Steve Kiner, just as I found him impossible to figure out.

When I first met Steve in August of 1971, he was on the verge of stardom. On the field he could do his thing with the best of them in the National Football League. Away from it he was different ... incredibly different. I doubt that he knew what he would be doing in the next five minutes. His mood could change with a fingersnap. And if he didn't know his next move, how could I possibly outguess him?

And that's the way it was with this so-called free spirit, who in truth wasn't free at all. He was trapped within himself and unable to escape. The things he wanted most were those he seemed most intent on destroying. He wanted to be a great football player, yet he did things that caused his coaches to wish he would disappear. And soon after, he usually did.

Which in part explains why Tom Landry unloaded Kiner at Dallas, after a fine rookie season, and sent him to New England for a fourth-round draft choice. The year before, 1970, he had been the best player on the Dallas specialty teams, making tackles all over the field as the Cowboys plowed their way to the Super Bowl. He was labeled a star of the future, another discovery, another triumph for computer scouting. The Cowboys have long been regarded as the foremost practitioners of machine science in football.

But computers can't read what is inside a man's heart or his head and soon the Cowboys, a very straight outfit, realized they had a product of the counter culture on their hands.

Kiner was restless, independent and uninhibited. Tom Landry was composed to the point of being icy, rigidly self-disciplined, a devout man who devoted long hours to the Fellowship of Christian Athletes. Let us say that the atmosphere in Dallas was not one in which Steve felt he could freely express himself. "All Tom Landry ever talks about is two things," he would tell me later, "football and religion. That's all. Just football and religion."

Landry, who had the reputation of being the most patient man in football, could take only one year of Steve Kiner. I never learned what, if anything, was the final blow. Landry showed little emotion, I am told, when Kiner parked his own car in Tom's designated parking space, at least once during a heavy rain, when his coach walked silently into the office, dripping wet. I don't believe it was because Steve got busted for drugs in Dallas, or because Duane Thomas, another labeled troublemaker, was his best friend and roommate.

Maybe it was because Steve didn't like some of the less glamorous features of football, such as practice. "The only thing I like about the game," he would say, "is playing. The rest of it is a waste of time."

For Steve, as I would find out later, statements like that are a week's conversation. He didn't like small talk. Some people can communicate volumes with nods, glances and shrugs. Steve preferred to stare. It could be very disconcerting, and scared my wife Anne the first time she met him.

Have you ever been introduced to anyone who just eyeballed you for two minutes without saying a word? That was Steve.

But good people became attached to Steve, sensed something original in him, and it was through one of those that I came to know him. He was in camp with the Patriots on the campus of the University of Massachusetts, at Amherst, a little New England town in the foothills of the Berkshire Mountains.

I received a call that summer from Tom McEwen, the respected sports editor of the Tampa *Tribune*, who had known Steve since he was a schoolboy football star and the street-fighting champion of downtown Tampa. He had a reputation as the toughest kid in the county and he fought all comers, regardless of size or age or convictions. Tom had followed Steve's career at the University of Tennessee, where he was an All-American, and in his rookie season in Dallas. Lately, he had learned from the grapevine that Kiner was fouling himself up, being tagged an eccentric and not watching his finances.

"Bob, you'd do me a great favor," said McEwen, "if you went up there and tried to help this kid out. I told him I'd ask you to get in touch. He's really a good kid. I just think he needs some decent advice."

So I drove to Amherst, through some of the prettiest farm-land in all the colonies. I was eager to meet my new client, and my first impression floored me. We shook hands, spoke maybe half a dozen words and instantly I felt a flash: *"Hey, this fellow is on dope or something."* The curious part is that I had never seen anyone on drugs before, at least to my knowledge, and really didn't know the signs. But that was exactly how Steve Kiner struck me.

He had a look about him I had never before encountered, almost Christ-like. His hair was down to his shoulder, his face divided by a wild mustache. His countenance was ethereal, almost serene. And those eyes—they were like laser beams, just looking right through you. I'd say something and before he responded, he would give me the stare, as if measuring every word, mine and his. In the time he took, he could have traced the Latin derivatives.

We decided to take a long, private walk around the campus; strolling through the fields, just wandering aimlessly as he pieced together as much of his story as he cared to tell me. It was not a new story. Basically, the world was against him. They were no damned good, none of them, anywhere. His college, the Cowboys, his agent, a business partner in a store in Tennessee, had all used and deceived him. He had no money and no friends, none worthy of the name, anyway.

The more we walked, and talked, the more I found myself drawn to this suspicious and unconventional young man. I have spent the better part of my life being touched by people with troubled histories. I told myself, "Robert, if you're ever going to do a job for a young man, this is it. This one needs help."

I went directly to Upton Bell, the general manager of the Patriots, determined to plead his case. I was only mildly disappointed to find the effort unnecessary. Bad times were upon the Patriots and Bell would have taken the Boston strangler, if he had lateral quickness. They needed Kiner.

"Bob, you've *got* to get this kid to play for us," said Bell, who only the day before had sent Kiner's friend Duane Thomas back to Dallas after an abortive trade. In a separate deal, the Patriots had acquired Thomas and appeared ready to reunite the old Dallas roomies but Thomas was now gone.

They were one grand set of salt and pepper shakers. Dallas had traded Thomas—had *attempted* to trade him—after refusing to renegotiate his contract. Whereupon Duane had blasted everybody, but especially Tex Schramm, the general manager, whom he described as "sick, demented and completely dishonest." Schramm had responded, "That's not bad. He got two out of three."

Soon after that the deal with New England was arranged. But Thomas refused to take a physical, did not find John

Mazur's coaching to his taste, and was sent back post haste. Duane had some of the personality traits I was finding in Kiner. He preferred to stare, instead of talk, one of the reasons the two of them got along so famously.

"We didn't have to talk to understand each other," Kiner once told me. "One time we spent a month down in the Caribbean, and didn't say a word for two weeks. We just knew what the other was thinking, so we didn't have to talk about it."

Bell and Mazur never did know what Thomas was thinking and, after seventy-two hours, they no longer cared. He was gone. Bell gave me a puzzled look. "I never before had a guy just sit and stare at me for an hour," he said, pouring us both a soft drink. "Have you ever heard of anything like that?"

I just smiled, sympathetically, not wishing to tell Upton that I knew another one very much like that. Instead, we sat down and worked out a contract for Steve that was quite fair. The meeting lasted until 2 A.M., and I was pleased, even more so when I went up to Kiner's room in the dormitory to wake him and tell him the figures.

"I can't believe that anyone would stay up this late working for me," he said, his voice almost meek. He shook my hand. "Thanks."

His attitude struck me as sincere, almost penitent. I told him that I'd be glad to have him as a client, handling all his affairs, if that was what he wanted. He said it was. Though to myself I added, I didn't know if it was what *I* wanted.

Steve was spectacular in camp and went on to a splendid season, twice being picked as the NFL's player of the week. The writers who had covered the Patriots for years said he was the best outside linebacker the team ever had. He was a highly visible performer each Sunday, because the Patriots believed in the blitz, which Steve loved. They came with two or more linebackers thirty percent of the time and, against certain formations, breezed in maybe fifty percent.

He was colorful, too, saying what he thought, when he said anything at all. The week before the Patriots were to play his old team, the Cowboys, he was quoted as saying that quarterback Craig Morton could be "intimidated." This is the stuff of bulletin-board ammunition, the kind coaches dread for the opposition to get their hands on, and isn't the sort of comment players are expected to make in public. Kiner shrugged off the stir it caused. "If he can be intimidated," he reasoned, "my saying it isn't going to change things."

His lifestyle hadn't changed. He still looked like a hippie and talked like a monk. I'd invite him over to the house, with some of the other players, to watch the Monday night football games, and Steve rarely said a word. I lined up a free car for the season, in return for which the dealer asked only that Steve make one appearance at his showroom. On the appointed day, Steve never showed.

Another occasion he went on local television, miffed because he felt the fee was low. When the announcer asked a question he didn't like, he simply stared as the cameras rolled on, the air filled with ominous silence.

He had the ability to lose himself totally in thought, without respect to time or place. Once, while with Dallas, during a game he braced himself for the play—arms up, knees bent, the usual linebacker pose. As he waited, staring into the line, the ball was snapped. The flow of the play moved completely away from him, to the other side of the field. Bodies collided and scattered. And Kiner never budged. He just stood there, alone, arms up, knees bent, waiting for a play that had already been run. It must have been interesting when the team and coaches viewed the game films the next day.

Still, he was playing well, even though he missed most of the practices at the end of the season with a groin pull. The Patriots wound up 1971 with a big win in Baltimore, and Steve decided to drive home to Florida from there. He rented a car, headed south and stopped off in Tennessee to visit friends. Back on the highway, outside a town called Benton, Steve was stopped by state police for speeding.

When it developed that he had no valid driver's license—

it had expired three years before—the officer told Steve to follow him to the Polk County jail. Cheerfully, Kiner obliged. He followed the police car to the station and when the officer pulled up to the curb and parked, Steve kept right on going out the other side of town. Naturally, a chase ensued and the errant linebacker was apprehended again. Sometimes, the wheels of justice can travel at speeds up to one hundred miles an hour.

Angrily, the cop walked over to the car. "Didn't I tell you to follow me to the station?"

Steve nodded. "That's just what I did."

"But you didn't stop."

"Oh," he said, innocently, "you never said anything about stopping."

A search of the rented car turned up a quantity of pills and white powder, later identified as cocaine, about which Steve said he knew nothing, the car not being his. The next morning he telephoned my office and told Len Shapiro, one of my assistants, what had happened.

Len was upset for him. "This is terrible," he said. "Did you spend the night in jail?"

"Yes."

"How was it?"

"Groovy, man, groovy."

I contacted Ray Jenkins, the brilliant Tennessee attorney who gained national prominence in the Army-McCarthy hearings of the early '50s. Ray took over the case and, eventually, got Steve cleared of the drug charges.

The case made newspaper headlines in Tennessee at the time, owing to Kiner's previous status as an All-American at their state university. But some months later, while I was speaking at a luncheon in Knoxville, I discovered that Steve had not exactly left loving memories at the school. When I mentioned that he was a client of mine, instead of the applause I had expected, they booed his name. Later, I was told by a prominent alumnus that the *folks* around there felt he had turned on the university, after they had done so much for the boy.

When I discussed this with Steve he had his own version. "Until my junior year," he said, "I was Jack Armstrong, the All-American boy. I had the short haircut and everything to go with it. But when I let my hair grow, and tried to be myself, they took away my scholarship."

There are three sides to every story—yours, mine and the truth. Somewhere between the Tennessee version and Kiner's, Steve's life started to go haywire. Although we never discussed it, I felt then—and later confirmed—that this was when his involvement in drugs took him over the cliff. It didn't, of course, happen overnight.

"I started into drugs the summer after my freshman year," he was to say later. "I loved to get high and ride horses. I went back to school my sophomore year and told myself, 'I'm so good I can totally dedicate myself to football during the week and get high after the game, Saturday night and Sunday.'

"My junior year I told myself I was so good I could get high *every* day, as long as I was ready to play Saturday. My senior year, I thought I was so good I could be high for a game."

I'm no doctor, psychologist or clergymen, and I have no set lecture about how drugs ravage the body and the spirit. But there is a progression here that simply cannot be ignored.

"I went to Dallas," said Steve, "and became the focal point of the drug scene. I guess because I *was* the drug scene in Knoxville. Grass. Speed. Mescaline. Cocaine."

The longer I knew him, the more I saw Steve Kiner deteriorate. The first time I ever knew, positively, that he was using drugs was the spring of 1972, when he flew into Boston to attend a weekend training session for the veterans. He walked into my office flying so high I refused to let him go to the stadium. I called Upton Bell and advised that, under no conditions, would I allow Kiner to practice that day. If it was obvious to someone as naive as me, it would be obvious to anyone.

That was also the day I saw what effect drugs were having on Steve's thought processes. When he had left at the end of the '71 season I felt we were close—that he trusted me. Now only a few months later he was standing there in my office, shouting that I was no damned good, that I was just like all the others, out to take his money. He was so irrational that at one point he blamed me for the money he lost in a store in Tennessee, by not protecting his interests.

That was all I could hold. "Steve, what the hell are you talking about?" I shouted back. "You made that deal, and blew that money, a year before I ever met you."

But that's how whacked-out he was. The next day he got himself together enough to appear at practice, but he wasn't ready to work. His groin injury still hadn't healed.

At that point Upton Bell called. "Bob," he said, "Steve must be into heavy drugs. The doctors say that something like that just won't heal if a guy is using drugs."

As time went on, and I guess his usage stayed high or even increased, Kiner became even less rational. When he reported back to camp that fall, I had waiting for him what may have been the best contract of any linebacker in the NFL. He refused to sign it.

"I want the money tax free," he said.

"No one gets money tax free," I argued.

But he insisted on that, and other extraordinary clauses just as far out of line. By now he had bought his own bus. I mean a *bus*, not a station wagon or a van or a trailer—a used Greyhound bought for $14,000, converted into a mobile home, with bedroom, bath and kitchen. He parked it right outside the stadium and lived in it.

Meanwhile, John Mazur, the conservative ex-Marine and Notre Dame man, was talking to himself. The other players came and went to practices without a ripple. Kiner stayed in his bus, nursing his injured groin, his contract unsigned.

He did attend some of the squad meetings and, at one, Mazur growled, "Some of the hair is getting too long around here. I want it cut by dinner time tonight or there will be fines."

Everyone knew this was directed at Kiner, and the Patriots couldn't wait to get to the training table that night. As usual, Kiner came in last, wearing a hat that had become one of his trademarks, a peaked, Amish-style hat. But, lo and behold, no hair fell down to his shoulders. He did have a neck. Even ears. "Way to go, Steve ... way to look, baby," applauded some of the team's veterans, as Kiner assembled his tray of food and went off quietly, to eat alone in a corner.

When he finished and started to move out of the room, someone yelled, "Hey, Steve, take off the hat. Show us how you look in short hair."

Kiner stopped, smiled and lifted his hat, exposing all his long hair braided neatly into a bun. He hadn't cut a single strand. He simply tied it up.

Mazur couldn't take any more and neither could Bell. They wanted to unload Kiner and, even though he was coming off a nearly all-star year, it wasn't easy. They couldn't cut him outright, because he was injured and could sue for his full salary. And they couldn't trade him instantly, because the word of his "problem" by then had spread around the league.

Finally, Bell prevailed on Don Shula, a buddy from their days together in Baltimore, to bring Kiner to Miami. Upton genuinely liked Steve and was convinced that if Shula couldn't salvage him, the job was hopeless.

In order to make the deal, the Patriots had to trade their finest defensive player of the year before—Kiner—and a seventh-round choice in the '73 draft, in exchange for Miami offensive tackle Bill Griffin, a player of taxi-squad experience who lasted exactly one week before being cut by the Pats.

It wasn't until I realized how little he had to lose that I understood why Shula even bothered to make the trade. One of the great men in sports, Shula doesn't tolerate disruptive forces on his team, which is why Kiner didn't figure.

Steve lasted about three weeks in Miami. As I understood it, the Dolphins tested his urine daily—yes, the same test given to race horses to see if they've been doped. He kept telling

Shula that he had kicked it. "I told him," Steve said, "he didn't know a damned thing about drugs and that I had been into them for six or seven years. He told me to clean up my act. I told him it was already clean."

If football is a jungle, and sometimes it can be, Steve Kiner was still tripping over tangled roots. He cut his hair—twice, he said, to please Shula—and told reporters he was off drugs and had changed his way of life. The day the story appeared was the day Miami released him.

George Allen signed him to the Washington taxi squad, where there were no games to break the drudgery of practices. He had time to think about his past, where he was going, if anywhere, and about the career he had so nearly ruined and wasted.

He had learned that he really wasn't so talented that he could stay high and play. "My weight got down to 185 from 215," he said. "I felt I was in great shape when I wasn't. I finally decided to get my head on straight. I'm not opposed to drugs. But I don't recommend them, either. I get excited about things now that I never even used to notice."

The Redskins gave him his release in October of 1973 and, for the second time, the New England Patriots picked him up. This time they had a new coach, Chuck Fairbanks, and a new system. Kiner lasted the rest of the season, which by his recent standards practically amounted to job tenure. By February of 1974, the Patriots had sent him on to Houston for a ninth-round draft choice.

He had taxied a season, missed camp and had to adjust to a new role in a defense that turned out to be the weakest in the league. When the Patriots let him go, again, he said he wasn't bitter, but he couldn't understand why he had been tossed around like an old sock the past two years.

But he *did* understand. He explained it himself: "I'm a quality football player with a bad reputation." And he knew the label was self-inflicted and he knew the source of it: drugs. Steve Kiner isn't the type to go around making speeches at high school auditoriums, but his story makes a rather dramatic case history.

So he wound up in Houston, for what he described as his last chance, and there the comeback may have begun. "I had gone through a stage of trying to identify with all my peers," he said. "Now all I have to do is please the people around me."

I hoped he meant that. I wasn't able to help Steve Kiner and I regretted that, and still do. He was in some ways an attractive fellow, with the kind of confidence and fearlessness that, properly channeled, are the qualities of great athletes.

He was never one for pretense, and I liked that. I remember being appalled, the year Ed Marinaro of Cornell came in second to Pat Sullivan, the Auburn quarterback, in the Heisman Trophy balloting, and declared that he felt the honor should have been his and he was rooked, in effect, by the voters.

That week, by coincidence, Kiner walked in as I was thumbing through a recent NCAA football guide, and I happened across his name. I looked up and, with some excitement, said, "Steve, do you realize that the year you graduated you came in ninth in the Heisman Trophy balloting?"

"Yeah." He nodded. "I should have won the gawdam thing."

I realized then that Marinaro's popping off was simply an expression of the faith every fine athlete has in himself.

Steve Kiner apparently never lost that belief in his ability to play, but he grew as a man in the eyes of many people when he looked at his own character and found it lacking. At twenty-six, his career was certainly one of the strangest in pro football. He had been with six teams, counting the Patriots twice, and had moved around more than a guy selling phony uranium stock.

Yet by wising up, and I like to think that he did, he may have performed a major service. He may have given a human, though slightly oddball, dimension to the drug problem.

When you put the word drugs in the same sentence with pro football, an alarm system rings all over the country. It is the one issue, besides gambling and point-shaving, the public will not accept as negotiable. Big Daddy Lipscomb, one of the game's most popular players in the 1960s, died of an overdose of heroin. In 1974, the sport was stunned when the commissioner fined eight members of the San Diego Chargers for using drugs. And in early 1975, a woman of dizzy and unsavory reputation caused a near panic by claiming to be the courier for a nationwide drug ring operated by pro athletes. Her charges were proven to be completely unfounded, but the publicity attached to them, the suspicions they raised, were a yardstick of the problem.

It's a scary scene, not only because the athletes who take dope damage themselves, but because they betray the fans, who have the right to know if their heroes are performing on something stronger than emotion.

Luckily for the future of sports, the problem is, I think, self-liquidating. The Steve Kiners have demonstrated that players can't abuse their bodies and still perform, and they are learning that even if they could coaches won't tolerate it. In today's regimented camps, the gamble has grown too great to offer a shelter to those bent on causing trouble.

12

My Two Amigos

---

1 9 7 1 W A S A Y E A R in which campus leaders were tearing their T-shirts and screaming about causes and justice and relevance. Inevitably, they had called into question the importance of athletics—especially football.

What *was* football? What did it contribute? Character? Competition? Entertainment? Or was it a waste, when vital things were ignored?

That year, in the fall of 1971, I met two young men who were the walking answers to the quetsions that had, at times, bothered many of us. They were out of California, out of Stanford, and their stories seemed to celebrate all the promise and all the cornball values that coaches call forth each winter at the football banquets.

Jim Plunkett had won the Heisman Trophy, the most famous award in sports. He had quarterbacked Stanford to the Rose Bowl, throwing touchdown passes to a toy-size receiver named Randy Vataha. Plunkett was the first player chosen that year in the pro draft. He was hot copy, but for a reason not entirely related to his considerable football gifts. He was a Mexican-American, the son of blind parents, a background the slick magazines and the feature writers found irresistible. The publicity, though much of it was well-intentioned, made Plunkett uncomfortable.

His friend Vataha, at 5-9 and 170, was not exactly the classic dimensions for a wide receiver. His major claim to fame was that he had spent one of his college vacations playing Bashful, one of the Seven Dwarfs, at Disneyland. It was type casting. No dwarf had ever made it before in pro football.

I didn't know either one of them when the pros reported to camp that summer. Jim was represented by Wayne Hooper, the respected Oakland attorney, who had been hand-picked by a group of Stanford alumni close to Plunkett.

Randy didn't need an attorney. If a last-round pick—which he was—had walked into a general manager's office with a lawyer, they'd have given him a trophy for chutzpah. The Los Angeles Rams had drafted Randy, a local boy, from Garden Grove and cut him after the fourth preseason game.

In the meantime, Wayne Hooper had called me when he brought Plunkett to Boston to negotiate his contract with the Patriots. Hooper is one of the people I admire in this profession. His clients have a way of becoming friends, not fees. He asked me to keep an eye on Jim, if I could, and help him get settled in the city.

Over the years Boston had been blessed with a parade of superstars—Cousy, Russell and Havlicek with the Celtics; Orr and Esposito with the Bruins; Williams and Yastrzemski with the Red Sox. But none had come in with the gusto of Plunkett.

From the beginning, the Patriots had been a losing concern. It had been five years since the team won more than four games in a season. This was a reflection of their management, which had to dig very hard for a dollar and could be best described as in a state of constant chaos. To compound matters, the ownership kept threatening to pull out, and remove to any town that had a plausible pro stadium.

Boston University, Fenway Park, Boston College and Harvard all had provided a home field for the Patriots, who, because of scheduling problems, had once played a "home" opener in Birmingham, Alabama.

Now the renaissance was at hand. Jim Plunkett was coming, thanks to the vision of Billy Sullivan, the team president, who stood fast even as the offers for that precious Number 1 pick kept getting more and more tempting, up to an hour before the draft.

At the same time a modern new stadium, in suburban Foxboro, housing over 60,000, with the Patriots as prime tenant, was being readied for the 1971 season. The fans had been waiting for a Plunkett for 12 years. They had seen the Rose Bowl become a showcase for his talents, in Stanford's dramatic upset over Ohio State. They had read and heard what a rare fellow he was.

Curt Gowdy, the noted telecaster, a New Englander, had watched him linger on the field for an hour after the Rose Bowl had ended, patiently signing autographs, and decided: "This kid is going to take Boston by storm."

A few days before the end of his first training camp, Jim Plunkett called. He still hadn't found an apartment in the city. "Tell you what," I said. "Come live with us until you find your own place. We've got the room. Then you'll have plenty of time to shop around and find the right place, rather than rushing into something."

From the Woolf family point of view, it turned out to be an inspired idea. Our own live-in hero. But there was another dividend. If it is true that you never really know someone until you live with them, I was to learn now who my clients really were, and what made them tick. I had dealt with some of the biggest names in sports for six years. I enjoyed most of them, grew fond of several and even understood one or two. But I hadn't fully realized what a roller coaster the pro athlete's life is, how their emotions flash and change like psychedelic lights. The glory. The pressure. The pain. The joy. And the frustration. Jim Plunkett, soon to be joined by Randy Vataha, together would be my post-graduate course.

Vataha had fought his losing battle with the Rams, who were well stocked with veteran pass catchers and didn't have room on their roster for a rookie—least of all, one who reminded them of Mickey Rooney. Randy thought his playing days were over. He was quickly waived on by every team in the NFL. No one wanted him. So he went home to find that his parents and friends were taking his failure harder than he was.

"I had to get away," he told me later. "I had accepted the fact that I wasn't going to play pro football. But everyone else was so low, they were making *me* depressed. So I lined up a job coaching at my old junior college, and I took off for a few days."

While Randy was vacationing, events were taking place nearly 3,000 miles away that would change his future dramatically. In the Patriot training camp, Plunkett was having problems throwing to young Al Sykes and Ron Sellers. The rhythm, the chemistry, the confidence, whatever it is a passer must share with his receivers, wasn't there. It showed in the preseason games.

For one of the rare times in his career, Plunkett tried to tell a team its business. He went to the front office and suggested that they bring in Vataha. He convinced Bell and Mazur that it was worth a try.

There was a touching scene at Logan Airport, in Boston, when Vataha's plane landed. Jim Plunkett was at the gate, waiting for him. Randy remembered a time, three years before, when he flew into Palo Alto to be recruited by Stanford. The player the coaches sent out to meet him was Jim Plunkett.

The next morning, Upton Bell, the general manager of the Patriots, walked through the offices and noticed what he assumed was an office boy sitting idly in a lounge chair. He motioned to his assistant, Peter Hadhazy: "If that kid's got nothing to do, get him the hell out of here."

Puzzled, Hadhazy glanced around the room. Then he grinned. "That's no office boy," he said. "That's Randy Vataha. You just got him from the Rams, remember?"

One could sympathize with Bell's problem. He had inherited

a franchise in turmoil. His coach, John Mazur, was new. And he was new. They were practically signing players off the street And his rookie quarterback talks him into auditioning a wide receiver who is 5 foot 9. One couldn't conceive of a less likely candidate.

So now I had two house guests living in the lower level of my split-level ranch home. I found myself worrying more about them than I was about my own law practice.

Plunkett was being besieged on all sides by people trying to use him. A survey of the sports pages in 1971 had revealed that his name appeared in print more often than any other athlete in the land. It was the year of Jim Plunkett. They wanted him for public appearances. For radio and TV shows. For interviews. And to endorse their charities. Finally, I had to say, "Look, Jim, let my office sort out all of this stuff for you, and keep those people off your back. You have enough pressure on you as it is."

Those were difficult days for Plunkett. He admitted later that there were times, in that first preseason, that he doubted himself as a quarterback. As with any rookie—particularly one playing on a poor team—he was having his troubles coping with the sophisticated zone defenses in pro football. He was also having a problem mechanically, because his offensive line was practicing its "look out" blocking technique. That's the one where the defensive lineman roars right past the blocker, who informs the quarterback of impending danger by screaming, "LOOK OUT!"

There was a preseason game against Atlanta that year when he was nearly annihilated. In one sequence, John Zook, a defensive end, hit him so hard that he must have left the imprint of his helmet on Plunk's rib cage. A couple of plays later he got it from Claude Humphrey, pouring in from the other side.

"Nice tackle," Plunkett told Humphrey as they unpiled. "Thanks," said Humphrey. "I'll be right back." He meant it, too.

Randy was living his own kind of nightmare at the time. He

didn't believe he was going to make the team. From the start of training camp, under Upton Bell's renowned revolving-door system, the Patriots had tried thirty-six different wide receivers in a span of just six weeks.

"Why don't you give Anne your laundry?" I'd say to Randy.

"Not until Tuesday," he'd say.

Tuesday is by tradition the day in pro football when you find out whether you stay on for another game or not. If a team keeps a player on its roster after Tuesday, it must pay him for the week, so all the cuts are made then. Randy was always afraid to look at the bulletin board for fear his name would be on it.

One point the average fan should comprehend is that a player doesn't make the team simply by signing a contract. As a rookie, Vataha didn't get paid a cent for playing in preseason games. He would receive his first check when, and if, he was lucky enough to make the forty-man roster. Then he would draw his salary after each regular season game—fourteen games, fourteen paychecks.

Most fans, I find, are under the impression that a player is assured a year's salary when he signs. He isn't. In some years a team will sign as many as 120 players, knowing that only one out of three will survive the cut. In reality, the standard contract in pro sports is the most one-sided agreement known to law. Every contract has a clause which states that a player must maintain the degree of proficiency expected by that team, in order to get paid. In short, they can get rid of him anytime they wish if, in their opinion, he isn't doing the job. The only exception is in the case of a player with a no-cut contract, and few get those anymore in the NFL.

This is why Vataha was so worried about making a big mistake or having a bad game. At any moment he could be cut and, whatever his effort, his bruises, the ache in his bones, he would be paid for none of it.

The days leading up to the opener were nervous ones. Plunkett was named the starting quarterback, which, in a way, I viewed with mixed emotions. Mike Taliaferro (pronounced

TOL-iver), another client of mine, was his competition, and the circumstances were unique.

When training camp opened that year, Plunkett was in Chicago playing for the college squad in the annual all-star game. Back in camp were Joe Kapp and Taliaferro, who kept his bags packed. With Kapp on hand and Plunkett coming, Mike had to be going. He expected to be traded with good reason. Upton Bell had told him he would be.

But a hitch developed. Joe Kapp, the highest paid player in pro football, and one of the more colorful, was ordered out of camp by Commissioner Pete Rozelle. Joe had steadfastly refused to sign a "standard" NFL player contract.

The year before, Joe had played out his option with the Minnesota Vikings, a team he led to the Super Bowl in 1968. For the first two games of the '70 season he sat at home in San Francisco, watching the action on television, when Bill Sullivan moved in.

Sullivan made a deal with the Vikings for the rights to Kapp, then flew to the West Coast, where he signed Joe to the most lucrative contract ever given in the NFL. Kapp got $200,000 a year for three years, with a mutual option between himself and the club for the same amount for a fourth year.

It was all transacted in a hurry and, due to the tax ramifications of such a package, Kapp signed a "memorandum of agreement." This deal—approved by the league office—would allow Kapp to play until his taxes were squared away. At that time he would sign the regular NFL contract.

Yet, when the time came Joe said no. He refused to sign a standard contract because that would bring him under the jurisdiction of Rozelle and the NFL. He argued that if the "memorandum of agreement" was good enough in 1970, it should be good enough for 1971 and beyond. When Rozelle didn't accept this, Kapp left the team and in due time filed a multimillion-dollar suit against the league. A Federal judge in San Francisco ruled in his favor in the middle of 1975 and the NFL attorneys filed an appeal. But no matter how it comes out,

Kapp threw away the last and richest years of his career. After a while he surfaced as an actor, appearing in westerns and bad-guy roles in movies and television screenplays.

I didn't agree with his decision. Joe had made a bargain and then reneged on it. But moral issues aside, his action turned the Patriots and maybe football upside down. Before Kapp decided to split, Mike Taliaferro had been treated like a fifth wheel. The Patriots had made it clear they were going with two quarter-backs—Kapp and Plunkett. Now, suddenly, they needed Mike.

Plunkett was still in the all-star camp in Chicago. Kapp was in Los Angeles. Taliaferro was the only one left in the camp at Amherst who knew how to throw a spiral. Mike, the forgotten man, was now golden.

Luckily, he hadn't reached terms for the new season, and immediately Upton Bell invited me to training camp to work out a contract befitting the new Number 1 quarterback of the Patriots.

Part of the bonus arrangement I worked out for Mike called for a $7,500 payment if he started *any* game during the regular season. Just one out of fourteen and, the way it looked, he al-most had to start the opener.

He didn't though. Jim Plunkett was too tough and too good to hold back. He would start and finish every one of the fourteen games, the first rookie quarterback in NFL history to do it. Taliaferro never got on the field for a single play during the season, which isn't exactly the hardest way to earn $50,000.

There were many times I thought Mike was going to collect that bonus. Plunkett, despite leading the Patriots to a succes-sion of upset victories, was being hammered. Jim would come home at night with welts all over his body. He was taking a fearful punishment. In any game you expected to see him trot over to the sideline, shaken, holding his kidney in his hand.

I could tell what day of the week it was by the way he walked. On Monday he couldn't. On Tuesday he hobbled. On

Wednesday he limped. By Thursday he was starting to jog.
Friday he could sprint. Saturday he could run again, only to be
slammed and battered all over again the next Sunday.

But those were joyous days in the fall of '71. On the eve of
the season's opener with the Oakland Raiders we all had dinner
with another of my clients, Raymond Chester, Oakland's great
tight end. The Raiders, coming off a string of five preseason
wins, all against class NFL teams, were ruled a 14-point favorite.

Plunkett stunned them the next day with his clutch passing
in the second half, and sent the huge crowd home delirious
when he fired the winning touchdown pass to Vataha.

"Gee, Bob," Randy said later, "if you've got a client on every
team we play we can eat dinner with them the night before and
win them all."

Yes, those were delicious times in the Woolf household. The
Patriots were playing well and my new lodgers were the toast
of the town. I was bursting with pride in them. There was
fun and laughter around the breakfast table as we looked over
the glowing writeups about Jim and Randy.

Our own kids delighted in the atmosphere, and had an un-
canny knack for being part of the scene when the network TV
cameras came out to shoot film of the resident heroes. The kids
really didn't have to scheme. Jim and Randy went out of their
way to make sure all of us had a piece of the limelight. Whenever someone came for an interview, they wanted us around.

But the quiet times were the nicest. The best pictures would
have been the ones of Plunkett holding our baby, Tiffany, in
his lap, or Randy playing pool in the game room with Gary
and my daughter Stacey. You can't pose that type of scene.
It was real—filled with warmth and affection.

The Patriots didn't win them all, but they did collect six
victories in a schedule the experts said was the toughest in the
league. Plunkett set a modern record for touchdown passes by
a rookie. Vataha broke three Patriot all-time receiving records.
And, as in a storybook, they ended the season with a spectacular,

88-yard touchdown pass from Jim to Randy that knocked the Colts out of first place in the division, and had the Patriot fans hungering for 1972.

"They're going to have to invent a new league for Plunkett," decided Bubba Smith, then of the Colts. "He's something right now. But wait until he realizes how good he is. Then we're all in trouble."

As sweet as '71 was, '72 was just as sour. Plunkett was butchered, mentally and physically. Vataha was relegated to the bench. A team that was happy and spirited the year before now was torn apart in losing.

I was reminded again of the swiftness with which fortunes change in sports. Lillian Hellman once wrote that failure in the theater is more public, more brilliant, more unreal than in any other field. Sports is like that. It was a crushing season, 1972, and we all learned from it.

Randy had married his college sweetheart during the off season and had leased his own apartment that second year. Plunkett had found what he was looking for, a one-bedroom apartment in the Chestnut Hill section. Both lived nearby, so they were still very much a part of the Woolf household. At times, as the season washed away, it seemed as though I were conducting weekly wakes. There were no more good times at Ken's Steak House after the game. It was back to my home for a quiet evening of grief.

The ritual was nearly always the same. Plunk's first move would be to call his mother on the West Coast and assure her he was okay. No matter what happened, his first thoughts always were with her. This love was so pure, so special, that even now I am uneasy writing about it, the way a stranger might feel at a train depot, watching families embrace, wanting not to look but looking, admiring their tenderness, respecting their privacy.

Plunkett's story is just so far removed from the climate of sports, so easily twisted into something maudlin, that he resists having it told. His mother, Carmen, has been sightless since she was twenty. His father, William, was legally blind, the result of an eye disease, but he ran a newsstand at the post office and worked until his death, in 1969.

Jim is proud of his parents and sensitive to stories of their disabilities. He is offended by those who indicate, by word or attitude, that he was deprived: He never felt deprived. They were super parents, self-sufficient, and they gave him a sense of values.

My wife and I stayed in touch with his mother, a beautiful lady. We would call after a game, when Jim was out of town, and she would say: "Oh, I just *saw* him on television."

We were their guests in the summer of 1975 in their new home in San Jose, and Mrs. Plunkett was still adjusting to the furniture and design of their one-level, ranch-style home. She would sometimes lose her way, and Jim would walk into a room and find his mother standing in a corner, confused. It never embarrassed her, and Jim would kid her gently.

Plunkett is proud of the home his football earnings bought. He loves to show his friends the clock that softly and uniquely *announces* the time to his mother: "It's nine o'clock."

They treat each other with great tenderness. When Plunkett came home his mother would touch his face, and hold his head, and I have heard her say, in the voice of mothers everywhere, "Oh, son, you need a haircut."

Once, Jim flew to the coast during the preseason and returned in a couple of days. Anne asked him why he would take such a long trip for so short a stay. "I just wanted to be with my mother," he said, "to be near her, to ride to the airport with her next to me in the car."

That second season of 1972 I saw Jim, for the first time, start to get down on himself. It was our habit to meet at my office every Monday, and walk down Newbury Street, and just commiserate. We would stroll past a line of fashionable shops, talking, sorting things out, trying to get his mind off his latest defeat, the newest problem. Often, as we came to a curb, accustomed to helping his mother, he would unconsciously take my elbow and, in the middle of a sentence, say "Up" or "Down."

For a sensitive young man like Plunkett, the season opener against Cincinnati, and their wily old coach, Paul Brown, would be a portent of what was to come. A week or two before the opener, Brown had picked up two former Patriots, Taliaferro and defensive back Daryl Johnson. From them he acquired most of the Patriot plays and their system of numbering plays.

Brown then drilled his defensive unit to recognize these numbers when they heard them. But how were they going to hear them when plays are called in the huddle? Easy. Make Plunkett check off as many times as they could with unusual defensive alignments. When Jim had to change the play by calling an audible—bingo.

"Every time I checked off," he said later, "one of their linebackers would yell, 'It's coming right through here,' and point at the hole where the play was going. One time I checked off to a quick pitchout, and their defensive end nearly caught the ball before our back did."

It was all a part of the education of Jim Plunkett. The Patriots won only three games. Mazur would quit. Bell would get fired. The team would decay. Their failures became a kind of town joke. One day, as I walked into the stadium a few minutes before the kickoff, a friend rushed past me and waved: "Can't stop," he said. "Don't want to miss the opening fumble."

Plunkett blamed himself for the defeats. When you win, your mistakes are forgotten. Lose, and every one of them is magnified. For the first time in his life, Jim Plunkett found himself labeled a loser. I got all kinds of phone calls from his "fans" of the year before, telling me: "That kid has really changed. Something must be bothering him." Plunkett hadn't changed. The fans had.

The Patriots were beaten by adding-machine scores (52–0 by Miami). Jim was sacked 44 times. His own linemen sniped at him in the papers. "He takes too long to throw. He's releasing the ball too quick. He isn't setting up fast enough."

It was a revelation to me how a team that seemed so together the year before now turned on one another. Everyone was copping out. It was always someone else's fault. This, I learned, was the lament of a loser. Winners will assume their share of defeat. Losers look for an excuse. Victory has a thousand fathers; defeat is an orphan.

Vataha was also having his problems. After reviewing the films of the year before, opposing teams realized that the only way the Patriots could hurt them was Plunkett to Vataha. Take that away and you had them. And this was what they did, double-covering Randy whatever pattern he ran.

Plunkett was under orders from the coaches not to run, except as a last resort. If forced to scramble he was to take a dive when anyone got near him. Jim followed orders until the second Miami game played in Miami. The Dolphins were undefeated, on their way to winning them all, and Jim wanted to beat them badly, as he had in that first season, at Schaefer Stadium.

It was still a close game in the third quarter when Jim faded to throw on third down and, as usual, was trapped. This time he ran and didn't take a dive. He wanted the first down and tried to hurdle a linebacker to get it. He was hit in mid-flight and his knee buckled.

"Something popped," he told me after the game. "I've got something wrong with my knee."

In the same circumstance, most players would have cashed it in for the season. But not Jim. He played the remaining games and, then, a month after the season, he stepped out of his car and the knee gave way. He had to have the cartilege removed a few days later.

Plunkett was to suffer through two years of despair; not a long time as adversity is measured in sports, but it is if you're living it. The Patriots won five games in '73, another year of long walks and lonely nights. I had begun to search my own conscience. I wondered if this were the time to do something I had never done before: suggest to a player that he ought to be traded.

I have never felt that it was my job to look for that kind of an out, but now my own feelings had gotten entangled with my commercial judgment. I felt so close to Plunkett . . . I didn't want to see him waste his whole career, buried in the second division, all that promise unfulfilled.

Then there was another consideration. A new coach, Chuck Fairbanks, had arrived in 1973, out of the college ranks at Oklahoma. One of his first moves was to announce that he would send in the plays from the bench. Plunkett was shaken. He prided himself on reading the defense and controlling the tempo of the game. He didn't like standing on the field, waiting for the play to come in. It made him fidgety. At the bottom of it all, he felt it reflected a lack of confidence in him. Meanwhile, Fairbanks was said to be toying with the idea of installing the wishbone-T, an offense that had won big for him at Oklahoma.

There was one catch. The wishbone demanded a running quarterback, which Plunkett was not. The speculation didn't exactly subside when Chuck traded for Jack Mildren, then established as a pro safety, but remembered as an Oklahoma quarterback.

Fairbanks is a tall, good-looking example of midwestern virtue. He is an organized, disciplined coach who doesn't try to get by on charm. His personality is not what one would call ingratiating, but it isn't unpleasant. He simply doesn't reveal himself.

So the question in Boston was: how would Plunkett get along with Chuck Fairbanks? Jim was wondering, too. In the summer of '74 he felt he had to clear the air. Fairbanks was vacationing in Michigan. Plunkett went to him, prepared to put his future with New England on the line.

Plunk poured out his feelings, his resentment of having the plays called by the bench, about the wishbone rumors, even the coldness of his coach's personality. Fairbanks listened politely. He promised to give it thought. When the season started Jim still wasn't certain where he stood, but he was calling his own plays, and there was no more talk of the wishbone-T.

And then the miracle. The Patriots jelled, they became a team, they made a strong run at the playoffs, bowing out in the last two weeks. Plunkett threw 19 touchdown passes and Randy had an equally successful season.

It's a strange, almost sad thing to say, but to the victor go the spoils. I find it distasteful in our society that we credit only those who win. Trying isn't enough. We had gone through it with Jim, who kept his dignity either way, treating success and failure alike. It is a point of pride with Plunkett to come off the field with his head high, even after he has thrown an interception.

In his rookie season, wherever he went, people fought to pay his checks and fussed over him. The next two years he picked up his own checks. Then, in '74, the pendulum swung again. Life was a holiday. He was even the guest of honor one night at the ballet, where we sat in the center box with the president of the company, Jim sleeping through the first half while I slept through the second.

The media gave him the full treatment. National magazines such as *Time, Newsweek,* and *People* sent writers to do cover stories, some of which never appeared, being overtaken by events. It isn't easy to describe the pressure of having three or four reporters follow you around, for days at a time, all looking for an angle, all wanting to be unique, all searching for the *real* Jim Plunkett.

You realize they have a job to do. And the exposure, you remind yourself, can't hurt. But I have seen Plunkett, and others, exhausted from answering questions, and more questions. I mean, drained. Then the magazines go to press . . . and the editors have decided at the last moment to go with something else on the cover. The story, the one the reporters lived with you a week to get, ends up buried inside—if it isn't delayed or canceled altogether, depending on the latest score-board.

But the point was, the Patriots had fielded a winning team, opening the season with five wins—a glorious streak that included the Dolphins and Rams. They would lose to Buffalo twice by three points, and finish with a record of 7 and 7, but the world was right again.

Until it happened, I hadn't imagined 1974 as a turning point, a fork in the road, for Jim Plunkett. It didn't appear to me that the Patriots had improved themselves, and I had begun to look at the options. The World Football League, in its early noisemaking stage, had made an inquiry, at the league level. Would a million dollars, over five years, tempt Jim Plunkett? No, I told them, it wouldn't.

But once the Patriots got a whiff of the WFL's interest, they suddenly were eager to renegotiate his contract. The ironic part was that they let it be known they would prefer to deal with Wayne Hooper. "We don't need Woolf in this," they assured him. Wayne laughed when he repeated that. He said I should think of it as my badge of honor. It was their way of acknowledging that Plunkett's new contract would cost them. Wayne immediately went to work on the contract and we conferred several times in Boston as to a fair figure. I can say flatly that Jim Plunkett, before he is through, will be one of the highest paid players in the history of pro football. The bottom line, I expect, will prove him the greatest quarterback the game has known. I base that partly on personal prejudice, partly on expert opinion. George Allen, among others, has already called him "one of the finest pure passers ever."

He will achieve all this despite one of the cruelest handicaps in sports: he has no vices. He isn't flamboyant. One of his roommates on the road, Ed Philpott, a linebacker, told of the time he returned to their hotel room to find Plunkett propped up in bed, near midnight, studying his playbook.

"Every other guy on the team was out having a few beers and a little fun," said Eddie, a happy-go-lucky sort who had the misfortune of scoring a dubious triple play—released, divorced and bankrupt in the same year. "The playbook was bad enough," Eddie went on, "but when he called his mother before going to bed I knew it was time for a new roomie."

The funny thing is that Plunkett isn't comfortable with that image. If he had the constitution for it, he would love to be Off-Broadway Jim. But he is what he is. Two beers and he's looped.

I should pause here for a moment of confession. Part of the pleasure of sport is in rediscovering the boy in all of us.

The habits of a lifetime die hard. So it was that I, Bob Woolf, entered into a competition with Jim Plunkett and Randy Vataha, in a kind of pentathlon—basketball, golf, billiards, tennis and bowling. This was long before the "superstars" were getting paid for it on TV. Don't think it wasn't serious. It was for the *world* championship.

Golf was the first event. I should have won, being the best golfer, but Randy, who is superb under pressure, slipped in. I finished second, Plunkett third.

Perhaps this is the time to make a point about Randy Vataha. If someone said to me, Bob, you *have* to be someone else in this world, you can't be yourself, who would it be?—if I faced that choice, becoming someone else, assuming his looks, build, disposition, integrity, sense of humor, intelligence, compassion—right down the line—there is no question in my mind: Randy Vataha. And as I reluctantly warned Anne, if his gorgeous wife, Debbie, happens to come along in the deal, so be it.

With that scrubbed face, and the blond cowlick, he looks like a page at King Arthur's court.

I disqualify Plunkett, on the grounds that it would be too much responsibility to have all that size (6-3, 210), talent and decency. Also, during our world championship tournament, I discovered a streak of meanness in Jim I didn't know existed.

In the one-on-one basketball series, which we played in the backyard of my home in Florida, I had Plunkett down, 9-0. Once a shooter (Boston College), always a shooter. But then

Jim started getting rough. He pounded me right into the ground and rallied to win, 10–9. He denied it, but the fact is he was all over me.

The tournament may take years to finish. It is my prerogative —part of my handicap—to schedule the remaining events. As part of my basic strategy, I plan to wait until they are both hurt and then call for the tennis competition.

13

Going Hollywood

———

I N T H E A U T U M N of 1974 I picked up a letter from the pile on my desk, skimmed it and realized with a rush of excitement that it was an invitation to speak to the Harvard Law School.

Phrases leaped out at me: "... you are invited to appear ... we have been honored in the past to have such distinguished guests as Winston Churchill, John F. Kennedy, Fidel Castro, Madame Nhu ... a reception will be held in your behalf ..."

Then, as I reached for the phone to share the glad news with my wife, I noticed the letter was addressed to:

> Mr. Derek Sanderson
> New York Rangers Hockey Club
> c/o Robert Woolf Associates, Inc.

I do not wish to overdramatize my reaction. But after I picked myself up and restored my swivel chair to an upright position, I thought to myself, "*My God*, Derek Sanderson is going to stand at the podium where once Winston Churchill and John F. Kennedy stood? I mean, if the legal profession can learn from Derek Sanderson, who needed Watergate?"

Not long after that, Derek dropped by my office and I handed him the letter. He read it with a bemused smile. "What the hell am I gonna tell them?" he said, cutting right to the heart of the issue, as he so often did. The invitation was gratefully declined.

But the experience served as yet another reminder—if any was needed—of the respect and adulation lavished upon today's breed of professional athlete. In a society that creates instant stars, needs and nourishes and often destroys them, the superplayer has become in many ways what the movie idol was in the heyday of Hollywood in the 1930s and '40s.

Take the sports superstar of today and what picture do you see? Namath and his llama rug and airline hostesses. Ali and his fleet of Rolls Royces and antique cars. Wilt Chamberlain, now retired to his palatial hilltop home outside Los Angeles, with the retractable roof over the master bedroom, so Wilt can sleep, or whatever, under the stars.

This kinship with Hollywood isn't new. Years ago athletes often appeared in "beauty and the beast" type movies. Douglas Fairbanks, Sr., once cast a picture that called for the most sinister-looking character his talent scouts could find. They produced a wrestler named Luigi Montagna, who had once chopped wood in Italy for eight cents a day. Wrestling paid better than that, but even greener fields opened to him now. He went on to a long career in films, mostly westerns, under the name Bull Montana.

Of course, that's part of it, the eternal quest for more cash and brighter lights. But that doesn't explain how they got there, who wanted them and why. Sports today is the language of art and politics. Athletes are running for offices higher than sheriff: a former Big Ten center, in fact, made it to the White House.

In many ways, the superstar athlete has taken over as the glamour boy of the American public. To verify that, all you have to do is check out the commercials on television. You didn't see Robert Redford warming the popcorn by the fireside, or stretching languidly in his pantyhose; it was Joe Namath. You didn't see Michael Caine knocking himself silly in an aftershave spot; it was Joe Frazier. And there was Chamberlain, touching himself up with Brut; Bob Griese running around in popular-priced slacks; George Blanda singing the praises of a pickup truck; Willis Reed spooning down yogurt.

Why do companies hire athletes, who are not trained for it, to sell their products in front of the TV cameras? The answer is simple. The athlete has become more credible to the viewing public. And they know him. He isn't just another pretty face. He has the advantage of looking sincere and not reading his lines too smoothly. And youngsters still revere him.

So for better or for worse, the sports idol has become the movie star of the '70s. He has it all: the entourage, the fan clubs, the autograph seekers, the groupies, the con men hoping to exploit him, all the sundry pressures of a public figure—as well as the opportunities to cash in: endorsing products, making personal appearances, writing his autobiography, hosting his own TV and radio shows, being the subject of film or TV dramas, and investing in sweetheart deals.

All of which has complicated my life considerably. As a sports attorney, I have had to become knowledgeable in each of these areas. If we were talking about a commercial, or a show, to be produced for television, was it to be cleared for network, regional or local exposure? Were single or double residuals to be paid? If a product endorsement, what was the guaranteed advance and percentage of royalty? What were the marketing and distribution potentials? Was it a quality product? Was the company legitimate?

The fringe money in sports is no longer on the fringe. It has become an industry of its own. Unfortunately, in our society it only goes to the superhero. The other 95 percent of the athletes who never endorse a product or see their smiling selves on television are out of luck. Meanwhile, the hot athlete can profit from a dozen sources, with his price rising, as his reputation grows.

A decade ago, some of the best-known athletes in the country would make a public appearance for $100. Today, for $100, if you want a speaker who is close to the home team, they will send out the boy who carries the Gatorade. When Bill Russell retired from the Boston Celtics, he did so knowing that he was going to make at least $100,000 the next year outside of sports. How? A booking agent had lined up 100 speaking engagements for him around the country—mostly before college groups—at a minimum of $1,000 a program. The kids wanted to hear Russell, and others like him, because he had the tell-it-like-it-is reputation so admired these days by the younger generation.

What could better illustrate the phenomenon of sports "going Hollywood" today than the story of Bill Russell and Ron Watts?

In the mid-'60s, Ron Watts was briefly a teammate of Russell's with the Celtics and they became devoted friends, who amused each other endlessly with needling insults. Watts was a rarity, a Jewish pro basketball player out of a Baptist college, Wake Forest. A knee injury ended his career. He became an insurance salesman in Washington, D.C. I bought one of his first policies. Once he had been my client and now I was one of his.

When Bell Telephone asked Russell to film a commercial for them, he brought Ron Watts with him for company. Between takes, Bill and his old pal reverted to their usual pastime of trading barbs. The agency people were fascinated. And the rest, as they say, is history. They turned on the cameras, filmed the pair doing their thing, and out of those ad libs came a commercial that soon established Ron Watts, former obscure pro bench warmer, into a minor celebrity. From around the country, questions poured into the phone company offices and into newspapers, wanting to know who was the guy with Russell? Did he really play for the Celtics? Did he, as he claimed, teach Russell all he ever knew?

The commercial was so popular that, within a few months, Bell Telephone had hired Ron Watts to head one of its departments, the aptly named WATS Line, promoting their special, flat-rate, monthly long-distance service.

It was a charming success story, of a kind that almost *never* happens to the marginal athlete. Or the marginal coach. But when you find that rare coach who is larger than life, and bigger than his team, then you have the new breed of superstar. The late Vince Lombardi was one of the most sought-after men in the country for endorsements, sales meetings, even training films, during his great years at Green Bay. Miami's Don Shula was the next to move into that role.

Ironically, I see the same thing happening at the management level in sports as in the movie industry. Nowadays the director is often the "star" of his film, that is, the box-office name. Federico Fellini, Ingmar Bergman, Mike Nichols—these men make films in which their personalities surpass that of their actors, just as the Shulas and the George Allens put together great teams.

Even so, the average fan identifies not with the coach, but with the performer in the arena. When they watch Chris Evert serve an ace, or Jack Nicklaus drop an 18-footer for an eagle, or Bob McAdoo pop one from the circle, they are projecting themselves into the accomplishment of that athlete. The average fan, in fact, on his good days may do some of these things. (On the other hand, it is a little harder to see yourself standing in the pocket, while the offensive line breaks down.) But the identification on the part of the fan is there, and the athlete is made, sometimes reluctantly, into what the fan wants him to be.

The athlete pays a heavy price for his split, show-biz personality. He is expected to play the role of the big shot and pick up every check. He is expected to let the public and the press have little pieces of him and not fall apart. All of which places a strain on any man's emotional stability. He can't run into the locker room and hide all the time. He has to come out and face these people who, in a real sense, have made him what he is.

Different athletes react to these pressures in different ways. Bill Russell eventually refused to sign autographs. When he was badgered for one, Bill would demand: "What do you want it for? What are you going to do with it?"

Another who rejected autograph seekers was Mike Marshall, the scholarly relief pitcher for the Los Angeles Dodgers, an off-season college professor. "Let them ask their teachers for an autograph," says Marshall. "When they start looking up to their teachers, I'll give autographs."

Autograph seeking to me has always been a curious occupation. I have never met anyone who actually saved those signatures for any length of time. Nor do I recall anyone asking for themselves, but always for a little brother, cousin, niece, son or neighbor. I have my own personal theory as to why people seek autographs, and some psychologists have agreed with it. The fan is really searching for the undivided, personal attention of the star, even though it might be only for ten seconds, while he signs the program or scorecard or notebook. The autograph seeker knows that for that period of time, the star has given up a portion of his life, no matter how short, to him. It is further remarkable how rude, almost demanding, the autograph seeker can be, often not allowing a star to finish his meal or enjoy a theater play without interruption, sometimes making the star feel as if it were his *obligation*.

Popular sports fiction of a generation ago held that pro athletes spent most of their time visiting little sick kids, were married to baton twirlers and addicted to nothing stronger than chocolate brownies. That they now smoke, drink, swear in public and on occasion cheat on their wives is more or less assumed by sophisticated fans, though not socially acceptable to some. Morally, the average ball player isn't that different from the average businessman, except that the athlete has more pressure and more opportunity; he is exposed to more women and is, sometimes, the pursued rather than the pursuer.

Every town has its own particular corps of sports groupies—young girls, and some not so young—who not only want to meet the players, but carry them off to paradise. Some of them keep lists. Some work their way through an entire roster. A few legendary ladies have tried mightily to seduce an entire league, but as far as any historian knows, time and the rapid turnover in personnel combined to make it impossible.

Understand, a groupie is not a normal young lady with healthy instincts, who happens to be smitten by an athlete and succumbs to his charms. Rather, she has a fixation, dedicated not so much to a man, or men, as to a cause. One baseball player repeated to me a revealing conversation he once had with such a groupie in Milwaukee, when the Braves were still the town heroes. She was in love with the National League. She swore to him that she only went to bed with baseball players, National Leaguers, in season.

"No football guys?" he asked, incredulous.

"No football guys."

"What do you do after the World Series ends?"

"I do without."

"When do you start again?"

"When the baseball season opens."

"Man," he said, shaking his head in amazement, "that's *loyalty*."

Such casual ladies frequently make life difficult for the shallow player who fails to reckon the consequences of his frolic. I know of one rejected girl friend who got even by planting a pair of her stockings in his suitcase, at what was to be their last rendezvous. I would have enjoyed hearing him explain that to his wife.

For many of them the motivation isn't really sex, they just want to be a part of the player's world, and tell their friends about it. They don't expect a wedding ring, they don't expect fidelity, and most don't mind being passed around to his friends. They want only to bask in whatever limelight they think attaches to a pro athlete. Sex is just a way of making that happen.

They'll use any approach to accomplish this goal. One girl

on the hockey circuit—there are different groupies for different sports—phoned players in their rooms and told them she wanted to come up to say a rosary. It wasn't hard to figure out that she wanted to prey, more than pray.

By and large, the girls do not meet the kind of resistance offered by the defenders of the Alamo. I know of one player who maintained four or five girl friends, and a wife. He had to organize his afternoons after practice like a dentist making appointments. He also had to get five or six complimentary tickets scattered throughout the stadium for home games, so that none of his playmates bumped into each other and started comparing notes.

All things considered, the percentage of athletes who settle for groupies, or other offbeat ladies, and wind up with problems is small. I wish I could say the same when it comes to con artists, the self-appointed "financial advisors" who get close to an athlete and whisper into his ear, softly, about all those wonderful, foolproof schemes they have for making him rich.

My strongest concern is with the type of people my clients meet. You can't screen them all. You hope, as you would for your friends or your own kids, that they cross the paths of only decent human beings. But they won't, because the law of averages is against them. And this is one reason why I urge my clients to let me be their buffer, to get between them and the idea man with something to sell. When they are approached, I want them to smile pleasantly and tell the promoter two words: "Call Bob."

You begin with the fact that no one likes to pay taxes, not even heads of state apparently. But they are a necessary evil, required by law, and if you want to argue with the U.S. government you better go out and raise your own army. Yet young men just out of their teens, and making huge sums of money for the first time, blanch when they realize that a good part of their pay is going to Uncle Sam. In steps the con artist: "Lissen, I can show you how to make even more money and beat the taxes with a 'can't-miss' tax shelter." In the usual course of things, the young man not only blows his investment, but the IRS rejects the tax shelter and he loses twice.

Shake any tree in America and a dozen idea men will fall out, each holding a briefcase that contains a plan, a work of art, really, explaining how to strike it rich. Unfortunately, they don't have the cash reserves themselves, you understand. But the athlete does.

The emerging star, the bonus baby, is the magic ingredient, and the con artist is going to show him how he can buy a night club; or franchise some restaurants; or back some new invention that's going to make a million.

The temptation is tantalizing. It draws every ounce of avarice and greed into the open. This is where a player representative, if the player has one, must step in and say, wait a minute. Don't be a damned fool. At best, this is the longest of long shots and not worth the risk.

There is no such animal as a sure thing. I have been burned myself, and I try to pass my experience along to the players. Look at it logically. If the investment had low risk and great potential, the con man wouldn't come looking for the athlete and his money in the first place. What the happy hustler wants is to take the gamble with someone else's money, with little or no risk to himself.

The fact is, I spend more time attempting to prevent the exploitation of an athlete than I do in generating funds. I figure they will come out well ahead, if I can help them keep what they have earned. The vultures are always out there. Not a week goes by that I don't receive a frantic phone call from the West Coast, invariably at 2 in the morning, Boston time. It is only 11 P.M. out there and the nectar is probably just beginning to flow good. He is calling from the Red Garter Concert Hall and Saloon, where a friend of his, whose name he can't remember, has offered to cut him in on something BIG.

All he wants me to do is wire him $5,000, and in six months, or less, he'll get back $50,000. At that point, it is my sad duty to inform him that the banks are not open in Boston at 2 o'clock in the morning. Then I go back to sleep.

These con men are bred by the successes of a few athletes— the ones who have the talent, or the looks, or a genuine story to tell and who have attracted legitimate offers.

I have found that every big-time athlete has his own "Hollywood" story. One of the more amazing is that of Ron LeFlore, who came to the majors from a background one couldn't imagine. Until 1970, *he had never swung a baseball bat.* No sandlot ball, no Little League, no high school. Nothing.

That year LeFlore and two buddies had held up a small store in a Detroit neighborhood, emptying the cash register into a brown bag. They were arrested a few blocks away, even before they could count it. A first offender, only seventeen, LeFlore was given a sentence of five to fifteen years.

In the beginning, he was an incorrigible, and placed in solitary confinement. To overcome the intense boredom, he started doing push-ups and sit-ups by the hour, in order to get himself tired enough to sleep. After six months, his body became incredibly powerful. When released, he decided to exert his energies in a more positive way. He directed his attention toward sports and picked up a baseball for the first time. Before long, he was impressing his prisonmates with his extraordinary feats. He was nearing parole when the Tigers sent out a good-will party, headed by the then Detroit manager, Billy Martin, to visit the Southern Michigan State Prison. There the other inmates kept touting Martin about the speed and talent of LeFlore, their star athlete, and a tryout was arranged.

In 1974 he was playing centerfield in the American League, with less than one season in the minors and three years of prison ball behind him. I believe Ron will make it. Pulling for him are a great number of people who feel he has paid his debt, and earned the right to rise above his street-corner classroom.

I have already received publishing offers for Ron to tell his life story, and even inquiries about a movie and TV drama.

(I've had similar offers for Jim Plunkett; the image-makers find athletes highly salable.)

My nomination for the next player to rate this media treatment would be a New England Patriots rookie named Russ Francis. Negotiating a Patriots' contract for Russ may have been a waste of time. He is 6-6 and weighs 245, with the kind of looks that Faye Greener, in *The Day of the Locust,* described as criminally handsome. He will probably wind up in the movies. But if he does stick with the Patriots, he will be the most colorful rookie the league has seen in decades.

He is from Hawaii and wrestles professionally, the son of a pro wrestler. He drives a Maserati, flies his own Beechcraft Sierra 200 airplane, sings and plays a guitar and claims that he likes to wander out to the pasture and serenade the cows. "The cows," he says, "think I have a great voice."

Extraordinarily, the Patriots selected Francis even though he didn't play college football the previous year. He quit after one season at Oregon, because he thought the firing of Coach Dick Enright was unfair. There is no doubt in my mind that he has the natural talent to establish himself in the pros, if that's where his interest is. Persuaded his last year in high school to go out for the track team, Francis set a world record for the javelin throw. In his first year in the NFL he was a starter and was voted runner-up for Rookie of the Year.

By 1973, with the Russ Francis types coming, and the movie-star syndrome growing, I was approached by International Creative Management, the largest talent firm in the world. They too saw the trend, most particularly Marvin Josephson, their visionary president, who negotiated the sale of the television rights to the 1976 Olympics to ABC.

They offered to make available to my clients the same opportunities they had traditionally offered their own, including people of the stature of Dean Martin, Brigitte Bardot, Burt Reynolds, Raquel Welch. We soon became associated, one more indication that our two worlds overlap.

But the major question that these digressions all raise is,

why are so many athletes, so early, thinking about these other directions?

In a sense, this "Hollywood" kind of life offers an escape from the stifling pressures that confront a player every day. In what other occupation does a man have to prove himself to his boss each time he goes to work? In what other job does a man get booed when he makes a mistake? How would any of us enjoy reading in the papers, or hearing on some talk show, that we were incompetent, a bum, or worse, and ought to be traded?

The pressures of sport are often cruel. The player not only has to beat the other team, he must compete first against his own teammates, often friends, to win a job.

So an athlete builds walls. He changes. For most of his life, the exceptional athlete has been protected and nurtured by his coaches, from the peewee leagues on up. And this is where the system creates a monster. At the age of eight or nine, when young men first display some talent, they are all too often babied through Pop Warner Football or Little League baseball. The parents coddle them, and thus begins the star treatment. It continues in junior high. If he lives in a big city, the promising star might have three or four high schools competing for his services. The school that gets him then has to treat him *right*, so he doesn't transfer out the next season to a school that will treat him better.

In high school he gets the star packaging, from the coaches and even the faculty, who keep him eligible. Imagine the number of grades that have been changed over the years, so that a star high school athlete wouldn't flunk off the team.

Next, the colleges come to call, pinching his biceps and telling him what a splendid human being he is. They make sure he takes the right courses.

And, finally, the pros arrive, behind an advance guard of agents promising a piece of the moon. The young man is now twenty-one. For the past twelve years he has been told that the world was his oyster, waiting to be opened with a flick of the knife. He has grown conditioned to the idea that, yes, you *do* get something for nothing . . . if you can run or throw or do tricks with a ball or shove other bodies around.

But once he hits the pros, they take the security blanket away from him. Now he's on his own, and exposed to forces and temptations and phonies he never knew existed. The effect is often traumatic. His standards change. He gets confused. His personal relationships suffer. Maybe for the first time he fears failure. He dreads the thought of being cut or getting hurt or going back to his hometown a fallen hero, to be asked a thousand times, "What happened?"

So sometimes he changes. He adopts a carefree, colorful personality which is supposed to let the world know that he's cool, really hip, it's just fun and games, man. And inside his head there is chaos.

I have known several players who have come very near to nervous breakdowns because of this two-faced existence. Jimmy Piersall, a popular Boston outfielder during Ted Williams' last decade at Fenway Park, did crack up. His story became a best-selling book, *Fear Strikes Out*, and later a movie. Maybe an actor can switch from role to role without problems, but many athletes can't cope with this dual role. They're out of their element.

This is my only objection, actually, to the way sports has gotten married to show business. It's fine for those who can handle it. It means more income and the opportunity for a better life. But for those who lack maturity there is danger. When they get the big money they lose the hard edge of desire. I once obtained a long-term contract for a player in *seven* figures, and less than a month into the second season I received a phone call from his general manager. "Bob," he said, "that son of a bitch is laying down on us. He got the big money and now he doesn't want to put out. He thinks he's got it made."

A lot of players think they have it made, that the golden stream goes on forever, when in reality all they have is a very fragile moment. If they misuse it, they'll find themselves on an empty stage, with the orchestra gone home, the fans filing out, and Madison Avenue looking for a new face.

Even so for every athlete who abuses, or loses, his chance, five will seize the opportunity. They make valuable contacts, save their money and prepare for the future. They'll never be afraid to look the credit manager at the bank in the eye. They will manage their lives.

And, sometimes, quietly, professional athletes do good deeds the public seldom knows about. One of the best examples I know involves Joe Namath, whose business interests included a string of Bachelor Three night clubs around the country. In Boston, Jimmy Colclough, the ex-Patriot receiver, managed the club. When Derek Sanderson became associated with the clubs, I got acquainted with Joe and Jimmy. In December of 1971, Colclough's wife, Jo-Ann, died after a brave four-year battle with cancer. That same day Namath, playing a football game in Dallas, took such a physical beating he had to be carried from the game. Yet, the next day he arrived in Boston, without any fanfare, to pay his respects.

A few months later, at the annual meeting of the Bachelors Three stockholders, it came time to discuss the Boston franchise. Namath, who had been quiet throughout most of the meeting, surprised even his closest friends on the board when he said, softly: "I gave all my shares in Boston to Jimmy Colclough." That was a handsome gesture of friendship.

The good guys are not the ones you read about, of course. Better known are the stories of Denny McLain, the Detroit pitching star who got involved in a network of shady deals, including a bookmaking operation that stopped his career at its crest; and Lance Alworth who lost his money in outside investments. Lance had taken a $175,000 loan from the San Diego Chargers, lost it in a fast-food franchise, and asked the team to float another such loan to cover his loss. When the Chargers wouldn't come through, there were hard feelings on both sides. This is why I don't believe in clubs making loans to players. The team is not a bank. All it should be paying the player is a salary based on his performance.

McLain and Alworth both went through failed marriages, one of the hazards, if not the product, of what I consider the Hollywood syndrome in sports. The noises on the fringe, the attention, the dazzle, the distractions. Some can handle it; some can't.

14

The Spirit of St. Louis

––––––

"I WON'T PLAY for less than a million dollars. I'd rather go to work in a factory."

That line was symbolic of the haywire thinking in sports. I would have thought it funny except that the young man who said it was someone I represented.

Marvin Barnes had said it—at the wrong time, to the wrong audience. On the day of his graduation from Providence College in 1974, reporters had descended on the campus hoping to learn how high the bidding would go for one of the nation's most desirable basketball recruits. That week, he had been claimed by Philadelphia as the first player taken in the regular NBA draft (Portland had won a coin-flip several days earlier for Bill Walton). Denver, which had tried mightily to sign Barnes the year before, still owned his rights in the ABA.

The talk about Walton was that he would command so much money that his contract would resemble a foreign-aid bill. The guesses ranged up to $3 million, for five years—and Walton, who didn't believe in haircuts, ate only fruits and nuts and natural foods, and shopped for his clothes at the Army-Navy store, could live on seventy-five cents a day. My client wasn't that far behind him in talent, but had much more expensive tastes.

Such was the background the day Marvin Barnes met the press. Later, he assured me he was only clowning, responding in kind to what he felt was the mood of the questions. When someone asked what he would do if he didn't get his million, he simply let the microphone drop from his hand and stood there, slack-jawed, as if in shock.

But his wisecrack was going to be on every sports page in America the next day, and no one would read a smile or a wink into it. It had the unmistakable stamp of Famous Last Words.

On occasion, athletes tend to confuse honesty with tastelessness, leaving their lawyers or representatives to clean up the mess. When Mark Spitz gave up the wet look to turn actor and TV pitchman, he was quoted as saying: "People know me. I'm already a marquee name that will draw customers. I'm going to have to work harder on my acting the first couple of times, but I'm ready to face the problems. I want people to eat their hearts out because I've accomplished things in such a short time."

Such conceit fosters the impression that athletes today are overpaid and overpublicized. I knew the same reaction was going to hit Marvin Barnes hard. And it did. In the summer of 1974, the economy was in trouble. Unemployment was soaring. There was not much sympathy for a recent college graduate who demanded to be paid a million dollars.

But, in the meantime, writers were calling my office to ask if I thought he was worth a million and would he get it? Marvin was asking, too. So I had to go along with it. Of course, I said. He would get that and more, I said, because *fair market value* was the essence of any negotiation. However, I stopped short of predicting that Marvin would work in a factory if the money was less. I had been in factories. Workers punch clocks there, and being on time was not one of the things Marvin did best.

It would take more than one incident to make me lose my faith in him. It would take, in fact, a broken contract, Marvin's strange disappearance, and the intrusion of a wild character who claimed to have cosmic powers. Compared to those hijinks yet to come, Marvin's statement to the press was just an innocent lapse.

One did not make easy judgments about Marvin. I had observed him at a time when he showed his maturity: Denver was trying to lure him out of college with an offer of $200,000 a year. Under the hardship rule, he could have turned pro as a junior and suffered few stings and arrows of criticism. Such a move on the part of a college junior had become acceptable, by 1973, and his family was heavily in debt. Marvin and his mother, Lula Barnes, met with Alex Hannum, the Denver coach and general manager, who made Marvin an offer. They were tempted, but Lula called and asked if I would advise them. She wanted to know if I thought the money would still be there a year later.

That was really how I came to be involved. Marvin didn't need a lawyer at the time. Actually, he had two of those, defending him against a charge of assaulting a teammate with a tire iron. Nor did he need an agent, because under the college rules that wasn't allowed. What he needed was a friend. Lula had asked around, and came up with my name.

So I was elected Marvin's advisor, at no charge. There was, of course, the prospect that I would represent him when he turned pro. Suddenly, that option was available to him a year early, and I found myself in a position to push him in that direction.

Would the money be there a year from now?

That wasn't an easy question. My gut feeling was that it would be there, that the leagues were not going to merge. But what if I was wrong? Even so, in the end, Marvin said he had given his word to his coach, Dave Gavitt, that he would stay in school, and he walked away from a contract worth $200,000 a year. *That* showed me some character.

The Denver offer, incidentally, had been for five years. Clowning or not, Marvin felt he had his million coming. So that's where we were, in 1974, when the 76ers made Barnes their first draft choice. Of course, going into the final hours of maneuvering, I had to cope with the usual NBA infighting. I was being pressured by Jerry Colangelo, in Phoenix, one of the league's more charming rogues. I was fond of Jerry. He's a mover, handsome, wavy-haired, well tailored. But I had few illusions about honor among NBA general managers.

Phoenix owned the fourth pick in the draft and Colangelo thought they might get Barnes, if he could hold off Philadelphia, who were desperate for a center, or a power forward, both roles Barnes could fill, and they would be picking first. The 76ers, in fact, had won only nine games two years before and still needed just about everything.

Colangelo's play was to urge me to call the 76ers and discourage Gene Shue, their coach and general manager, who had begun a huge rebuilding job, from drafting Marvin. All I had to do, he said, was tell Shue that Marvin would refuse to play in Philly, that he preferred Phoenix, and not to waste his pick. "I've talked to Marvin," Jerry assured me, "and I know he feels that way."

I checked with Barnes and he denied saying any such thing.

I wasn't about to play games. I called Shue and told him that contrary to anything he might have heard, if the 76ers drafted Marvin they would have an even shot with anyone else. My real concern was Denver. The Rockets, soon to be renamed the Nuggets, still held his ABA rights. But the team had undergone a management change, the club was up for sale, all I had heard from Colorado was silence, and it was fundamental to any negotiation that we had to have a bid from both leagues.

Gene Shue of the 76ers came in quickly with an offer that was exactly half what Marvin wanted—$500,000 over three years, plus certain incentive bonuses. Gene wanted to return to a system where a player would be rewarded *if* he produced. I agreed with this philosophy and admired him for it, and I respected him as a coach. But if he was going to introduce something new to contract bargaining, I was reluctant to let him start with my client.

About this time in June I had to appear in Denver, where I was to speak at the law school on a program with two attorneys of recent distinction—Archibald Cox and Arthur Goldberg. I had good feelings about the trip. I was impressed with the city, and with the new Denver management, Carl Scheer, the general manager, and Larry Brown, his young coach.

Moreover, Denver is, for several reasons, a very desirable city for black athletes. The living is easy, the lines are blurred, there is a very casual attitude toward matters of race. Philadelphia, on the other hand, was ghetto-ridden.

So Denver looked promising, except for one catch. The Nuggets had no interest in Marvin Barnes. They read his character as less than what they wanted, and they were already in the process of signing two expensive rookies, Bobby Jones and Bill Van Breda Kolff, the coach's son.

As I reflected during the flight back to Boston, I knew I had a problem. Barnes would be curious as to when he would visit Denver. How could I tell him that they hadn't invited him? My tactic was to tell him we had to nail down Philadephia first.

I met Shue, Irving Kosloff, the owner of the 76ers, and their head of player personnel, Jack McMahon, in Bookbinder's, one of Philadelphia's historic eating places. Gene wouldn't budge from the figure of $500,000, and I was treated to a lecture on morality, about people proving themselves, getting paid for how they perform, and not on their potential, and a few added observations on the American Way of Life.

The 76ers knew there was no competition for Barnes, and they were honest enough to say that openly to me. But all through lunch I insisted on the *fair market value*. I knew that Denver only days before had signed Bobby Jones for $1,700,000 over seven years, which works out to $235,000 a year. Ernie DiGregorio, a former teammate at Providence, had signed the year before for $2 million, although payment was spread over many years. Was I going to tell Marvin Barnes, the second pick in the nation, that he was worth less than half what Ernie D. and

Bobby Jones got, and a number of others drafted after him?

I left that meeting feeling depressed. The merger talk was getting hot. For the first time, Larry Fleischer, general counsel of the National Basketball Players' Association, said he would not bring suit to stop it, if the two leagues reached an agreement. I had to do something, I felt, and fast. So I called Frank Goldberg, the Denver owner, with whom I had been friendly. I said, "Frank, I realize you probably don't need Marvin, but the ABA has a very good shot at getting him. And this is a player of some stature. I'd like your permission to speak to the commissioner, and just say to the league, if any team wants him they are going to have an open negotiation and a very good opportunity." Goldberg said he'd get back to me.

While I waited several days to hear from Goldberg, Gene Shue and I were on the phone almost daily. An appealing and active fellow, Shue was usually telephoning from a tennis court, or a health club. He has a charming mannerism. When he is impatient, his voice slides down a sentence as though he were going down a musical scale. "Bob," he'd say, "whyyy don't you let him signnnn? Why don't you just come on downnnn? What are you waiting onnn?"

And I would always answer, "Gene, I just can't recommend it to Marvin. Not when the other top players are all getting between two hundred and two-fifty."

So it went. After a number of calls around the ABA, luck struck. The Carolina Cougars, who were bankrupt, had been purchased by a group of investors from New York, who had arranged to transfer the team to St. Louis and rename it the Spirits. The principals were Donald Schupak, a young attorney; Harry Weltman, who had been an executive with teams in both football and hockey; and two brothers, Ozzie and Danny Silna, both fans and well funded. As part of their deal, they obtained the rights from the commissioner's office to Marvin Barnes.

That was the bargaining power I needed.

I had told my ABA contacts that we would entertain an offer

of $1,500,000 for five years for Marvin. Weltman, who was to become the team's general manager, called to say they were interested.

Now Philadelphia got wind of St. Louis's interest. There are so many coaches and front-office people who have worked on both sides, the word *always* gets out. So Gene Shue telephoned to ask that we meet again, and I agreed to fly to Philadelphia.

But not before Weltman and Schupak hurried to Boston. In my home, we worked out a contract that would pay Marvin $2.1 million over six years, with provisions for deferred compensation, a home for his mother and a $15,000 Cadillac for him. He would take $100,000 of it in cash, as a bonus for signing.

In Philadelphia, Gene Shue came in with his final offer: $1,100,000 for five years, which was now quite respectable, except for two points. Gene in his conservatism didn't want to guarantee the payments (part of the money was still tied to performance), and we now had a more lucrative offer.

I explained the offer from St. Louis to him. He was flabbergasted. He didn't see how the ABA could pay such figures, particularly in view of the fact that two weeks ago no team in the league was even willing to bid.

When Gene made it clear that his figure was firm, I asked if he would mind repeating it to Marvin on the phone. "I don't want any misunderstanding," I said. "I don't want him asking me later if I'm sure that was as high as you'd go." I placed the call and Gene talked with him gladly. He told Marvin they wanted him, repeated what they were willing to pay, and cautioned that the offer did not include a no-cut clause and he still had to make the club.

Marvin said, in so many words, "See ya later."

Of course, one has to be realistic about the 76ers. Was he worth $300,000 a year to their club? They didn't have a player on their club, pending the return of Billy Cunningham, making half that. Marvin wasn't the kind of dominating center who could turn them around, who could become The Franchise, as

Abdul Jabbar did, as Portland hoped Walton would. So I'm not convinced that Gene Shue made a mistake, other than losing a draft choice, and a potential "problem" draft choice at that.

But at that moment, with a firm, lucrative offer from the midwest, all problems, real and imagined, were forgotten. I hurried back to New York to complete the deal with St. Louis, and a few days later it was announced at a press conference in the Americana Hotel. The new owners, hoping to take the sting out of his factory crack, had Marvin walk in wearing a hard hat and carrying a lunch pail, with the contract tucked inside.

Lula Barnes was there beaming with pride. He had been roasted in the press for saying he was worth a million, but his mother told every writer she could reach he was worth *three* million. Terrific. For a while, everyone was negotiating but Woolf.

I had tried to reason with her. "Lula," I said, "three million, that's more than Wilt Chamberlain makes." And she responded, "My son is better than Wilt Chamberlain."

But now everyone was happy: Lula, Marvin, the owners of the Spirits, me, even the writers, who saw that Marvin had a sense of humor. They were going to St. Louis, Marvin and his mama, and we said goodbye in a shower of hugs and handshakes and fond wishes.

Two days later, on his way to St. Louis, Marvin detoured by my Boston office to drop off a gift: his most valuable player trophy from the East-West game at Dayton, one of three such awards he won in three separate all-star games. He had prepared a touching little speech to go with it. "Bob, I want you to have this trophy because, as far as I'm concerned, *you're* the most valuable player on *my* team."

Months later I would have reason to remember with mixed feelings that moment and that sentiment. But at the time I was touched. I felt lucky to be representing this talented young fellow who was so easily misunderstood. I placed the trophy on the ledge of my favorite window, with its view from the 45th floor of the Prudential Building. The scene below was tranquil. Sailboats glided by on the River Charles. Harvard and M.I.T. were visible in the distance, a fitting background for Marvin's trophy.

In fact, my entire life was for a time tranquil. Marvin occasionally called with minor problems, but nothing cataclysmic. He was twenty-two, 6-9, strong, eager and unpredictable. He could be open and generous. He would take his friends anywhere with him, when he was flush and when he wasn't. If he was invited to Hawaii for a basketball game, he'd bring along four pals. He still worshipped his mother, a queenly lady who had worked all her life to support the family and now was a nurse at the state hospital in Providence. His relationship with his father had been strained.

I saw these seeds of character, and yet I had reason to wonder who was the real Marvin Barnes. He was chronically late and often thoughtless. In college he had cut classes, missed practices and found himself in frequent mischief. Once, his temper got him into something more than that. His fight with a white Providence teammate, Larry Ketvirtis, had almost landed him in jail.

Marvin pleaded guilty to a charge of assault and accepted a one-year suspended sentence, with three years of probation. He feared that to prolong the case might jeopardize his pro career. Ironically, his plea came on the very day of the NBA draft.

When the 1974–75 season opened, Marvin got off to a brilliant start. Off the court he had gone through $115,000 in cash in two months, a spending spree worthy of an Arab prince. But to his credit he had paid off all of his and the family's debts, totaling $70,000. He had also traded in his Cadillac for a $35,000 Rolls Royce, a purchase he had neglected to discuss with me. I was thankful I had paid off his taxes ahead of time.

Weeks passed and Marvin was not in my thoughts, except indirectly, when I spoke to the Columbia Business School in

New York in November 1974. As part of my speech, I made the point, as I often did, that my biggest headache was preventing the exploitation of an athlete.

When I finished my talk a call was waiting. A reporter for a New York paper wanted my reaction to the latest Marvin Barnes rumors. He said an agent in Los Angeles had telephoned that day to say Barnes was broke, penniless, and that his contract was invalid. The agent said he had advised Barnes to renegotiate it.

Quickly, I tried to collect my thoughts. I had not talked with Marvin in a week. But I *knew* he had a binding contract, he was free of debt and had a $4,000 paycheck coming in every two weeks. I couldn't imagine what the difficulty was.

I made no attempt to reach him until a few days later, when the Spirits were in New York to play the Nets. The first appearance of a new team and a new star in the Big Apple always generates a little extra excitement. This is true nowhere else. The Spirits were aware of it. One of the team's new owners had invited five hundred friends to see the team, and its celebrated rookie center, make their New York debut.

I telephoned Marvin at the team's hotel on Long Island. It was immediately obvious to me that someone else was in the room. He mumbled that he was busy; he'd call me right back. That was the last time we talked.

Later that night, in Boston, I went to Symphony Hall with Jim Plunkett and Randy Vataha to attend a concert by José Feliciano. During the program I was paged for an emergency call. It was the Associated Press.

Marvin Barnes had disappeared.

He had not appeared for the game against the Nets. He had left word that he would not play under his existing contract. Then he disappeared.

Over the next several days the story was to take the most bizarre turns I had ever encountered in sports. In my career I had dealt with all kinds: kleptos, nymphos, militants, vegetarians, acid freaks, flower children and Republicans. But this was the first time I had ever been exposed to the mysteries of the occult.

At this juncture enters Marshall Boyar, a Los Angeles agent whose phone call had first alerted the press that something was afoot. Slowly, I pieced the facts together. When Marvin had complained about being short of cash, and having to pay taxes, a teammate, the veteran Joe Caldwell, had put him in touch with Boyar. A little-known character who lives in Beverly Hills, Boyar had been an associate of Al Ross, the agent who had helped smuggle Spencer Haywood, Jim McDaniels and John Brisker out of the ABA and into the NBA.

What I didn't know was how much nonsense Boyar had pumped into Marvin's ear, an inviting target. Nor did anyone know where Marvin was, including Lula Barnes, who called me on the verge of panic. She had heard from this Marshall Boyar person, she said. He had assured Lula that her son was safe, was in fact with him, but he wouldn't reveal their whereabouts.

She quoted Boyar as saying that he had "special cosmic rays running through my body that enable me to dominate people."

Well, what does one do upon hearing sad news? For one of the few times in my career, I felt truly helpless. My sense of humor was fading fast. Boyar was calling reporters around the country issuing outrageous statements. "The American public," he said at one point, "will be surprised when it learns how shabbily Marvin has been treated. The American public will not tolerate it."

I had a notion that the American public had a few other matters on its mind, such as the Mideast, inflation, the energy crisis, the Nixon pardon, busing. But all the while, Boyar was claiming that Bob Woolf had negotiated a contract that somehow cheated Marvin, and further, a contract that wasn't legal.

Boyar's unjustified indictment of me stung. I had negotiated some 1,200 contracts for athletes, so there was really little mystery to it. But here was some stranger with a telephone who was threatening a reputation I had spent a professional lifetime in building. He was accusing me of being dishonest and incompetent. "As far as Marvin Barnes is concerned," Boyar said, "he has no contract with the St. Louis ball club." Promises had not been kept, he said. Taxes were unpaid. Money had been spent without being accounted for.

It was that ultimate sensation of being bitten to death by ducks. I had built a business that depended on my credibility, on the faith of my clients and the respect of the people with whom I dealt. So I wrestled now with my feelings. How could anyone make such unfounded statements? How could the press print them? How could Barnes listen to him? The papers were filled with it, each new edition adding more confusion to the previous day's headlines.

There was still no sign of Marvin. Lula had taken the precaution of telephoning the New York police and filing a missing persons report.

I had finally released a statement of my own saying that if Marvin intended to renegotiate his contract, he and I had nothing to talk about. As a practical matter, I wasn't certain I still represented him any longer. But I didn't want to see his career destroyed, and I was concerned about Lula. So, I invited her to drop by my office and review the contract, to satisfy herself as to what was in it. I encouraged her to bring anyone she wished.

Lula told the wire service and reporters in Providence that she was on her way to my office, accompanied by her husband, and one of Marvin's college coaches, Jim Adams, to read the contract.

"I have faith in Mr. Woolf," she said. "I've known him for three and a half years and he has been fair and honest with us. I don't know that other man. I don't know what he wants from Marvin. All I know is that Marvin is doing the wrong thing, leaving his team on the advice of some stranger. Marvin has been in trouble all his life and I've stood by him. I'll stand by him again if he's been wronged by somebody.

"I don't believe in the way he's handling this. If he has a

question about his contract, he should go like a man to Mr. Woolf and talk to him, like a man."

They read every word of the contract and Lula left my office satisfied that it was just as I had described it to her.

I woke up on the morning of November 23 feeling as if I had been haunted by Marshall Boyar all of my life. It was a small shock to realize that only three days had passed since Marvin had gone into hiding.

That morning the papers reported that he had surfaced in Dayton, Ohio, at a pool tournament Boyar's wife, a photographer, had been assigned to cover. The story had now spread to four cities: New York, St. Louis, Providence and Dayton.

In the meantime, Lula Barnes had fallen ill, heartsick over her son's unexplained antics and suffering from high blood pressure. The next day, the twenty-fourth, the St. Louis *Post-Dispatch* reported that Lula had finally gotten in touch with Marvin, using a ruse to get past the security watch mounted by the suspicious Boyar. She enlisted the help of a friend, who telephoned Marvin in Dayton.

The first call was intercepted by Boyar, who had two hotel rooms registered in his name. When the friend advised him that Mrs. Barnes was ill, he assured her that this was not his problem. After a few angry words he hung up.

Next the ladies called the front desk at the motel and asked the clerk to send a note to Marvin's room. Within a half hour he called back, and his mother, between tears, described what had happened. According to Lula, Marvin was furious. "Nobody," he fumed, "is going to keep me from talking to my mother."

Time was running out on Marshall Boyar.

Declaring he was *his own man*, Marvin flew out of Dayton the next morning and was soon on his way to Providence. The last anyone saw of Boyar was later that week, when he appeared in New York State Supreme Court during the trial of the ABA's suit to prevent Billy Cunningham from returning to Philadelphia. Boyar was wearing white boots and a blouse open to his belly button. As far as Barnes was concerned, Boyar no longer existed. One moment he was there, the next he had just vanished in the night. Marvin was already in the process of taking on a new agent.

His revolt and disappearance had lasted barely a week, from November 20, the day he went AWOL, until the day before Thanksgiving, November 27, when Harry Weltman announced that the Spirits had reinstated him. Barnes went on to become the ABA's rookie of the year, leading his team into the playoffs and a stunning upset of the Nets in the first round.

A St. Louis paper later reported that Marvin figured out that Joe Caldwell had been behind his problems. Earlier in the year, Caldwell had been quietly going to management and urging that they clamp down on the rookie, whose tardy habits were as evident as ever. When the team fined him, Joe then buddied up to Barnes and told him he was being misused. He also confided that he knew a fellow who could manage his affairs properly.

One can't help but wonder what motivated Caldwell. Jealousy, perhaps. Resentment. Possibly a chance to make a few dollars at the expense of a rookie who had displaced him as the team's big man. At any rate, according to Marvin, the plan was for Al Ross to become his agent, collecting a straight ten percent. Boyar, who had a real estate license, would get his money to invest. No one knew what Caldwell's cut was to be.

But Caldwell's cut, as it turned out, was from the St. Louis roster. The club suspended him indefinitely for his role in the affair, an action I applauded. All the more so because they suspended Caldwell even though they really needed him. It was one of the few times I had seen a team do the honest and gutty thing in a situation of that kind.

A postscript to the whole zany episode appeared in the December 2 issue of *Newsweek*, in a column by Pete Axthelm, whose writing is highly respected.

"The Barnes case," he wrote, "puts the agent problem in sharp perspective. Marvin's lucrative deal with St. Louis was engineered by respected Boston attorney Bob Woolf. As in 1,200 other contracts he has drawn for athletes, Woolf hammered out details that would protect Barnes' family, avoid top-heavy taxes—and also make Marvin as wealthy as possible. And once he had extracted a fair deal from the team, Woolf expected his own client to be fair and stick to the agreement: Woolf has never tried to renegotiate a contract. Marshall Boyar, a non-lawyer from Beverly Hills, doesn't play by these rules...."

Boyar had convinced Marvin, among other things, that he should not have to pay taxes. Marvin had also decided that his salary should be guaranteed against an injury *off the court*. I had argued for that clause, but relinquished it when it became obvious the Spirits would not budge. Not many teams, if any, will on that point.

Slowly, I put it all behind me. The experience was, I thought, a commentary on the times. How easy it is for those with elastic scruples to poison an athlete's mind, especially one as susceptible as a Marvin Barnes.

There was no defense against Marshall Boyar. When the St. Louis team threatened to bring a suit against him, he laughed at them. "Go ahead," he told owner Donald Schupak. "I *love* lawsuits. Got half a dozen of them against me right now. Got one for $11 million. Hell, when you called I thought it was my ex-wife, looking for more alimony."

There will always be players who refuse to honor their contracts and agents who encourage them. A handful of agents have hurt sports so terribly much, a few bad actors who need to show how clever they are, to the detriment of the athletes and the teams they serve.

So I had come to the end of my erratic association with Marvin Barnes. No more the worrisome headlines, the small, pesty phone calls. But I hadn't quite heard the last of him.

Two weeks after I had closed my files on her son, Lula Barnes called the office and left a message with Jill Leone, who is the ideal secretary. She is pretty and loyal and has a sense of decorum, the proof of which is that she didn't giggle when she delivered the message to me:

"Tell Mr. Woolf that Marvin isn't mad. He still considers him his friend. Marvin wants to know if he can borrow a thousand dollars from Mr. Woolf, and he'd like his trophy back."

15

The Men Who Would Be Czar

———

INSTINCTIVELY, we brace ourselves when the voice on the other end of the line recites the words, "Hello. Your name was given to us by..." Either something flattering is forthcoming or...

This time the voice identified himself as Tedd Munchak, owner of the Carolina Cougars, and a member of a select committee to hire a new commissioner for the American Basketball Association. I leaned back in my swivel chair to listen. Munchak went on to explain that fifteen men, involved at various levels of major league sports around the country, had been asked to nominate five candidates as a possible commissioner. My name, he said, was on every list. I was naturally flattered, a reaction that lasted right up until Mr. Munchak's next sentence.

"Tell me, Bob," he asked, curiously, "just what *do* you do? I've never heard of you before."

Traditionally, professional leagues in this country do not select commissioners; they grope for them, like a drunk trying to put on overalls in the dark. Even Pete Rozelle, the ablest administrator in sports, was anointed only after thirty-two

ballots, as a compromise candidate, by the visionaries of pro
football. He had to hide in the washroom while the owners
tried to think of reasons to vote him down. Every time a reporter entered his self-styled sanctuary, the uncomfortable
Rozelle busied himself at one of the wash basins. This gave rise
to the line that, when at last Pete was awarded the commissioner's office, he came to it with clean hands.

But no one who had involved himself in sports as much as I
had could be unmoved by the idea of running an entire league.
I was, to put it modestly, intrigued. This could be the biggest
challenge of my life. From the moment of that call, in May
of 1972, I considered the role for three solid months. In the
process, I discovered a good deal more about owners than I ever
knew or suspected. As an attorney representing athletes, I had
met with many of them and dealt as an adversary. But as a
prospect for the commissioner's job of one of the major leagues,
I saw another and revealing side of the men who move the
pieces across the chessboard of sports.

Of course, I didn't exactly go into this negotiation as a
debutante. I knew all the negative factors. I understood the
problems, I thought, more realistically than some of the men
who were screening my credentials. It has been a curious fact
that since the election of Pete Rozelle, no league has been able
to rest easy with its leadership. Jobs have gone begging. Good
men have given up out of frustration; and weak choices inevitably have been discarded.

In the mid-'60s, baseball hired as its commissioner a retired
Air Force general named William D. Eckert, who had never
even *seen* a big-league game. He was hired to do nothing, and he
did it so well they fired him. Eckert was a forlorn and sympathetic figure who never seemed to remember anyone's name,
perhaps a hangover from his military days, when he addressed
subordinates by rank.

When the name of Buzzy Bavasi was mentioned as a possible
successor, the former Dodger executive, then running the new
San Diego franchise, declined immediately: "I'd rather pump

gas," he said. "At least, if you do something for a customer you might get thanked."

The old gadfly, Bill Veeck, recommended Michael Burke, on the grounds that he once had experience with the Ringling Brothers circus, "and is used to working with clowns."

Perhaps from these anecdotes you will get a sense of the esteem with which the owners hold their membership. I knew all that, and more, and yet the idea of being considered as the commissioner of a major sport still appealed to me. I certainly didn't *need* the job. It would have meant substantially less income than my own practice provided. But it seemed a rare opportunity to test some theories, and to correct some wrongs. What missionary could resist that?

I found myself caught up in a series of phone conversations, interviews and meetings. The new relationship was a refreshing change. This time I wasn't sitting across someone's desk, hammering out a contract. We exchanged views, philosophies, concepts. In the end we very nearly got married. To explain why we didn't, I must tell you about the courtship, which will help you to understand the suitors.

For men who seemed so determined to drive themselves out of business, whose public gestures seemed so consistently unsound, I found the ABA owners to be paragons of charm, grace, power and wealth, with more than a dash of ego. They were intelligent in many ways, but in matters that went to the heart of the problems of sport, I found them less than astute.

But just who were they, these owners? Not only in the ABA, but in every other pro sport? Why do they get involved, when they have success and financial security elsewhere? What is it they seek, what music do they hear?

I found the typical owner to be a man who had made his fortune in unrelated fields, and was now searching for something that would produce fun, recognition and prestige.

Fun. More atrocities in our culture have been committed under the cloak of that word than anything short of war. Somehow the idea was perpetrated that a sports franchise would be the greatest fun—pregame cocktail parties and sitting on the bench and complimentary tickets for your friends and huge tax writeoffs.

And for some it actually worked that way. Sonny Werblin, who built the New York Jets and helped establish the American Football League, was one of the most powerful businessmen in the country for two decades before he bought into pro football. He ran a company called Music Corporation of America, whose clientele included such figures as Frank Sinatra, Cary Grant, Liz Taylor.

But until Sonny Werblin brought Joe Willie Namath to Broadway, he was little known outside of his own business circles. Then Sonny himself became a star.

Phil Wrigley, the wealthy owner of the Chicago Cubs, whose product exercised the jaws of Americans for three generations, marvels at the same process. "I make a multimillion-dollar deal in business," he said, "and I get two paragraphs in the *Wall Street Journal* the next day. I fire Leo Durocher, and it's front page news all over the country."

Wrigley, a private man, almost a recluse, became a celebrity in sports in spite of himself. Small wonder that those who seem to seek the spotlight always find it. Once, the owner was someone who stayed in the background and let the "experts" run his business. They came around maybe once a year to accept a plaque from the Chamber of Commerce, or to check and see if anyone had stolen the ballpark. But now there is a new breed and most of them love to get involved. They are often more flamboyant than their players, and if people recognize them in public, they are ecstatic.

One of the most perceptive comments I have ever read on this subject was that of the late Aristotle Onassis, who once said:

"I have come to the conclusion that the way you get to be a celebrity is to get control of the people's playthings. It's a little like children and their toys. You do not become a celebrity by controlling the people's money, their banks, their national resources, their raw materials. . . .

"If I had remained just a shipping man, I would have remained relatively obscure. But the moment I bought Monte Carlo, that was something else again. I then controlled one of the people's playthings. I was like a man who owned motion picture companies, or a television network, or a racetrack or horses or a ball team.

"They are all celebrities, and since I controlled the most famous casino in the world, I became one of the most famous men in the world."

Any discussion of ownership leads inevitably to Charles O. Finley, the colorful and irascible owner of the Oakland Athletics, who dramatize their contempt for Charley by winning the world championship every year or so. Charley O. was a grassroots Midwesterner, making a living selling insurance in Indiana. But then he plowed into sports, first with baseball, with his mule and his softball uniforms and his giveaway days and his mustache days, his hirings, firings and rehirings, and his appetite for controversy.

It isn't every day that an owner fires his second baseman in the middle of a World Series for making a couple of errors. Most owners go to the other extreme; they like to get close to the players, particularly their stars. I have always liked to negotiate with an owner, directly, when it came to the contract of a top athlete. They tend to worship their superstars and consequently tend to be generous.

This attitude has always existed in sports, the father's love an owner feels toward a special player, but it hit a benchmark in Philadelphia, in the early 1960s, when Wilt Chamberlain was raising the salary scale in pro basketball. Partly because Wilt demanded it, and partly because Irv Kosloff wanted to show his affection for his temperamental seven-footer, the Philadelphia owner gave him the first $100,000 salary in the NBA, at a time when no one else in the sport was within $25,000 of that figure.

Meanwhile, the Boston Celtics were winning all the NBA

championships, so what could Red Auerbach say when Bill Russell strode into his office and asked, pointedly, "Shouldn't I be getting paid more than Wilt?" Of course, Red had to fork over $100,001. That extra dollar was a symbol to Russell, who always had to feel he was a little better than Chamberlain.

Then there was Carl Yastrzemski in baseball. Yaz was earning around $50,000 in 1967 when he led the Boston Red Sox to the pennant. He was given a contract the next year for $100,000, because owner Tom Yawkey wanted to show his appreciation.

Yawkey had been the first to pay an athlete the magic sum —a hundred thousand—when he gave that much to the incomparable Ted Williams in the early 1950s. But Ted was a different breed of athlete from the players of recent vintage. In 1958, when he failed to hit over .300 for the first time in his career, his salary was $125,000. That winter the Sox sent him the same contract. Ted sent it back, with a note that read: "I'm not worth that much. I only want to get paid what I earned. I won't sign this contract until you give me the full pay cut for having a bad year."

So Ted Williams docked himself approximately $30,000 in salary because he didn't feel he earned it. Where did that kind of people go?

In the late '60s, Red Sox first baseman George Scott, then one of my clients, hit a lusty .181 and was a holdout the next spring. The Sox had offered him the same salary, but he was demanding a raise. George asked me to negotiate for him. "George," I pleaded, "you're lucky as hell they're not trying to cut you. Take the same contract before they change their minds." He did.

Many people ask me, "Where is the fairness in a system that no longer seems geared to performance, but only to fluke market conditions? How can a club pay a $200,000 salary, when it is losing $600,000 at the gate?"

A strange paradox, at first glance. However, you have to understand that the owners are in a unique position of losing money while winning in other ways. Take those ABA franchises which originally sold for $25,000, and have since been resold, some of them, for $2 million or more in cash, even though the teams have lost money for years.

The original American Football League franchises also went for hamburger money, $25,000 each, in 1960. Although most teams lost heavily for the next seven years, the franchises appreciated wildly in value through the largesse of television and, in time, merger and realignment with the NFL. In 1975, expansion franchises were sold to Tampa and Seattle for $16 million.

But there *is* a catch to all this. The teams could continue to survive, while paying out more in salaries than they were taking in, only so long as they had those crucial other ways to win, that is, TV and expansion money. But by the mid-'70s there were signs that a day of reckoning was at hand. The economy was in trouble, the tax laws were being reexamined, player demands were escalating crazily the cost of doing business.

I thought I saw those trends coming, and the ABA commissioner's job offered a chance to do something about it. I kept playing scenes in my head, what I would do if it were offered and I did accept. In terms of my own interest it made no sense, and maybe not in the owners' either, but I could see myself bringing the owners and the players together in a new healthy relationship.

But there is one drawback, maybe a fatal one, to restoring reason and order to professional sports. Before a man can decide how to improve his business, he must first understand the business he is in. And I've learned from experience that the men who run the sports establishment today have only the slightest idea what it is they are selling.

It's not untypical to hear an owner declare, *"I'm a hardnosed business guy. Just show me the bottom line. What works in the plumbing supply game will work in sports."* Yet they consistently forget that their product isn't an inanimate object, but faith and emotion, without which the fans would cease to exist.

And something else. Major decisions in sports are made so

slowly, with such effort, for one basic reason: the owners do not trust each other. Ethics that are taken for granted in a more conventional business are abandoned altogether when games are involved. Owners will raid each other's talent, cheat on rules, and look for an advantage at the risk of ruining a league. All of which was impressed on me again when I found myself a contender for the ABA commissionership.

As I met individually with some of the owners, I began to get a sense of what they were seeking. It was more obvious to me than to them. In a nutshell it was leadership, someone to unite them in a common cause. I seriously questioned whether I had the credentials, even as my enthusiasm continued to build.

Finally, in August, I was asked to come to Chicago for the final interview. I was told that the selection was down to three, and each of us would appear before a meeting of all the owners, general managers, coaches and officials of the league. I had heard that Bob Carlson, the attorney for Roy Boe of the New York Nets and a counsel for the league, was one of the three finalists.

On the eve of the meeting, before leaving for Chicago, I placed calls to a few friends around the country who held high positions in the major sports. I sounded them out, looking for advice, discussing the positive and negative aspects of such a move.

One of my last conversations was with a man I respected deeply, who, because of his position as a top executive in one of the pro leagues, might help me focus my own thoughts and feelings. We talked for over an hour. I literally poured out my soul to him, my doubts, my ambitions, all the information I had, the rumors I'd heard. He was very pleasant and made several suggestions, which I appreciated. At the end of the conversation I confided that the list was down to three, and I thought that Bob Carlson was one of the others.

"I'll let you know," I said, "whatever happens in Chicago. I'll call you as soon as I know how it's going to turn out."

"Bob," he laughed, "there's something I've got to tell *you*.

I'll be seeing you in Chicago. I'm number three."

I was apprehensive when I walked into the conference room and faced all the ABA people at that final meeting. My adrenalin was flowing. I had mixed emotions, because I wasn't at all sure I wanted the job. Yet it had become a competitive thing and now I was in the finals.

It was a curious feeling, sitting down and looking around the long table into the faces of Charles Finley, who then owned the Memphis team, Adolph Rupp, the renowned Kentucky coach who was running it for Finley, and Alex Hannum, a great player and winning NBA coach who came to the other league to build a franchise at Denver. The atmosphere was friendly and dignified.

I was determined that my presentation would stick exactly to what I wanted to tell them, and not what they wanted to hear. I wasn't going to con them in any way. Actually, I would offer them a deal they probably couldn't afford to accept—but one with which I could live if it became fact.

To begin with, I told them that I felt their league was no different than any other, that what it needed was a sense of direction. I informed them that I favored cleaning up all of basketball, and doing away with the practice of stealing players from the NBA; signing underclassmen; inducing players to break contracts, and fighting with each other in public. I told them that I would try to negotiate a truce with the NBA and get all the parties in both leagues to respect each other as gentlemen. I went on to say that honesty would be my best policy.

I realize now, as I see those words on the typewritten page, how much of a Pollyanna I must have sounded to those tough, driven men who considered themselves in a business inhabited by buccaneers. The questions came quickly:

"What would you do about underclassmen?"

"I wouldn't sign them."

"Why not? The NBA does."

"The NBA does because they don't trust this league. If they

thought you wouldn't go out and take juniors, they wouldn't either. The mistrust here is what is causing so many problems. If I get the job, the first thing I'm going to do is tell everyone that we're not taking underclassmen, and we're not going to entice players to jump from the NBA."

Their faces were impassive. I felt as though I had walked into a Republican caucus and advocated wider welfare payments.

I pushed right ahead. "The next thing I'm going to do," I said, "is announce that I'm going to make every effort to bring the players and the owners closer together in this league. It shouldn't be the owners first, and players second. If you have happy players, you're going to have a healthy league."

That one almost caused a few coronaries. Some reacted favorably. But most didn't. "Screw the players," retorted one of the owners, "they don't think about us."

Another asked, with pretended innocence, "What would you do, Mr. Woolf, if you were the commissioner and, say, Earl Foreman signed an underclassman?"

Now this was a loaded question, because I had been Julius Erving's attorney in 1971, when he quit college to sign on with Virginia, and Foreman, in his junior year.

"In the first place," I answered, looking across the table directly at Foreman, "Earl and everyone else knows I was never for that. But in answer to your question: I'd jump on the first plane to Virginia and hit Earl over the head." We all laughed over that one. That's not quite the way I would have really handled it, and I was sorry I had phrased it that way, but they got the message.

The owners probably thought I was either radical or naive. I am neither. The cause of most problems in sports, I feel, is the fact that no one trusts the other fellow. Yet I have no doubt that if the commissioner of the ABA would make public the sentiments I supported, within days Walter Kennedy of the NBA would have taken a similar stand, and much of the chaos would have been swept from basketball, and some mutual trust would be established.

And yet, the problems of league-jumping and raiding school-yards were still rampant in 1975. By then, the NBA had already spent a full year of searching for a successor to the retiring Kennedy. The league spent untold thousands of dollars to hire a market-research firm, to interview and screen candidates. Then the board of governors met twice, and once cast ballots for two days, and still the position went unfilled.

Really, I wonder if it had to be that complicated, if it has to take a market-research study and a year of looking to find the right man. Part of the difficulty is in what the owners expect of their candidates.

Baseball, for example, wanted a commissioner who knew who Henry Aaron was, made a nice appearance, and had the guts to discipline anyone who tried to throw the World Series. They were lucky to wind up with a good man, Bowie Kuhn. Originally they showed the measure of their confidence in him by giving Kuhn a one-year contract, but in the summer of 1975, he survived a small revolt and justifiably earned a long-term contract.

The NBA was looking for a lawyer who knew management and marketing and had friends in Congress. Hell, both political parties were looking for a man like that. And the ABA once wanted someone with television contacts, who could get them national exposure. So they hired Jack Dolph, an executive with CBS, and Jack couldn't give the games away.

And that is why we had come to Chicago, where the ABA owners had gathered again to choose their man. I'm quite sure I clinched my own rejection when I advised them that I would want to establish the league office in Boston, for two good reasons. First, I felt that there was an advantage in having the commissioner's office in a neutral city. And, two, I had no intention of moving.

I was treated well and with courtesy by the owners, but to no one's surprise, they selected Bob Carlson. He stuck it out for roughly two years—very roughly—and was followed by Mike Storen and by Tedd Munchak, who accepted it on an interim basis. By the spring of 1975, they were again in the market for a new leader. It was one of those coincidences that so enliven sports management that both professional basketball leagues should be trolling for a commissioner at the same time.

At a time when 16 million Americans were unemployed, pro basketball had two jobs open and could fill neither of them. Finally, both leagues found their men, and they were good ones. The NBA hired Larry O'Brien out of politics, and the ABA turned to a resourceful young man who had moved through every level of the game, Dave Debusschere, a coach at twenty-four, a general manager at thirty-two, a commissioner at thirty-three. One was completely alien to sports, the other had grown up in it. Both, I think, are excellent choices.

I developed instant hopes for O'Brien after his swift and decisive response to the New York Knicks' illicit signing of George McGinnis, whose contract he voided. The Knicks were heavily fined, as were the Atlanta Hawks, a late but appropriate response to their tampering with Julius Erving (an echo out of my own past).

Interestingly, Dave Debusschere was the fourth commissioner appointed by the ABA since I had been interviewed for the job in 1972.

In my statements to the ABA bosses, I had stressed a principled code of conduct. If that sounds naive, foreign to the scene of sports today, then I can only mourn for the games that used to be. The role of a commissioner, which was created in baseball more than half a century ago, centered largely on one mandate: to safeguard the integrity of sports.

That need grew out of a national scandal. In 1919, a gambler named Arnold Rothstein wished to make a wager on the World Series. And to protect his investment he took out an insurance policy in the form of eight Chicago White Sox whose services he purchased. They did such a sloppy job of fixing the series that the scandal broke quickly into the open, and the game itself was threatened with collapse. So, in a moment of desperation, baseball hired a crusty and respected federal judge named Kenesaw Mountain Landis to bring integrity back to the game. He did so with unyielding discipline, and the help of a fellow named Babe Ruth, who began hitting home runs at regular intervals. Between them, they made people forget about the Black Sox scandal and baseball began an era of new riches.

Today I fear that in our preoccupation with tax deferments and pension plans and TV contracts and lawsuits, we have forgotten that what we most need to protect is the purity of sport. I still believe that, and the balloting by the ABA people indicated to me that at least some of them agreed. I was told by Munchak that through nine ballots I led, five votes to four, and finally lost to Carlson on the thirteenth ballot.

In retrospect, my only regret is that I lost a chance to make a major impact on professional sports. I would have tried to make the ABA an example of decency and honesty in sports, with the hope that it would have a kind of domino effect among other leagues. As it was, I like to think that I stirred a few ripples in the minds of those men who, I hope, someday will use their influence to bring the tides of change.

At least, that experience gave me a better insight into how commissioners are, and should be, selected. From the beginning, all commissioners have been hired and paid by the owners, exclusively. Yet this man is supposed to be a neutral arbitrator, looking after the interests of player and owner alike. How can he, when he is really only indebted to the people who gave him the job?

I feel strongly that the commissioner should be selected by both the owners and the players. The funds for his office should also be supplied equally, by both groups. In this way he could be a true commissioner, partial only to the needs of the sport.

This may seem a modest step, but antagonism between management and labor will continue, in every sport, until it is resolved. Once both sides can look to the top of any league and say that the appointed leader is indeed neutral, the inevitable minor skirmishes will no longer turn into all-out wars.

In the meantime, commissioners will still be picked in the random and mindless way that the country has so often picked its vice presidents. Baseball's stumbling search in 1969, before it ended up with Bowie Kuhn, is a kind of classic example. At the height of the hunt, some writer on a light news day happened to ask Vince Lombardi, the former Green Bay football coach, if he had any objections to being commissioner of baseball. Lombardi made some harmless reply, like, it was an interesting thought and I played a little sandlot ball as a kid. The next thing anyone knew, Charley Finley had declared Lombardi the leading candidate for the job.

16

Brave New World

———

THE WORLD FOOTBALL LEAGUE was doomed to failure because its founders committed a fatal error. They treated it not as sport, or a cause, or even as business. They saw it as a way to traffic in franchises. In the words of the well-known television analyst, Don Meredith, it wasn't football. It was McDonald's.

Let me make it clear at the outset that I favored the World Football League, liked its chances, prayed for it and, when it arrived, welcomed it. This was largely a matter of good business, which isn't ruled by the heart. I represented players whose value would be enhanced dramatically by the presence of a second pro football league. Beyond that, I felt there was room in the country for another league. And I thought the time was right.

What wasn't needed was a burlesque that included phony attendance figures on a scale seldom practiced before, franchises going broke and moving, or going broke and not paying their bills or their players, and, finally, the spectacle of players being treated to free lunches by townspeople touched at their plight. Lawsuits spread like crabgrass. Uniforms were repossessed.

Cities sued teams for back taxes. One owner was indicted for falsifying his bank statement.

Other owners blanched at the sight of their own red ink and scrambled desperately for "local investors," a euphemism meaning someone who lives in the city that has been granted the franchise, who wants to look good to his neighbors and is willing to pick up the losses. All the while, Gary Davidson, the commissioner, was running around the country trying to remember where he had left all his franchises.

A pretty picture, isn't it?

We all wanted the WFL. We gave it the benefit of every doubt. Where did it go wrong?

Let us begin at the beginning. I had first heard rumors of a new pro football league in the fall of 1973, through sources in the World Hockey Association. Many of the people involved in the WFL had been connected with other expansion leagues —the WHA, the ABA and World Team Tennis, all the brainchildren of Gary Davidson. A young attorney of boundless ambition, Gary had a kind of prep school charm and a Robert Redford, California surfer look. He had built a reputation by aiming high, moving in and leaving early.

With a touch of bravado you had to admire, the WFL scheduled a league meeting for Los Angeles, the second week of January, 1974—the day the Super Bowl was to be played in Houston, pairing Miami and Minnesota. It may seem odd that I left Houston that Sunday morning, missed the game, and wound up watching it on television with a group of men who claimed to be creating a rival league.

It had started with a phone call in Houston from two of the new franchise holders, Bill Putnam of Birmingham and Tom Origer of Chicago. They invited me to attend the meetings. They wanted to discuss the availability of my clients. I had received so many inquiring calls from players I represented, I told them, I thought I ought to learn more about what they intended, and agreed to come. To my surprise, I had received a number of inquiries from coaches, as well. And not just assistants. I was amazed at the names of some of the NFL head coaches who phoned and said, "Bob, if you hear anything I'd appreciate your looking out for me." I suspected then that most of them were woefully underpaid, when you consider the responsibilities they have and the fact that, in some cases, they are coaching players who outearn them by a considerable amount.

So I gave away my Super Bowl tickets and flew to Los Angeles. I wanted to meet the people behind the new league, hear their plans, assess their credibility. I needed information. For weeks, everywhere I went I was being interviewed about the WFL. On the "Today" show. The Howard Cosell show. I needed some answers.

They were meeting in a suite of rooms at the Marriott Hotel. The game was on when I got there and the scene was not to be believed. Keep in mind that the Super Bowl today is the premier sports event in America, viewed by 80 million fans. I found myself in a room with eight other people; whose league existed at that moment only in their minds. We sat there watching the game, only to hear periodic outbursts, such as: "I want that fellow right there." And someone else would say, "I'm going to take this one and that one." And John Bassett, the wealthy Canadian, kept saying, "I love that Csonka. I'm gonna get that Csonka."

Here was the biggest spectacle in sports, and here was this small group of strangers, over highballs and potato chips, dividing up the very treasure of the NFL. It would have been laughable, except that within five months some of it had started to happen. Bassett got his Csonka as well as Jim Kiick and Paul Warfield, the pride of the Dolphins.

One thing Bill Putnam mentioned that day, however, made me uneasy. Putnam was no stranger to pro sports. He owned an interest in the Atlanta Hawks, and he now had the rights to one of the WFL's franchise plums, Birmingham. "Bob," he asked, "what do you think the average salary is in the NFL?"

I said, "Oh, somewhere between $27,000 and $29,000."

Bill nodded. "That's good. I think we can afford to double that."

I sat down to think about that. My god, he was talking about a 100 percent increase in salaries. I wasn't sure pro football could survive that, if it came. There just wasn't that much margin of profit, not for the amount of investment that was required.

Even so, I left the meeting feeling that they had a good shot at making it. Forces were at work that weighed heavily in their favor. For one thing, the salaries in pro football were then the lowest of any major sport. While basketball salaries had risen out of sight, and hockey's had improved radically, pro football interestingly had held the line since the bonus days of the last great war between the leagues.

At that time there were ninety basketball players earning at least $100,000 a season (some four and five times that); there were approximately sixty at that level in hockey and some forty in baseball. In pro football there might have been half a dozen: all the more criminal because professional football was the nation's most popular sport.

I have found that a very real misconception exists about football salaries. Larry Csonka was making $50,000 a year when the WFL came after him, at a time when he had emerged as the symbol of the game's power and clout. Paul Warfield, the supreme wide receiver, was making $65,000. When I first took Buck Buchanan as a client, he had been an all-pro for eight years and was earning $32,000. Duane Thomas had a superstar year as a rookie for a salary of $18,000.

What the public didn't know was that as late as 1973, first-round draft choices were signing for $20,000 per year and under.

So this was the major issue behind the famous football strike of 1974, which related importantly to the WFL. Money, not principles.

This turned out to be the major miscalculation of the players' union, their failure to present a valid case honestly, instead of hiding behind so-called freedom issues, abstractions that few fans understood. This in turn led to another misconception. The players' union failed to realize that the most important people in sports aren't the athletes or the owners or the people who control the stadiums. *It's the fans.* When they lose their loyalty, when our games create more problems than they take our minds off, attendance will dwindle, and if the evolution continues, there will cease to be a sports industry.

The strike of 1974 failed because it was ill conceived and badly explained. No one could relate to the freedom demands —no curfews, no fines, more *social amenities*—not when they thought the players were earning huge sums of money for six months' work. A nation beset by inflation, unemployment and scandal didn't know what the football players really wanted.

Yet an inequity in pro football pay did exist, compared to other sports, and had they focused on that issue the basic fairness of the fans would have won them a hearing. The sympathy of the fans would have been an immense influence on the owners. Instead, the players went to management with an unreasonable group of fifty-seven demands, abstractions that made no sense to the fans. Even the use of the word *demand* turned off the fans. The country was weary of political ultimatums.

Behind the scenes of the strike, two not-so-subtle pressures were at work. At some point the strike divided along racial lines, with blacks taking a more militant attitude toward staying out of camp, and holding tight on the freedom issues. Then there was the baiting of Pete Rozelle by the director of the union, Ed Garvey, who seemed bent on showing the NFL how much muscle he had. This attitude was reflected in the doomsday threat of Alan Page, the Minnesota player representative who announced: "We have the capacity to destroy the National Football League."

The thrust of several of the player demands was to reduce the power of the commissioner's office. In their naiveté they committed the foolish error of turning the strike into a personal clash, and they picked the wrong man. In my experience in sports, Pete Rozelle has been the ablest administrator of all. In time he will no doubt belong in the pro football hall of fame, and deservedly so, because no man has done more for the sport. I believe he has handled his office well and fairly, even though I happen to disagree with the Rozelle Rule, which allows him to fix compensation in the case of a veteran who has played out his option. My disagreement is with the system, not with Rozelle, because you are not always going to have a Pete Rozelle, with his sure instincts, making the ruling. In June of 1975 I testified to those very sentiments in a courtroom in Minneapolis, where the Rozelle Rule was on trial.

So, when you consider all of these factors, the signs were there that indicated the World Football League had come along at a time that was right. The strike had disrupted the NFL, and thrown into confusion its training camps and early schedule. The players were rooting openly for the upstart league. There seemed to be no way they could lose. The WFL and the player's strike were oddly interdependent.

Obviously, I was sympathetic to the players, who were tied, I felt, to a clearly one-sided contract. The fans, on the other hand, are not so knowledgeable about how easily a player can be fired, his income lost, his pride shattered. Or how quickly an injury can end his career. I know of few businesses where the pressure on the performer is so constant.

The player never quite loses identity with the proverbial actor who kept dreading the day he would be fired from a play, a notice that usually came by telegram. Then one day a Western Union messenger appeared backstage. His heart sank. For a long while he couldn't bring himself to open the wire. At last, with trembling hands, he did. He let out a joyful whoop of relief: "Guess what? My mother just died!" So the advent of the second league offered two hopes: leverage at the bargaining table, and a haven in case the wrong telegram did arrive.

In my time with sports I have gone through the original football war, as well as the hockey and the basketball ones. Through them all one reality remains constant: the war develops a player's market. Without the existence of two leagues there was just so much I could do for such Number 1 draft picks as Walt Patulski and John Matuszak. We had nowhere else to go. We had to rely on the sense of fairness of the NFL owners. Which was not always easy.

So the birth of the WFL meant a new deal: no-cut contracts; the money guaranteed; full payment in the event of injury; and a new wave of six-figure salaries. It was boom time again. The WFL, having opened the bank, was also promising to match the NFL standards—pension plan, insurance, all the programs.

There was no doubt in my mind that the new league would be able to entice a significant number of key players. There was simply too much discontent in the ranks of the NFL. It hadn't mellowed their attitudes to read that Gordie Howe, at forty-six, signed for a million dollars to play hockey in Houston. Or that Bill Walton negotiated a $3 million contract to play basketball in Portland.

Yet the average football player was playing for $30,000 in what purported to be the Number 1 sport in the land. So, with the fat boiled out, the freedom issues came down to money and security. When it began to look as though the WFL could offer both, the bandwagon so common in sports was on its way.

But even as the WFL was starting to score—signing the Miami trio, landing a television contract—I was feeling the first shaky vibrations. Behind the scenes it was turning into a circus. With a few exceptions, the people I met in California were no longer the ones who owned the teams. By the time I had checked out one set of investors, they had sold the franchise to someone else.

And this gets to the crux of the problem. There was a rush into professional sports by those who were merely promoters and entrepreneurs, in the poorest sense, and their impact was disastrous. It is crucial that an investor have at least two qualifications: deep pockets and a healthy attitude toward sports. But the WFL originators—hit-and-run boys—apparently had neither.

For months rumors of mysterious bankrolls backing the World Football League tantalized the sports community. First, Howard Hughes was whispered to be the angel. Then Japanese money was mentioned. Even Las Vegas, and Mafia money. And, late in the season, there reportedly was an infusion of Arab oil money. It was all a myth. The WFL was a league built on credit cards and promises. Only Bassett's franchise, Memphis (formerly Toronto), turned out to be adequately funded.

From the start, even the ones who wanted to stick it out frightened me with their cavalier, optimistic attitudes. I would ask them, "Are you prepared to lose two million a year for the first few years?" With no hesitation they would respond, "Of course, we are, Bob. But we're going to fool you. We expect to break even."

The confidence of the owners at that point was typified by Tom Origer, in Chicago, who told the press: "When my losses reach five million dollars, that's when I'll start to worry." A month before the end of the season, Origer announced bitterly that he was at the bottom of his resources. His Chicago Fire had lost over $800,000. To cut his losses, he took the unique step of canceling his team's final game and withdrawing it from the playoffs. Then he warned the fans that if someone didn't step forward with fresh money, he would have to put out the fire.

I was to have several strange experiences with the World Football League, but the one that took the prize involved Fran Monaco, the owner of the Jacksonville Sharks. One of my clients, Ron Sellers, a wide receiver of good reputation, who had played for Boston and Dallas and was now with the Dolphins, had been approached by Monaco and Danny Bridges, who was to be his general manager. Bridges had been a friend of Ron's since his college days at Florida. I suggested that Ron meet with them and get a feel for the kind of future they offered, after which I would confer with Monaco at his home outside of Daytona Beach.

I had been warned that Monaco's eccentricities were surpassed only by his imagination. But I wasn't overly concerned. As a class, the people in sports, conditioned as they are by the pressure to compete, are not exactly colorless.

But I simply wasn't prepared for Fran Monaco.

The moment Ron Sellers stepped through the door the sales treatment began: we'll give you anything you want, we'll make you a king, but you *have* to sign right *now*. Monaco rattled off a long list of Miami players on the verge of signing with him, including Nick Buoniconti and Bob Kuechenberg. He planned to announce them all on Thursday, he said—this was Tuesday—and he wanted to include Sellers in the package. He suggested that Ron stay over, as his house guest, until the press conference.

Sellers went to the phone and called me at my office in Boston. The bidding had started at $60,000 and was now, with Monaco doing all the talking, up to $130,000. "Bob," said Ron, his voice hoarse with excitement, "you better get down here right away."

I flew in the next morning and within an hour found myself in Monaco's living room, through which NFL players strolled as though he were holding an open house. This was my first exposure to Monaco and I took a moment to study him. He was about 5 feet 2, wispy, with glasses he wore near the end of his nose, peering over them like an irritated biology professor.

His conversations were given to sudden, emotional outbursts and long, painful silences. It was unsettling. At other times he rambled, as the salary under discussion swung wildly. At one point, out of the blue, he jumped to his feet and turned to Sellers: "You know nobody is interested in you," he shouted. "NOBODY WANTS YOU. I won't go over $60,000. Sign now." Then he went back to finishing his lunch.

Ron shot me a look that you would give a hitch-hiker in your car after you had heard on the radio that someone had escaped from the state mental hospital. By the time we had gotten the price back to $130,000 a year, I was trying mightily to decide if the offer was on the level. I had heard that Monaco was negotiating with a lot of players, but no one seemed to be signing with him. I soon found out why. He was giving no guarantees, no-cuts, or protection in the event of injury. No front money, no letters of credit, no personal endorsements. All you had was the word of Fran Monaco. With that and 10 cents you could mail a letter anywhere in the country.

In a dozen years I have not had another negotiation as frustrating and unpleasant as this. If you said something Monaco didn't like, he would suddenly fall quiet, and turn his back on you. He would begin sorting through his mail, pick up the phone, look at the wall. He might ignore you for the next two hours.

I spent the night in Daytona Beach with Ron and planned to meet again with Monaco in the morning. Sellers had already shown me his class by insisting that he wouldn't sign until he had returned to Miami first, and discussed the offer with his coach, Don Shula.

When I called him, Shula, already stung by his losses to the WFL, reacted sharply. "Bob," he said, "if you let him sign with Jacksonville I'll lose all respect for you. I can't believe you'd do that to me without giving me a chance to speak with him."

The next day resembled the second reel of a Marx Brothers comedy. Monaco kept telling Ron he had to sign right then. Shula was waiting for us in Miami. Next, Monaco was accusing us of using him to improve Ron's contract with the Dolphins. He wanted Ron to be a part of his blockbuster press conference on Thursday—tomorrow—when Buoniconti and the rest were to sign. By then I had checked my sources and knew he was bluffing. There would be no signings.

At that point I must have said something that offended him, because Monaco disappeared and when he returned, four hours later, he wasn't talking to me. I ran into him in the lobby of my hotel, where he had gone to meet some other guests. "Look,

Mr. Monaco," I said. "I don't know what's going on here, but I flew down all the way from Boston, and I don't expect to be treated like this."

"Oh," he said, "I didn't mean to show you any disrespect. I'll see you at my office in Jacksonville." With that he left.

Danny Bridges urged us to follow him. "I know it's insanity," he said, "but just play along with him. I know it'll turn out all right." We rented a car and drove to Jacksonville.

The offices of the legendary Jacksonville Sharks were bedlam. Monaco had cousins coming in to be assistant coaches and uncles coming in to work in the front office. And all the while this little man was running around, shouting orders, smiling one moment, angry and distrustful the next.

I slipped outside to a pay phone and called my wife. "Anne," I whimpered, "I'm in Jacksonville and I'm calling from a lunatic asylum. I can't even begin to explain to you what is going on here." She calmed me down, assuring me that no matter what happened I would still have her and the kids.

I went back in to face Monaco, and after a brief dialogue it looked as though we might get him up to $150,000. Ron, who had grown up in Palm Beach, was saying how much he had always liked Jacksonville. And my own avarice and greed were showing now. To myself I said: *I can't leave. This guy may be a nut, but he may be a nut with money.* Maybe he can back up all this.

Finally, Monaco agreed to give us two days to think it over. That week the Dolphins had scheduled a team meeting at the Fontainebleau Hotel, in Miami, the first chance Shula would have to address them since Csonka, Kiick and Warfield had jumped. I called Don and assured him Sellers would be there.

The bloody irony of all this is that we never did reach a final decision on whether to jump or stay. We were overtaken, I suppose, by events. By the time Sellers had his chat with Shula, I couldn't get through to the Jacksonville Sharks. Monaco couldn't, or wouldn't, take my calls. It soon developed that

Buoniconti and the others had signed again with Miami after having experiences similar to Ron's.

The Sharks were hopelessly confused. Monaco hired his old high school coach, Bud Asher, to build his team, hailing him as "the most brilliant mind" in football. Asher lasted about a month. Poor Danny Bridges didn't last much longer.

And here is the awful punch line to the whole episode: Ron Sellers wound up getting cut by Miami, and was out of pro football in 1974. And I have to live with that. Of course, Jacksonville was to fold at midseason, its players unpaid, and either way Ron would have lost. It was another graphic lesson in the cold uncertainty of professional sports.

In the meantime, the NFL owners were being led into a dangerous misjudgment. One way or another, the message got around the league to protect their draft picks. Suddenly, I was able to get more money for a second-round draft choice than I had for John Matuszak, the Number 1 pick in the country the year before. Where the two previous years, the Number 1 selections had signed for bonuses of around $60,000, I was able to get nearly double that for a player taken in the middle of the first round of the '74 draft, and a salary of $50,000 a year, twice the salary of the year before.

The owners will live to dread that day because there is no turning back. The NFL blundered, because the new league wasn't prepared—or able—to compete with them in signing rookies for big bonus money. The strategy of the WFL was to buy time, and publicity, by signing veterans for delivery in a year or two or three, by which time they had hoped to attract the new investors they were going to need. In short, they were fishing for the big money that would have to pay those salaries.

So the NFL was fooled into inflating its own payroll. Plus, they unconsciously put a cancer in their system. I represent a number of veterans. I know what the teams are paying rookies. How, in good conscience, can I allow them *not* to pay the fellows who have done the job?

To compound matters, the NFL fought back by calling in certain key players and signing them to four- and five-year contracts. Now, for the first time, they were asking players to come in and renegotiate, offering bonuses and—a sign of panic not seen since the last league war—they were considering giving no-cut contracts. At the start of the 1974 season, I doubt that there were six players in pro football with no-cut clauses. Of course, the best way to combat a new league is to tie up your best players for four or five years. But in so doing, you are making concessions you hadn't made before.

I could tell the threat of the World Football League—if not the league itself—had vanished by midseason. Suddenly, in the middle of negotiations with about twenty-five veterans, the NFL general managers were cooling down, telling me, "No hurry, let's think about it a while."

After fifteen games, with stories appearing daily detailing the WFL's financial problems, franchises moving in the night, and the latest legal embarrassment, the calls started to come in from players wanting to go the other way. One of them was Charley Harraway, who had signed with Birmingham for a salary nearly *four times* what he had made with the Washington Redskins. A fullback, he had been used primarily by the Redskins as a blocker for Larry Brown. In 1973 he had beaten out Duane Thomas to hold his position. His deal with the Americans had included a car, a no-cut, and all the guarantees.

Then one night he called, wanting to return to the NFL. Can you guess why? *He wasn't playing enough.* I am convinced that if there is any one thing that motivates a player more than money, it is his pride.

In retrospect, I would have to say that the signing of Csonka, Kiick and Warfield, one of 1974's biggest sports stories, hurt the WFL as much as it helped. The move escalated the salary costs wildly, and caused bitter dissension among the other owners. It was either ego or enthusiasm on the part of John Bassett, who signed them on behalf of Toronto (later Memphis). He could have learned, without too much research, that Csonka was making only $50,000 a year. Why did he have to pay $300,000, when he could have got any of them for half that? It was an impulsive move.

I happened to be in our old friend Fran Monaco's office that day when the teletype message came in, advising him that the Jacksonville club owed $47,000 as its share of the Miami refugee package. Monaco ripped the wire off and said, "Screw 'em. I'm not going to pay it. They didn't call me when they decided to sign them. It has nothing to do with me."

At the time, coincidentally, Monaco was sweating out bigger stakes. He had a large amount of money riding on the outcome of the NFL's latest expansion move. It developed that he owned the Florida rights in the WFL—for the entire state—and if the NFL did not go into Tampa, Monaco stood to make between two and three million dollars from a group in Tampa trying to swing a franchise. They were willing to pay that for WFL membership if the NFL rejected them.

"Boy," I heard him tell someone on the phone, "if they don't go to Tampa, if they go to Seattle, I'm home free. I make a cool two million, at least."

I was there when the news moved on the teletype wire that the NFL had selected Tampa as the site of its newest franchise. Fran Monaco had lost his instant fortune, and his dream of World Football League conquest. He wasn't sad or angry. He was catatonic.

Gary Davidson was another whose ambitions were jarred by the misfortunes of the long season. For a time, when the fake crowd figures were still being accepted, and the NFL strike had left the stage empty, Davidson was a hero. It began to look as though he had really pioneered something. The WFL owners hadn't yet started to resent Gary's slice of the pie: a six-figure salary, a piece of the TV money and a franchise to sell. When the league began to crumble, the owners—with Bassett and Origer up front—decided that Davidson had misdirected them. I don't believe he did, but he was fired. The final straw was the discovery that his firm had billed them for $400,000 in legal fees.

The Gary Davidsons often are entrepreneurs at heart, and not emotionally involved with whatever sport they invade. They bring in other people and then bail out, sometimes leaving behind bruised feelings and struggling ventures. But let me be the first to admit that Davidson has helped a lot of athletes, including my clients. The runaway salary explosions that often followed his intrigues made some of them rich.

Regrettably, the WFL added to the most serious problem facing pro football today—how it is perceived by the public. And it is all exposed in the media: the contract jumping, the drug problems, the law suits, the lack of candor.

It is not surprising then that the fans are growing more wary, more critical, less eager to offer their loyalty.

And yet I believed then, and still do, that room exists for another league—properly done. That means no stranger in a checkered vest, riding into town and selling a franchise. It will require a group attitude, a plan, strong, responsible leadership, a little class and, above all, tons of money and a will to survive. In 1975 the WFL, now known as the "new WFL" with its Hemmetter Plan, by which the players are paid a minimum and share in the profits if any, gave it a second try. And on October 22 it announced its own demise.

17

Comes the Revolution

———

TO A CONFUSED PUBLIC, it must have seemed that the New England Patriots had decided to celebrate the bicentennial a few months early. As odd as it sounds, that was part of it. The spirit of '76, the spirit of rebellion, was in the air.

Randy Vataha had said as much to me the night it all started. I had asked about the mood of the players. Randy said, "We just thought, what the hell, this was where the American Revolution began. This was where ours would begin."

When I first heard the news—that the Patriots had voted to strike a few hours before their last preseason game, one week before the 1975 season was to open—my first concern was not for football or the fans or what to do with my tickets. I thought about Randy Vataha. He was the New England player representative, a job not known for its longevity. Player reps have a history of getting traded and cut. I felt for Randy the concern you feel for someone who has done his duty and is going to catch hell for it.

I was at home that night, Saturday, September 13, when the phone calls came. The Boston papers and the wire services wanted my reaction. That was easy. I was dumfounded. For the second time in two preseasons, the pace of pro football had been broken by a strike, a wildcat strike at that.

For the first time ever, a team had defied its own union, as well as its employer, to walk off the job.

I felt a need, an urgency, to see Randy and find out what the hell was behind it. I knew the negotiations between the players' union and the owners on a new contract had gone slowly; they were, in fact, in their fifteenth month without results. But the strike a year ago had produced nothing but bitterness and stalemate. Why this? Why now?

It was about 9 P.M. when I slipped into my coat and told my wife not to wait up for me. I backed the car out of the drive and pointed it toward the stadium at Foxboro, where the Patriots had met twice that day to reach and affirm their decision. I had a feeling Vataha would still be there.

I saw him the moment I pulled into the parking lot. He was standing in front of the main gate, in the shadows cast by the parking-lot lights, listening quietly to two of the Patriot executives, Chuck Sullivan and Robert Marr. It struck me that they looked like a host and his guests standing in the doorway, drawing out their good-nights after a party.

As I walked up, I could hear Sullivan, distraught, pleading with him: "Randy, don't do this to us. Please. Don't let this happen."

Even in that tense and awkward moment, Vataha still had his sense of humor. When he saw me coming he lifted his chin and a smile spread across his boyish face. He knew the key word that would agitate me. "Ah," he said, "here comes Bob Woolf. Here comes my *agent*."

A few minutes later we were in my car, heading for the Red Snapper, a seafood restaurant a few blocks from the stadium. The striking Patriots were assembling there for another meeting. We were alone now and there were no more jokes.

"Randy," I said, "I just don't understand it. Where's the sense in it?"

He was tired and uneasy but still navigating on nervous energy. He gestured with his hands. "Bob, we just thought we had to do something. The owners have had fifteen months to make an offer and nothing has happened. We don't know what the Players' Association has been doing all that time either. We decided this was a way to find out. By Monday we'll know if we have a union or not. If we don't get any support, we'll be back on the field Tuesday."

"But why you? Why the Patriots?"

"I don't know," he said. "I can't answer that. It just turned out that way." And then he threw the line at me about the Revolution. At that moment, it made as much sense as anything.

Historically, this may have been the right team in the right place—a few blocks from Concord, where The Shot Heard 'Round the World was fired. How far would this one be heard? Well, at least in 25 other National Football League cities, and in the offices of every franchise in professional sport, where years of turmoil and unrest now seemed to be heading for a climax.

But this was no pageant, no reenactment of a moment in history. Even though my own sympathies had to be with the players, so many of whom I represented, I felt their timing was dead wrong. I don't mean that night or that week or that month. I mean 1975, a year when the average workingman and his family were squeezed by runaway prices and an uncertain job market, and great waves of despair were running across the land.

I waited in the lobby while Randy and the players retired to the banquet room to discuss their next moves. Soon, Sullivan and Marr and assistant general manager Pete Hadhazy appeared, and in a few moments we were joined by their coach, Chuck Fairbanks, grim and edgy. Now I thought about the human involvement. There was Fairbanks, trying to bring his team to a peak, and the night before their final tuneup game, against the New York Jets, they take a hike. For all he knew, his team and his season were down the drain.

And I thought of Jim Plunkett, waiting out a shoulder injury in California, cut off from the team and not a party to this decision, wondering what was going on. Wondering what would be left a month from now, when he was ready to come back.

Then the irony of Neil Graff, the Patriots' backup quarterback, hit me. A rookie, he was scheduled to make his first pro start the next day, Sunday, against the Jets, in New Haven's Yale Bowl, before a sizable jury of New York writers, on national television. It was a dream assignment. And now, in the interest of team unity, he had had to vote *against* playing the game, against his own start.

I understood the emotions as well as the morality of the position the Patriots had taken. But I didn't see the intelligence of it. It was everyone's war, but the players were going to furnish all the soldiers and shed all the blood.

What had developed, I learned, was this: Ed Garvey, the director of the Players' Association, had been in telephone contact with the player reps of the four teams involved in national television games that Sunday, September 14. New England versus the New York Jets, and St. Louis at Denver. Each had been assured that the other teams were prepared to strike the TV games, as a protest against the failure of the long negotiations to produce a contract.

But somewhere along the line there was a breakdown. While the Patriots were voting on Saturday to walk out, the other teams were making no commitment. The next day, the Cardinals and the Broncos went on as scheduled. The Jets took the unassailable position that since they had no opponent they wouldn't play, and they offered their moral support to the Patriots, stopping just short of voting to strike.

Soon the echoes were being heard throughout the league. The Patriots were in the curious position of holding the flag, while from time to time the other teams peered from behind their barricades to see if the Patriots were still upright. They were.

From the outset I felt the action was wrong, but it was obvious to me that the team would be soon swept along by events outside its control. At one point that night, the owners and Fairbanks were invited to speak to the team. I believe that there are two tactical mistakes you must avoid in the early stages of any negotiation—don't threaten, and don't get personal—and management made them both.

The players were warned that if they refused to take the field against the Jets, they would be locked out of practice and taken off salary until the contract dispute was settled, or a no-strike pledge signed. Then Marr, in what I can only describe as an emotional blunder, singled out Vataha.

"Randy is a great wide receiver," he said, "but as a player representative, I'm afraid he's terrible. I don't think he has done a good job of explaining all this to you."

If any division had existed up to then, it vanished. The Patriots walked out of the room a unified team, joined by their anger and the conviction that the heavy boot of the NFL was about to land on them.

I knew now that I had been right to worry about Randy. I felt for him, not just because he was a favorite of mine, but because I thought he was so unfairly in the middle. Listening to him explain the team's position, I sensed that Randy had attempted to act as a moderator, neither advocating nor discouraging the decision to strike.

His concern, it seemed clear to me, was that whatever they did, they did it together. But he was the spokesman, and the brunt of the criticism would surely fall on him. It wasn't long in coming.

Public sentiment was overwhelmingly against the players. The phrases that kept reappearing were "overpaid" and "over-privileged." One NFL owner, Carroll Rosenbloom, was quoted as saying that Vataha had been a student radical at Stanford, he was always a troublemaker, and that was one reason he had been cut by the Rams, the team that drafted him.

One of the first to rush to his defense was his old college

coach, John Ralston, now at Denver. "That's absurd," said Ralston. "Randy Vataha was, and is, one of the sweetest kids that ever played football."

Sweetness, of course, was not a quality that counted for much in the early, tumbling hours of a wildcat strike. Now the Patriots, and the fans, waited to see if the other teams would join them. Their cause looked shaky on Sunday, when the games went on, and CBS plugged in a video tape of the previous night's Chicago-Houston game to fill the dead air the Patriots had created for them.

When the players reported to Schaeffer Stadium at Foxboro Sunday morning, the gates were locked. It was back to the Red Snapper for a meeting, and an open-air press conference in the parking lot. The players were looking for friends, and not finding many. They were wound tight, and defensive.

"Bob," said center, Bill Lenkaitis, "how could you let us down? Why aren't you supporting us?"

He had seen an interview I had given CBS, which ran on Sunday, during the time the Patriots should have been on the field. I had said then that the decision disturbed me, I felt it was wrong, for the sport and for the Patriots. I had also expressed my concern that Randy Vataha's role would be misunderstood.

I repeated those feelings, there on the parking lot at the Red Snapper. And I added, "Now that the strike is on, I can only hope that something positive and constructive will come from it." All around the NFL, the teams were talking and meeting, and what the Patriots were getting was mostly lip service. The Patriots were beginning to look like Casabianca, clinging in his childish zeal to the burning deck.

Then on Tuesday there was a stirring. The Lions, Jets and Redskins voted to strike. Three or four others were leaning. Seven teams quickly voted no, one or two openly taking issue with the Patriots. The lines were being drawn.

That day I received a phone call from Wellington Mara, the owner of the Giants and a member of the Management

Council. He asked if I would talk privately to Randy, and persuade him, if I could, to speak by phone with W. J. Ussery, the federal mediator trying to bring the two sides together. "We're not asking you to influence him in any way," said Mara. "We're just not sure he's getting the right information from Ed Garvey, and we want him to hear it from Ussery. Then he can make up his own mind."

Again I drove to the stadium, where the Patriots were invariably drawn, waiting to see what would develop. I found Randy. After a few false starts, we reached Ussery. I don't know if it helped, but at least the lines were being kept open.

The next day, Wednesday, the Management Council offered a proposal designed to guarantee the opening-week schedule. The key points were no reprisals against the striking teams, and an offer to consider new proposals to modify the Rozelle Rule.

Here, of course, was the real trouble pocket in pro football. The issues are money and movement, and both are related to the Rozelle Rule, which requires that a team losing a player, whose option year has expired and who signs with another team, be compensated with equal value. When this can't be resolved by the two teams involved, the compensation is determined by the commissioner, Pete Rozelle.

The players want to be free at the end of a contract to negotiate with any team they please, a practice they feel would benefit them financially—as it would. The owners fear that such freedom would hurt the league's balance, and weaken competition, by allowing richer teams to stockpile talent—as it would.

So the Patriots saw the newest NFL management offer as just another evasion. They rejected it flatly, even as most of the other teams were indicating they found it acceptable. The Patriots were backing the entire league into a corner. Their reaction was a rather human one. They had taken the risk and caught the slings and arrows. They had earned the right, they felt, to approve the terms.

It appeared the strike would spread. Suddenly, the opening week games were in jeopardy, if not the whole season. Ussery went into around-the-clock negotiating sessions with both sides. In Boston, there was little sleep for Randy Vataha. His phone rang constantly, with calls from other player reps, from the press, from friends and critics.

When a compromise was reached—as one almost always is—the final irony was yet to come. Ed Garvey, members of the Management Council, Ussery and the player reps from *four* teams all flew to Boston to present the plan to the Patriots for their judgment.

Once more, back to the Red Snapper, where the little drama had first unfolded. The thrust of the new package was that the owners would submit a new and detailed and *meaningful* proposal by the first of October. On that assurance, the Patriots ended their holdout and agreed to return to the fold . . . with reservations.

But the crisis was averted. The opening games were saved. The fans, for the time being, were pacified. And the owner of the Red Snapper was delirious. He told me his business had improved by 1,000 percent.

So, if you really want to know what is happening in pro sports today, you begin with pro football, the scene of one owner lockout and two player strikes in a period of five years. This suggests something less than a serene and stable future.

Of course, the workers are rebelling in all sports, but the problems are more visible in pro football. The game is big and successful and the players are gaining.

What the fan has to decide is whether or not the players are simply correcting timeless wrongs, or if they are merely out to show who is boss. It would be an error to dismiss their cause as being without merit. Until the boom years of the mid-'60s, the ownerships controlled the athlete's job, his future and, to an unreasonable extent, his life off the field. He had no choices.

This was true of all sports. As well as anyone can determine, unrest among the labor class in sports is hardly new. One can research the subject and see that the problem goes back as far as 450 B.C., when Euripides wrote: "Out of the tens of thousands of ills in Greece, none is worse than the tribe of professional athletes."

Exactly what the issues were then isn't known. But they are not much clearer today. Most fans can't relate to the kind of money the players are demanding, and getting. The confusion isn't helped by the fact that sport continues to exist in a twilight zone between fun and business.

Whatever happens in pro football will be observed closely by those in other sports, because it will establish trends—and legal precedents—for all of them. By 1975 the players were battling the owners in court, challenging the Rozelle Rule as well as the option year—that limbo period during which they are bound to a team even after the contract has expired.

We have become a suing society, and the structure of our games began to change when the people who play them found out their grievances could be redressed in court. And sometimes only by raising the threat of a lawsuit. The players won some early legal victories, notably in the Joe Kapp case.

All of the maneuvers had one thrust: to loosen the grip the teams had on the player's destiny. The players have contended that Rozelle has made the compensation so stiff in previous cases, that teams are afraid to sign a liberated player for fear of what they might be required to give in return.

A case in point was John Williams, a fine offensive guard who in 1971 played out his option with the Baltimore Colts. Williams, in fact, was one of those involved in the original suit brought by the players' union against the Rozelle Rule. I had talked to several teams on John's behalf, but all were wary of what payment the commissioner might extract in return. Therefore, he really wasn't a free agent at all. There were still strings attached.

In time, the situation took an ironic turn. The Colts had been owned by Carroll Rosenbloom, who in 1972, in a most complicated move, sold the Baltimore franchise (to Robert Irsay) and bought the Los Angeles Rams (from the estate of the late Dan Reeves). Now, with the Rams, Rosenbloom turned right around and made a deal for Williams with the new owners of the Colts, paying him the kind of money in Los Angeles he had refused to give him a few months earlier in Baltimore.

In the strike of 1974, the players lumped their grievances together and called them freedom issues. At bottom, of course, the net gain would be economic: the right to sell their services to the highest bidder.

The moral issues were more subtle, not easily explained to the fans. To them a moral issue is whether or not a pass interference penalty is justified when our man jams a thumb in the pass receiver's eye. (It never is.)

But most of the unrest in sports in recent years boils down to one fact, and it is this: Only one occupation in America today binds a man to his employer for as long as that employer wants him. And that's in major league sports. If a plumber or an electrician or a chemist or a lawyer or anyone else so desires, he can quit an employer and try to make more money someplace else. Why shouldn't the athlete be granted the same freedom, one he supposedly has under our Constitution anyway?

It all began, of course, with baseball, whose exemption in 1922 from the antitrust laws triggered a moral and social confusion that has existed ever since. "It *must* be a sport," a frustrated Frank Lane decided after one league meeting. "No business could run itself like this." Lane operated a half-dozen big-league teams, fighting tradition on behalf of each one.

That initial Supreme Court ruling—at the time, baseball was the *only* major professional sport—held that the game was unique, and that chaos would prevail if the teams did not "own" these players. Football, basketball and ice hockey came along, following the guidelines set down by their older brother, with variations of their own, such as the option clause.

This was good enough for the players of that era, because the leagues were closed shops, and for a player to rock the boat meant he would risk being blackballed. With the coming of the new leagues of the past fifteen years—the AFL, the WHA, the ABA—there is not that fear of being forced out of their livelihood for all times.

In 1971, Curt Flood, an outfielder who rebelled at being traded by St. Louis to the Philadelphia Phillies, went to court to challenge baseball's reserve clause. He lost, but the decision was not clear-cut, and the legacy of Curt Flood will live on. He later moved to the Spanish island of Majorca, bought and tended his own bar, and withdrew entirely from the world of games. But the years ahead may prove that Flood left a greater imprint on sports than any Hall of Famer. I believe it is only a matter of time until the reserve clause, and other agreements like it, are knocked out of the box.

By 1975, many of the legal issues involving basketball and hockey had been resolved, or else were lying dormant. The major concern was simply how much higher salaries would rise, and could they be rolled back faster than franchises were threatening to move or fold.

I had my own experience with the legal drama of these times, when the National Hockey League sued Derek Sanderson and Gerry Cheevers, among others, when they jumped to the World Hockey Association. We intentionally kept the case out of the state courts. In reviewing other such cases, involving basketball players who had leaped from one league to another, we found that in every instance the local courts always ruled in favor of the home team. In short, the judges were "homers," and we knew that any state judge around Boston—no more than any other Bruin fan—wouldn't want to see Derek or Gerry take off.

Both players were nervous and discouraged in the weeks before we went to Federal court, partly because the Curt Flood ruling was still in the news. But my own pulse was strong. I assured Derek: "I'm convinced we'll get a favorable verdict. This is a different ball game. The Flood ruling pertained only to baseball as a ruling *peculiar* to that sport."

And we did. The judge turned down the injunction sought by the Bruins to keep their players from defecting. What happened to Boston, and the other NHL clubs, was that they failed to take the new league seriously as a threat. They acted as though their own reserve clause had been written on tablets. Instead, they found it was written in sand, and the sands were shifting.

Unrest in sports is contagious. Nor is it confined to the pros. Since 1972 we have witnessed not only strikes in baseball and football, but a boycott at Wimbledon, a "fix" in the Soap Box Derby, lawsuits against Little League baseball (now turned coed) and college football, and endless rumbles in amateur track.

The monsters we have created in sports are created early on. Once, a young client of mine told me he didn't even take his own college entrance board exam, because the coach recruiting him didn't think he could pass. The school used a professional "college board taker," who was employed on a regular basis, for $500 a test, to get the proper marks for some potential superstar.

I've also had clients who were paid *extra* in college for scoring touchdowns, blocking punts or making key tackles.

To me it is degrading for the top football coaches in the college ranks to have to beg a callow, teenage star to attend his university. Yet, that coach's job depends on winning, and that requires good athletes, and so he must do it. A month after he accepted the most prestigious college job in America, at Notre Dame, Dan Devine was pictured in *Time* magazine, smiling self-consciously, as he posed in the living room of a schoolboy he had just recruited. A proud man, with an air of quiet dignity, fresh from an unhappy experience in the pros at Green Bay, Devine could not have enjoyed that moment, and I felt for him.

I contrast these experiences with the sacrifices of the true amateur, such as John Thomas, the great high jumper, at whose wedding I served as best man. Night after night, I watched him prepare for the 1968 Olympics, straining through jump after jump, with only one goal in mind: to win the gold medal at Mexico City. When he didn't, when the gifted young Russian, Valery Brumel, outperformed him, John returned home and was humiliated in the American press. People called him a choke artist. The press judged him by the outcome. I judged him by his efforts. This was an athlete who had to work at three jobs to make a living.

How curious that we can become so obsessed with the infernal money wars of pro sports, when the John Thomases and other amateurs scrape and struggle to represent America. I consider this one more failing of the American sports system.

Some of these battles have gone on for years without resolution, even with the assistance of the courts. And there has been no single forum to which anyone could turn for answers.

So what *is* the solution? I am convinced the answer is in Washington, in the form of a Sports Regulatory Board established by Congress. To be sure, government control is repugnant to many Americans, who do not trust anyone in Washington, especially George Allen.

But to me there must be one authority capable of restoring and enforcing order among a sports society now out of control. All the conniving, the wheeling and dealing, the mindless growth, has to stop. In the end the one who pays the freight and bears the loss is the fan. When the owners and the players alike wonder where it will all end, the fan already knows: his ticket cost has doubled in the last five years.

If a Federal Sports Commission were established, I would hope it might consider a few of the points I once proposed in a five-year plan to the commissioners of each of the various leagues. Later, I included this plan in testimony I was invited to give to a congressional hearing on sports in Washington.

The key points I stressed are these: no player would be bound to a team for longer than five years, at which time his name would be included in a veteran's draft, making him available to other teams. If no agreement can be reached with the team then selecting him, his name would be resubmitted for a secondary draft.

It is, frankly, a compromise between what the players want and the owners are willing to give up. But some plan is essential. Legally, the tides are running high in favor of the player and, before chaos engulfs all of pro sports, some compromise, some kind of fair arrangement, has to be enacted.

As difficult as it may be to restructure sports itself, the human factors that must be dealt with are an even harder challenge. To me, one of the astonishing changes of the past ten years has been the status and attitude of the black athlete. A decade ago he was afraid to open his mouth. Now he's the revolutionary. At least, a Federal Sports Board would offer a tribunal where the black athlete might get the fair hearing he deserves that in turn would not encourage overreaction on anyone's part.

I believe I was the first sports lawyer in the country to have a large number of blacks as clients. At first, they were petrified by most contract and legal matters, and not without reason, since blacks had been shortchanged in our society for nearly two centuries. Until the 1970s, a black athlete had to understand two facts of life. First, there existed in sports a quota system, under which no owner wanted a predominance of blacks on a team. Second, no owner wanted a black who might be considered a troublemaker. (He didn't want whites of that label, either, but he was less quick to make a judgment.)

So the black athlete just went along, until his confidence was buoyed by what he saw happening outside of sports. He saw the changes that could come about when a group put its muscle together and started to force issues. This is what the black athlete did for himself. Soon he was speaking out, taking the lead, getting elected as player rep and taking an active role in the player associations.

Today blacks in pro football and basketball dominate the player unions and, with this new-found power, have asserted themselves as never before. I do think it's a healthy sign that he is finally getting the money, the exposure and at least some of the independence to which he, like any athlete, is entitled. When I first represented blacks, I found that beyond any doubt they were getting underpaid for equal ability on the field. For a variety of reasons—fear of being cut or waived or traded—he negotiated less vigorously than the white and accepted less, even though he didn't like it and brooded openly.

But the owner also faced a problem. He knew, and I'm afraid he *still* knows, that a predominantly black team doesn't help him at the gate. The fact is that middle- and upper-class whites buy most of the tickets to pro sports events, and the owner, who has the most to lose, doesn't want to turn them off.

Now, this is not an issue that any owner wants to deal with very early in the morning. No one talks about it, just as they didn't talk about it when the limit was two black starters in basketball, and football people thought blacks were fine as wide receivers and corner backs, and even farther back to a time when those in baseball dreaded the games when a black pitcher tipped the lineup, five to four.

Prejudice was, and is, a rotten problem in this country but it is a fact of life. A few fearless owners—or, more accurately, coaches—have fielded all-black lineups from time to time, in basketball, and on occasion in baseball (where the impact is softened by the presence of *Latin-American* blacks). But the owners quiver at the prospect of it becoming a regular, everyday practice—when their best players *are* black—and watching attendance fall off, and facing a brutal decision: let his business be ruined or let the makeup of his team be influenced by skin color.

Does it *have* to come to that? It may be too soon to tell, but the pendulum has now swung, ironically, the other way. The black athlete has become the toughest for management to satisfy. Reports of holdouts and the failure to honor contracts by black athletes have increased considerably in recent years. I dislike this almost as much as I dislike the unfair treatment the black player experienced in the past. I regret that some have confused their politics with sports, never a good mix. The ardent fan has always hoped that sports could remain a sanctuary from politics and other, alien influences. The stadium is where we went on an afternoon to relax and forget the disturbing news on page one. But now it has happened that, more and more, sports is a mirror of those problems. There is no relief in the sports section, once the readiest source of escapist literature.

In fact, there are so many legal entanglements on the sports page that the average fan has to know not only the difference between the T-formation and the wishbone, but also the difference between a temporary restraining order and a preliminary injunction.

Because of the black athlete's heightened militancy and intense desire for rights so long denied, many clubs find themselves made up of cliques, with the blacks separated from their own white teammates. You might see photographs, or TV scenes, of joyous locker rooms with blacks embracing whites, and vice versa, yet away from the field life is just as segregated as a South Boston playground. On buses, planes, in restaurants and locker rooms, most blacks still elect to be together. It's the same socially. I don't honestly think it has to be this way, or should.

Times have changed incredibly. When I first spoke to the big advertising agencies about using black athletes on endorsements, they reacted negatively. All that has changed, especially on TV, where you can flip the dial and see Bill Russell, Wilt Chamberlain, Willis Reed and Hank Aaron—as many black stars as white—performing in commercials. I have found this same change for the better at the negotiating table, although, in my own mind, there is still room for improvement. But gradually, the measurement of all athletes is approaching the same standard: what counts is on what round he was drafted, or how his line in the record book reads.

Yet, the black athlete will not have received full equality until sports teams have opened their coaching staffs and front offices just as freely as they have opened their lineups.

During the NBA playoffs, in April, 1975, a national television audience saw the following: before one game Bob McAdoo, of the Braves, received a trophy as the league's most valuable player from Simon Gourdine, the deputy commissioner. After another, Washington's Wes Unseld and Elvin Hayes were interviewed by Oscar Robertson, superstar turned TV analyst, while their coach, K. C. Jones, looked on.

The people mentioned in that paragraph all have one thing in common: all are black. I guess true equality will exist when no one notices. But we are not yet so blasé.

In the end, my advice is the same to the black athlete as to the white, and to those at every level of every sport. Let us establish a forum, in Washington—if all else fails—where any problem regarding sports can be aired immediately. Let us not resort to belting each other verbally in the media, or in court.

If a regulatory board had been in operation in 1973, I doubt that Charley Finley would have attempted to humiliate Mike Andrews as he did. Andrews was the second baseman Finley fired, after pressuring him to sign a phony statement claiming nonexistent injuries. Andrews had angered Charley O. by committing two errors in the same game.

By the same token, I believe this type of board would have prevented the firing of two American League umpires, who had been active in organizing a union. The dismissal of Al Salerno and Bill Valentine ranked among the worst injustices I have ever encountered in sports.

The two umpires had been fired as "incompetents" with one month left to play in the season, after both had worked in the league for years, and had been selected for prime assignments such as the World Series and the all-star game. The reasons for their dismissal are blatantly transparent.

It was clear that the American League office had gotten wind of their effort to organize the umpires into a union. They had been dismissed and their cases supposedly closed when Salerno and Valentine came to my office for help.

In a few weeks we had worked out an arrangement, I thought, to have them work in the minors for a month or so and then be reinstated in the big leagues, which was all they really wanted.

But for reasons that were never explained, the league office reversed itself and battled the case in court. Salerno and Valentine lost their appeal on a legal technicality, more than anything else. In my mind it will always be a case of two men who were punished trying to improve the working standards in their own profession.

All these grievances add up—ingredients of a time bomb, with devastating power, with no one to defuse it.

This is not, of course, the most opportune time for an appeal to the powers in Washington, who have had their own sportsmanship problems of late. But it didn't take Congress long to lift the TV blackout in pro football, and it would be pleasant to think that action just as swift could be available to remedy problems of even deeper import for the sports public.

It isn't just that we are made uncomfortable by the flow of financial, social and legal troubles we find in sports today. Worse, we are *bored* by it and, in the long run, that is the most serious threat of all.

18

Going International

———

I HAVEN'T THE FAINTEST IDEA what the question was, except that it probably had little to do with the answer it inspired. I only remember that Casey Stengel once assured a Federal sports commission that the Japanese would never be a source of supply for the big leagues, "because they got little hands."

For years the picture of *our* games being played by people of other lands, and other cultures, touched the American funnybone. One Japanese import, a young lefthander named Masanori Murakami, did pitch a few seasons in relief for the San Francisco Giants. The writers had a lot of fun with him, claiming that his favorite American songs were, "Herro, Dorry," and "Up a Razy Liver."

But today one doesn't hear so many jokes. This may be due in part to the rising financial influence of the Japanese—they are potential investors in our franchises—and the sharp improvement in the kind of baseball played there. But it hasn't been happening just in the Orient. While we were out to lunch, the games we thought belonged to us have gone international. The Russians have gotten damned good at basketball and hockey, as their Olympic teams convinced us in 1972. And Europeans have discovered knee-in-the-groin football, as played by American pros.

This is the wave of the future, as already seen in Japan, where baseball has gained in popularity until it ranks with judo, karate, sumo wrestling and rice wine. Within five years, I believe Tokyo will have a franchise in an expanded American major league, fielding a team composed largely of homegrown talent. And it will take an infusion of only three or four American players to make that team competitive.

It has been the practice for many years, of course, to make available our aging and fading veterans, looking for one or two more seasons with a little dignity and nice paydays. Owing to a kind of gentleman's agreement with the commissioner's office, the Japanese traditionally made no attempt to sign any American stars in their prime.

But it nearly happened after the 1973 season. The player's name was Carl Yastrzemski. I was an observer to what was nearly an international sports saga, one that illustrates how well our games travel.

I don't care to speculate what the reaction might have been if Yaz had jumped from the Boston Red Sox, not just to another team or another league, but clear across the Pacific. But that experience persuaded me, at least, that the Japanese are thinking big and they will be moving into the sports market in the same way they have cars and TV sets. The message to us is obvious. We must stop thinking of professional sports as our own little sandbox.

Japan beckoned Yaz in what seemed a quite innocent way, initially. My office had received some requests to have Carl film a TV commercial and possibly endorse a product. My first reaction was that they wanted him to promote a Japanese product to be distributed in the U.S. But, no, it was to be done there and released there, for home consumption. That was the first indication I had that figures in purely American sports were getting exposure overseas, and it was a revelation to me. As a rule, except for the heavyweight champion, and to a lesser extent a golfer as popular and traveled as Arnold Palmer, or an Olympic track hero, the athletes we turn into idols are for the most part unknown beyond our borders. Who would know Joe Namath in Tokyo, or Bill Walton in Rome? The best-known athletes in the world today are Pele, the soccer star, and Muhammad Ali, who is more than a sports celebrity, almost a legend, to millions of Africans and Muslims around the world. Ali, of course, was worshipped elsewhere even when his own country had mixed passions about him.

But the fact is, the fans in foreign lands have no reason to know about those who hit it big in team sports. They simply don't see them, or read about them, and it works both ways. We might hear of an occasional British soccer player like George Best, because he dated Miss Universe and strikes us as our kind of guy. But these are exceptions.

So it was against this background that we quickly packed our bags and flew to the Far East, Yaz and his wife, Carol, and Anne and myself. We stopped off to enjoy a few days in Hawaii. As chance would have it, in Honolulu one night we ran into Tip O'Neill, the white-haired, patrician-looking Massachusetts congressman. As the Democratic whip, he had helped establish the Judiciary Committee hearings that broke open the Watergate scandal. Carl is fond of him, and confided that he was going to Japan to discuss some *contracts*. When Tip returned to Washington, he mentioned casually to a writer that he had seen Yaz and me in Hawaii, and that Yaz had been offered a contract in Japan. The word spread to Boston and, by the time we left for the last leg of our trip, the papers were checking the story. We didn't know that, which was just as well.

In Tokyo, we went to the Imperial Hotel. We were told it would be better if Carl registered under an assumed name in order to insure his privacy. So he signed the name of our host, Herman Matsui. By this time we already had a suspicion our hosts wanted to talk about more than commercials and endorsements. In that attractively subtle Japanese way, in which one is never rushed and one's hosts never get to the point without taking a circuitous, but scenic route, it was hinted that if Carl liked what he saw something more permanent could be arranged.

Now let me clear up one detail. There really was, is, a Herman Matsui, and he lives in Tokyo and represents the Massachusetts Port Authority there. Somewhat of a mystery man, Herman is Japanese, attended M.I.T. and seems to know everyone, everywhere, including Yaz, whom he had met on one of his trips to Boston. He is one of those elusive men who appear out of a mist, and are gone, and you are never quite sure what they do or where, and he always knows when the phone is going to ring. The number of his USA Social Security card is *one*, if that tells you anything. That's all. One.

So Matsui-san arranged most of our trip, acted as our host, and introduced us to such Japanese dignitaries as Premier Tanaka, and Vice Premier Miki, later to become premier. And wherever we had a reservation for a party of four, and the name cards said Mr. and Mrs. Matsui, there sat Carl Yaz and his wife and their guests, the inscrutable Woolfs.

The first night there, we were invited to dinner at our hotel with the owner of the Nagoya Chunichi Dragons, a dapper little man named Takeo Koyama, and his general manager, Wally Yonamine, a native of Hawaii who had met Carl before. Somehow the local newspapers got wind of it, and when we left the restaurant we were greeted by the Japanese version of the *papparazzi*, as many as forty photographers buzzing around like fruit flies, snapping pictures from all angles.

We hadn't planned it but, we happened to straggle out of the restaurant in ones and twos, Carl and I leaving first. The next day, on the front page of the leading Tokyo newspaper, larger than life, there was a group photo of the two of us apparently in earnest discussion with Koyama and Yonamine. I learned later what had happened. The photographers didn't even know they were after Carl Yaz. All they knew was that a famous

American baseball player was in town. One of them went to the office of *Stars and Stripes,* looked through the files and found their man. Now they knew it was Yaz, and so they made up a composite of the pictures they had taken to get us together, and ran it with a story that said flatly he had signed with Nagoya.

Within twenty-four hours the story had broken in the States, appearing in the Boston *Globe* under the byline of Crocker Snow, Jr. A distinguished writer, Crocker had confirmed that we were, indeed, in Japan, and that Yastrzemski was rumored to be preparing to sign a four-year contract worth over one million dollars.

However, we had not done much more than smile at each other, all through dinner—Yaz and I, of course, knowing no Japanese, and our hosts speaking in halting English!

But the remarkable part of it was that we had all been captivated by Japan, the people, the culture, the charm, the smile coupled with genuine humility. What a contrast to find a land where crime did not seem even to exist. A young woman could walk in the streets of Tokyo at night, alone, without trepidation.

The Japanese are so unrelievedly considerate that if someone is stopped at a light directly behind your car at night he shuts off his lights, so the glare won't bother you. On the sidewalk, and in shops and stores, no matter how crowded it gets you are never jostled or bumped against. They are not obsessive handshakers but courtesy is an instinctive part of their philosophy, and their heritage, and none of us had ever been so exposed to it. Carl and Carol fell in love with the place and, suddenly, we all began to think, *Well, why not?*

Koyama invited us as his guests to Nagoya, a few hours by train from Tokyo, and now what had begun as a lark, and what even the Japanese had probably looked on as a publicity coup, had taken an unexpectedly serious turn. Was Yaz interested? Yes. He would at least have to listen. We were both curious. At that point, we were not really certain what our position was. I didn't know if the reserve clause even applied over here. There were more meetings, more interviews, and it seemed like 5,000 more photographers.

By now Carl was recognized, which really opened my eyes to the notion that sport had become an international language. People everywhere would shout, "Meester Yizminsky, Meester Yizminsky," and hold up three fingers, indicating the triple crown he had won in 1967, a fact they had already picked up from the newspapers.

In the midst of all this, even as we had decided to keep an open mind, Koyama was hearing from the commissioner of Japanese baseball, who had apparently heard from the office of his U.S. counterpart. The sense of the call was that further contract talks with Yaz would be looked on by the American authorities as not only unsporting, but quite possibly as a violation of the Geneva Convention and the infield-fly rule.

That, we thought, was *that*. My concern now was to avoid doing anything that would damage Carl's popularity in the Back Bay. The calls started coming from halfway across the world. So Carl and I caught the bullet train back to Tokyo, leaving our wives to do some shopping in Nagoya.

It occurred to me that we needed a reasonable explanation for our presence in Nagoya. I told anyone who asked that we had gone to Nagoya on a simple sightseeing trip, and to purchase some of the delicate pottery for which the city was famous. What the Japanese papers said was unfounded conjecture. Nothing else. Our wives returned the next day and we began to relax, with the knowledge that our adventure had ended.

That comfort turned out to be premature. The telephone rang, a voice said, "Hold rine for Koyama-san, preez," and the next thing I knew Koyama was asking when we could meet again to work out a possible Yastrzemski contract! I had assumed that the pressure from the States would have called them off. I was wrong.

We met at a private office of the Massachusetts Port Authority. Koyama showed up in disguise, wearing the little surgical mask that the Japanese don in deference to others when they have a cold. His hat was pulled down over his eyes. I think it's safe to say that no one recognized him, and we met in strict security.

Earlier, I had told them that for Yaz to consider leaving Boston, he would require a million-dollar contract over four years, his *taxes* and all living expenses to be paid by the team. We knew that Boston would pay him $200,000 a year, but the tax bite obviously is considerable. This package, if our hosts went for it, would be unmatchable.

Koyama and his people had countered with a figure of about $150,000, and we were still sparring on the other terms. I learned a great deal about negotiating with the Japanese, whose politeness adds another factor to the usual give-and-take. They say *yes* to everything.

A million dollars.

Ah so, yes. Everyone smiles.

They agree with whatever you say, because they do not wish to offend you by saying no. So they say yes, or they nod, or they smile, and when everyone goes home you realize the answer was no.

We had two or three more meetings, all arranged by the mysterious Herman Matsui. Each meeting was prefaced by minutes of bowing. Finally, I told them I could not budge from the figures I had quoted, and Koyama agreed that he would present them to his board of directors. The team was owned by the same company that controlled the largest newspaper and radio station in Nagoya. With that kind of support, I concluded that in three years "Carl Yastrzemski, of the Chunichi Dragons," could run for emperor. It surely had a great *sound* to it, something between a sneeze and an eye chart.

The negotiation continued by telephone between Boston and Japan, but it ended with Koyama making a final offer of $175,000, after taxes, with a free apartment and car.

We had spent nearly three weeks in Japan, returning home the week before Christmas, 1973. It had been a wildly entertaining trip: some of it spent trying to elude the Japanese papparazzi, catching high-speed trains, taking side trips to Yokohama, ducking in and out of buildings and all the while, the people were warm and admiring.

As enticing as the Japanese offer was, sentiment and Yaz's loyalty to Tom Yawkey began to work on him. Yawkey, the persevering gentleman who has owned the club during most of his lifetime, has always had a paternal attitude toward Yaz.

In the end, Yaz not only declined the offer, but out of respect for Mr. Yawkey, he didn't even mention it to him. As evidence of his feelings toward Yawkey after Yaz had led the Red Sox to the 1975 World Series, he stated: "I'd play my heart out for that man. I wish every club in baseball had an owner like that and I wish every player who ever came into the game had a chance to play for him."

Yaz is not a collector of souvenirs, but several weeks later, after our return from Japan, he appeared in my office looking for a copy of the Japanese newspaper announcing his signing. He wanted to have it framed for his den.

So, if I were to venture a guess, I would say that someday he may play in Japan. And why not? The money is there, a new stage and a new audience. Yaz—this athlete who has done it all, with talent and poise—would make a fine ambassador.

He might not have in him another year like 1967—a .326 batting average with 44 homers and 121 runs batted in—but few players do. The Japanese recognize class and they respect age, and it wouldn't be a bad way to go out, to the cheers of another public.

I consider it only a matter of time until all those in sports are thinking in global terms. International rivalries will dominate the scene within ten years, with crowds the size of a major city looking on. These competitions will evoke an Olympic spirit, and the kind of intensity that once was found in cross-town college football rivalries.

Depending on whether or not you think the passions aroused in people by sports are healthy, you may feel that either this kind of growth will promote international understanding or it will start World War III. For sure, what we learn about other lands, and other systems, can tell us a great deal about ourselves.

In the fall of 1972, just before I was to leave for Moscow to attend that year's famous hockey series between Team Canada and Russia, I was having dinner with Randy Vataha. Ever since he had learned of my trip, Randy had tried to imagine what the Soviet Union must be like.

"Bob," he said, finally, "when you think of traveling to places like Spain or France, you dream of it in technicolor. But when you think of Russia—everything is in black and white."

And that, I soon discovered, was the way it was in the USSR, stark, cold and chilling. The trip was a combination of business and pleasure. The business end began as a favor to John Mischa Petkovitch, the North American figure skating champion, then a student at Harvard.

John asked me if during my trip I could obtain the Soviet government's permission for their outstanding figure skaters to make a trip to the United States. An exhibition tour featuring the Russian and American stars would be arranged, with proceeds earmarked for charity. It would also give our people a chance to see, live, Russia's great skaters.

We were coming into the era of détente, a time of new channels to America's old Cold War foes, and sports had a curiously important role to play. It had created something called "ping-pong diplomacy," which took note of the fact that a U.S. table tennis team had been admitted to Red China, opening doors that had been closed for twenty-five years and leading to a somewhat freer exchange of ideas and people.

So I headed for Russia with a fine mixture of optimism and innocence.

The scene when we arrived in Moscow established the proper mood. Hundreds of hockey fans from Canada poured off the chartered flights and started into the terminal. As Vataha had pictured it, Russia is in black and white. A tension does exist. Almost everywhere one turned, there were men in dark trenchcoats watching and staring. Everyone was so nervous—and I mean frightened—that once inside the terminal, we sang the Canadian National Anthem, even the handful of Americans included in the entourage. It was spontaneous, the instinctive reaction of a crowd of people, who, uneasy in a strange and threatening land, needed to show they would not be intimidated. Someone began to sing, and the rest joined in, until the music filled the lobby. The Russians stood by, puzzled.

In Moscow, I went directly to the U.S. consulate—any business you may have starts there—and explained the purpose of my journey. The consular officials asked what my approach to the Russians would be, when we finally did meet with Mr. Piseev, head of the Soviet Figure Skating Federation.

"I'll explain to him," I said, confidently, "that their skaters would be given nothing but the best. Everywhere they went, and everything they did, would be first class. We'd make sure that they would not lack for anything."

When I finished, my hosts looked at each other and grinned, as though they had some kind of inside joke going. "Bob," one of them said, politely, "if you tell them that, not one figure skater will be allowed to set foot outside of Russia. They don't *want* their people to be treated first class. They don't want them to have a damned thing in the way of courtesies or comforts. If you told them you were going to give them nothing, show them nothing, they'd be happy. Because that's how it is here. No one is a star. Everyone is treated the same. No one has first-class treatment."

Given my background and profession, I was stunned. Imagine keeping our star athletes in second-class hotels and not giving them any spending money or entertainment. In five minutes they'd tell you what to do with your figure skates.

But the information was useful to me. And when I did eventually meet with Mr. Piseev—incidentally, a very pleasant man—I assured him the skaters would be treated in any way the Russian government would like us to treat them.

The Russians liked this attitude because they have their own particular way of looking at things. I got the feeling on my two-week tour through the Soviet Union that I'd never have to worry about opening up a branch office over there. They don't believe in the star system or high-paid athletes.

There were few pretenses of friendship on either side during the entire hockey series. As the Canadiens started coming back strong after early losses, the resentment between our hosts and ourselves became more open. At one game, I think it was the seventh, the Russian security guards tried to drag Alan Eagleson, the executive director of the Players Association who had arranged the series at the Canadian end, out of the arena bodily. During the game, the Canadiens scored a goal, but the red light failed to appear. Eagleson, greatly disturbed at this, jumped down from the stands and started shouting and gesturing his displeasure at the Russians.

They grabbed him, forced him into the aisle and were about to carry him out, when the players on the Team Canada bench spotted it. Every player in a Canadian uniform raced to the opposite side of the rink and started threatening the Russian KGB men with their sticks, until they released Eagleson rather than prolong the scene. After this, the players took him back across the ice and kept him on the bench the rest of the game.

The series was televised back to the U.S. and Canada and throughout the world. Many times since, I have been asked at various speaking engagements if I had thought any harm would have come to Eagleson. Yes, indeed.

At that same game one Canadian fan had been drinking, and he had the kind of raw courage that so often comes out of a bottle. He had brought along a bugle, the kind now popular in many American stadiums where the fans are excited with cries of "CHARGE!" He insisted on playing it, even though the Russians had told him not to. That was a costly mistake. When he persisted even after their warnings, they swept him out of the arena and off to jail.

He was arrested for drunkenness, stripped of every stitch of clothing and forced to stand under a cold shower for eight hours. They shaved off all the hair on his head and tattooed the bottom of both his heels to indicate he had been arrested in the Soviet Union. That will be with him the rest of his life, long after the memory fades, if it ever does.

A swift trial resulted in a fine of $260 and a sentence of one to three years in jail, beginning with fifteen days at hard labor. Only the personal intervention of the Canadian ambassador, who appeared in court to plead his case, kept him from serving the entire sentence. As it was, he stayed in jail four days until the series was ended, and then a police escort took him to the airport and saw him aboard a plane for Canada.

And that is why I suspect that Alan Eagleson might have come to some harm had the Russians insisted on taking him into custody.

The Russians do not like noise or disturbances of any kind. However, one enterprising fan taped the sound of an air horn on his tape recorder, brought the recorder to the game, hid it under his coat, and turned it up full blast every time the Canadiens scored a goal. It drove the Russians nuts when they couldn't locate the air horn.

For pure excitement, this series was the greatest sporting event I've ever witnessed. Team Canada was down 3 to 1 in games and had to win all the remaining games to take the series. To accomplish this on Moscow ice would be no easy feat. In virtually every game, though, Phil Esposito made the play that kept his team alive.

I'll never forget his extraordinary effort, which gave courage to his teammates and eventually led them to their spectacular victory. This series made Phil Esposito an international household word.

For me, the trip had a dual purpose. I was there to negotiate an American tour by the Russian figure skaters, but privately as a friend at court for the several players I represented. One was Vic Hadfield, then a star with the New York Rangers, who jumped the team in the middle of the series, to his everlasting regret. And mine.

I have always felt that had I learned of it in time, I could have reasoned with Vic and dissuaded him from a decision whose effects still haunt him. He did it on impulse, as athletes often do. He was having a bit of friction with Harry Sinden, the Team Canada coach, who did not seem very sympathetic to Vic's plea for more playing time.

It wasn't just that Hadfield felt misused. He needed encouragement. This is an old conflict. Every coach, at one time or another, considers it a weakness to explain to a player why he has made a certain move, or to give him hope, or a pat on the shoulder. When Vic asked for more ice time, I'm sure Sinden felt he was being challenged. "I'll play you when I feel like playing you," he said.

Hadfield brooded about that for a while and then he decided, what the hell, I might as well leave. And he took off, in an impulsive act. Vic was not just quitting on his team, but on an entire country.

I had returned from a side trip to Leningrad when I encountered Harry Sinden the next morning. "I guess you heard," he said. "Vic Hadfield has jumped the team. He's at the airport right now."

I couldn't believe it. My first instinct was to grab a taxi and try to head him off at the airport. But reality, and the Russian factor, quickly disabused me of that notion. You don't just dash out of a cab and go racing into the airport in Moscow, shouting and waving your arms.

Instead, I found a Russian official and had a call placed to the airport. The plane had just taken off. I had a feeling in the pit of my stomach as though I had swallowed a tin can. Vic was no schoolboy. He was established, a veteran, a fellow with a fine reputation. But it illustrates the emotional spins of even the best athletes. They're like children when their pride is hurt.

It has been my experience that no athlete, certainly not one who has reached the big leagues, can easily tolerate the idea of quitting, at any point. If they talk about it, threaten it, they are crying for attention. They are like suicides who leave notes lying around and call all their friends and put on their best pajamas.

Hadfield, I believe, had no intention of leaving Russia until he realized no one planned to stop him. When he suggested to Sinden that he might go home, Harry shrugged and said, "Go ahead if you want."

Vic hadn't any idea what was ahead. The press murdered him. He was booed by the crowds wherever he appeared that season. Opposing benches rode him.

Sinden was under enough pressure, I guess, without worrying about one player's troubled psyche. But I wish I had been there before it happened. I just would not have let Hadfield walk out, not if I had been forced to tie him up and lock him in his room. As it was, I marveled at the fact that he had gotten out of Russia so easily.

Anne and I had experienced again the tensions of travel in the Soviet Union on the overnight train from Moscow to Leningrad, while Vic was on his way out of the country. We shared a compartment with another couple, total strangers, from Montreal. When you travel by train in Russia, you are locked into your compartment at night. We were in our berths, trying to sleep, when Russian soldiers broke in and attempted to throw us all out. We were half asleep, half out of our wits, not understanding a word of what they were saying, but getting a fair idea from their gestures that they wanted our compartment. I insisted we all stay put, and after several minutes the conductor appeared, talked to the soldiers and led them away. All things considered, I could not really recommend Russia to vacationers seeking a place to relax.

Yet, if there is any real hope for breaking down the barriers, sport is a better bet than war or politics. I have traveled across two oceans, and to most of the continents of the world, in the interest of games and the people who play them. How well this kind of foreign exchange can work became apparent to me when I visited Italy to negotiate a basketball contract for a Boston College product named Terry Driscoll.

Terry was a 6 foot 7 forward drafted in the first round, the fourth player taken in the country by the Detroit Pistons in 1970. Like most players coming out of college at the time, Terry wanted the NBA, but he wasn't in love with the idea of playing in Detroit. The Pistons, it was said, had one of the poorest organizations in the league.

Still, I must admit that when Terry, my wife and I left for Europe to hear a proposal from the Bologna team, in the Italian *amateur* basketball league, it was mainly a lark. We went over for a vacation and to see the Continent more than anything else.

Our escort, guide and interpreter was a delightful man named Richard Percudani, a high school basketball coach in New York City at the time, who was a one-man scouting force for the entire Italian Basketball League in America. It developed that each team was allowed to have one American player and, of course, that fellow had to be the backbone of the club.

Upon arrival in Italy, we were given the red-carpet treatment. We were driven around in limousines, stayed in the best hotels, dined in the best places. Shopkeepers would invite us in off the street and offer us gifts.

We learned immediately that basketball was a very serious matter to the Italians. Although it was labeled amateur, the big companies in each town sponsored the team and made sure the players had *good* jobs.

The Italians were captivated by Terry right away. He was a big, good-looking, dark-haired kid who smiled easily and showed no sign of temperament. This hadn't been the case with many Americans who played in the league before him, and the people of Bologna sensed they might have someone special in their midst.

Our first negotiating session was held in a hotel room and grew so loud and menacing that my wife Anne, staying on the same floor, thought we had come to blows. To the team officials it was a market place. They were shouting, yelling, gesturing, all in good spirits—except, of course, when they heard our price.

But as the hours ticked by, they kept raising their figures until Terry and I could only shake our heads, in disbelief, at the sincerity and intensity of these people. The next day we were whisked to the coast and a beautiful resort town, Riccioni. The excursion was designed to impress Terry with what pleasant place this would be to pursue his career. In Riccioni we received an unusual request, by our standards, anyway. "Our team is working out at the local high school gym," we were told through our interpreter, Percudani. "We'd love to have Terry work out with them."

My first reaction was a negative one. I knew that Terry already had them on his side. But they kept insisting, and I could see he was itching to get out there. You never want your client to audition. But your client is a competitive player, and trying to keep Terry out of the game would have been like trying to walk a small child past a circus.

"Terry," I said, "there is only one way I'll let you play with these fellows. First of all, you haven't played in nearly a month and if you're lousy you can hurt our position here. You'll only play for five minutes no matter what happens. So while you're out there, put on a show. Give them everything you've got. A righthanded hook. Lefthanded hook. Behind-the-back dribble. Stuff the ball. And in five minutes. That's it. No more."

Terry nodded. He was like a young fighter going into the ring against an opponent he knew he could whip.

We walked into the gym and found it packed. Word of *Driscolloni*—Big Driscoll—had spread all over the small town and everyone wanted to see this Irish giant. He didn't disappoint them. He went to the hoop like Jerry West, Oscar Robertson and Abdul Jabbar all rolled into one. They were going nuts in the stands chanting, "Terreeee . . . Terreee. . . ." Then, like some high-powered Hollywood director, I moved onto the floor and waved my hands and told them, "That's it.

The show is over." They didn't like it, but I knew now they would give us anything we wanted.

What we wanted was six years of medical school, free. A rent-free apartment for a year. A new Maserati (they took us to the factory to show it to us). A starting salary equivalent to an NBA superstar. And all of it for a total of just twenty-two games. Once a week on Sunday for twenty-two weeks and that was it.

This was the package they agreed to, a dream package, and now the lark had suddenly turned into the golden goose. What made it even more tense was the Italian style. They wanted it *now*. Sign it *now*.

We were back in that hotel room. Terry had only to sign his name. But I wanted to be sure I wasn't selling him into exile. I stepped out of the room and made some quick calls to key people back in the States. Finally, I got Red Auerbach in his home in Washington. I knew I could get a straight answer here.

"Red, this is Bob Woolf," I said. "I'm calling from Bologna."

"That's just where you belong, Woolf, in Bologna," answered Red in his own picturesque fashion. Yet when he heard the offer, he told me, without hesitation, "Bob, Terry has to take it. He'd be crazy to turn down a deal like that."

Still, I wanted more time for Terry to weigh all the factors, all the adjustments. Our Italian friends didn't like it, but I told Richard Percudani, "We're going to think it over and be back in two days." And with that I grabbed Terry and my wife and took off for London. There Terry made his decision. Italy. "I'll never get a chance like this in my life," he said. "If I don't like it, if it doesn't work out, I can always go back to the NBA next year."

We returned to Riccioni and slipped unnoticed into our hotel. At that point, feeling a little mischievous, as people often do when a hard decision has been made, we played a little trick on Richard. He was a few floors above us in his room and when I dialed his number I told Terry to start walking upstairs.

"Richard, this is Bob Woolf calling from London," I said, holding the phone an inch or so away. "I don't know quite how to tell you this but Terry has gone back home. I don't know what to say."

While he was moaning and groaning and figuring out how he was going to break the news to his friends, he excused himself to answer a knock at his door. Even across the room, I could hear him screaming, "Woolf ... you dirty ... ," when he found Terry waiting at the door.

Driscoll played that season in Italy, enjoyed himself and learned from it. The next year he went for the larger challenge of the NBA, and has since drifted from Detroit to Baltimore to Milwaukee. His career so far has been somewhat marginal but, at least, for one year he was *Driscolloni*. And whatever feeling that gave him, he wanted more of it. In September of 1975, he returned to Italy, and to Bologna for two more seasons.

As I say, I have been east and west in pursuit of someone's sports dream, but one of the most unusual expeditions I ever made was Down Under. That was on behalf of the Sports Huddle gang of Boston, a radio show that requires some explaining.

In the late 1960s, three Boston businessmen—outwardly normal but, on the inside, seething sports freaks—decided they had a message worth delivering to the nation. The trio—Eddie Andelman, a real estate specialist; Mark Witkin, a lawyer; and Jim McCarthy, an insurance agent—began a radio show, which started locally and moved to national exposure.

They were an instant hit, colorful, comical and conscientious in what they felt was a personal crusade to protect the rights of sports fans across the country. They challenged the inequities in the pro sports world on, off and around the playing fields.

Once, in an effort to find a place-kicker for their beloved Patriots of the National Football League, they set up a contest in England to find some soccer-style specialist to bring back to New England. Out of this bizarre voyage came Mike Walker, a bricklayer who made the team two years later as the Patriots' regular place-kicker.

Emboldened by this triumph, they turned their sights on Australia, and the rugged sport of rouge football, in early 1973, hoping to discover a punter for the Patriots. The club had guaranteed them that if the "Kangaroo Kid," as the public now referred to him, could make their forty-man roster, he would be paid $25,000 on his first contract.

They got their man in a contest held in Melbourne. The winner was a young fellow named Des Ley, and when I talked to him about his contract I asked what he made for playing rouge football. "Five dollars a game," he said. "Fifteen in the big ones."

I couldn't believe there were still athletes left in the world, below the age of eight, who would risk their necks in a very rugged sport for that kind of money. Yet, on my visit, I learned that the Australian athletes have perhaps the best attitude of any in the world.

Mention Australia and you think of the Shane Goulds or the Rod Lavers or the Bruce Devlins or Evonne Goolagongs—great athletes. They compete with the best and rarely gripe. I've never seen an Australian get out of line in any sports competition. It's some kind of Australian tradition that you give your best and accept the consequences, good or bad. They won't tolerate bad manners, on or off the field, where athletics are involved. They are a cordial people, the Aussies, and in many of their towns there still exists a vigorous quality once found on the American frontier.

This is not to imply that the Australians have the "perfect" philosophy for sport. No one has, just as no government has the "perfect" system when it comes to politics. But I believe in sports as an international medium.

Some have come to think of the years between, say, 1965 and 1975 as the Golden Era of Sports. The expansion begun in baseball in the late '50s reached a climax with a mushroom cloud of new teams and new leagues. In 1959 there were sixteen baseball, twelve football, eight basketball and six hockey teams on the major league scene, numbering some 1,100 players.

By 1975 there were twenty-four baseball teams; thirty-eight to forty in football, depending on the pulse of the WFL; thirty in basketball and twenty-eight in hockey. Some 3,000 athletes had found employment. All of this, keep in mind, confined to one country and two or three cities in Canada. The true Golden Age, I think, is coming within the next ten years.

Then, when people talk about the World Series, they will not be talking about the National League against the American League. They will be talking about teams competing for a true world championship, teams from Japan, Mexico, Cuba and Venezuela. In time we will find the same development in hockey, and basketball, and there will occur a great surge of nationalistic feeling in every sport.

All of which will lead to a professional Olympics, in which every country will be represented truly by their best athletes. And the great ones will automatically become global figures.

So I believe in the future of international sports, and in "ping-pong diplomacy," just as I believe it should not be confused with the real world of politics. Take Red China, for example: Any country of 800 million people who claim their favorite indoor sport is table tennis would lie about other things, too.

Epilogue

Who Did You Used to Be?

IN 1969 a client of mine, a running back named Bob Gladieux, went to a party the Thursday before the Boston Patriots' season opener on Sunday and never made it home that night.

He was celebrating, in a traditional way, the fact that for the second straight year he had been the last player cut in the Patriot camp. At such moments, athletes often adopt the attitude of the singer Dean Martin, who was asked why he drank:

> "I drink to forget."
> What are you trying to forget?
> "I can't remember."

From all reports the party was still going strong, and so was Gladieux, when the football game intervened. Bob still had not been home to change his clothes when he drove to the Harvard stadium to watch, as a spectator, the opener between Boston and Miami. The Dolphins were making their debut under a new coach, Don Shula, late of Baltimore.

Bob had been assigned to the Patriots' taxi squad, a position that entitled him to see the game free. He had to buy a program outside the gate and point out his roster photograph to a skeptical ticket taker to get inside, but he did it. The kickoff was a half hour away when he settled into his seat, accompanied by a friend, an old drinking buddy.

"Harpo"—as Gladieux was then known, due to a resemblance between his curly locks and the Harpo Marx hairstyle—was still traveling on the fumes from the three-day party he had left hours before. But his friend went off to the concession stand to buy a couple of beers against the afternoon dryness. He was gone when Gladieux suddenly heard the public address announcer—he said later he thought it was God—boom out:

"WILL BOB GLADIEUX PLEASE REPORT, IMMEDIATELY, TO THE PATRIOTS' DRESSING ROOM."

That extra sense people have when they are cornered warned Bob that something was wrong. He looked down at the field and noticed Johnny Outlaw, a player who had been cut just before Gladieux, in uniform and standing in front of the Boston bench. (Outlaw had arrived earlier, been pressed into service, left the stadium to collect his uniform at the Patriots' practice field and returned a few minutes after Gladieux had talked his way in, to confront the same gatekeeper. The old fellow looked at the guy in the dirty uniform and threw up his hands. "I've seen everything now," he said. "I guess you're going to tell me you're one of the players, too." And he waved him in.)

Gladieux squirmed in his seat and tried to decide what to do. He was in condition to play only if you believed that the training theories of the last hundred years were dead wrong. Then he turned around and saw two assistant coaches, who had spotted him from the press box, heading toward him. With great misgivings, he rose and made his way to the locker room.

He was met there by Coach Clive Rush, who had a uniform waiting for him. Rush had created an opening by benching two regulars—while their ankles were being taped—for refusing to sign their contracts.

Meanwhile, Gladieux's pal returned to his seat, and assumed, logically, that Harpo had gone to the men's room to throw up.

Moments later the opening kickoff went whistling up the field, bodies meshed and collided, and the announcer intoned:

" . . . Tackle on the play by Gladieux."

His friend choked on his beer. Wildly, he looked around. He rubbed his eyes. With his little finger he excavated his ears. His immediate thought was that he had somehow lost an entire week. The poor fellow was so shaken that when he met Gladieux after the game, he said, "Bob, I was damned near ready to give up drinking."

Gladieux spent the rest of the season with the Patriots, was released, was cut by the Redskins—at least partly because of his long hair, I've always thought—and returned to the scene in 1974 as one of the rushing and scoring leaders in the World Football League. He was one of the fortunate ones who received most of his money (from the New York–Charlotte franchise).

But many times, over the last ten years, I have gotten the feeling that all of us were out for a beer when startling changes were taking place in sports. I am disturbed by many of these changes, the disloyalty I see, the blindness of big money, the new cynicism.

Maybe that sounds like blasphemy, coming from a fellow who may have negotiated more million-dollar contracts than anyone in sports. But the pendulum is swinging back now, as it was bound to do. I have watched it go from the point where the athlete was grossly underpaid, and treated unfairly, to the point where the athlete was in the driver's seat and management suffered. It is impossible in sports today for most teams to make a profit. I have seen the consequences of the greed and distrust, and the spectacle of checks bouncing, franchises folding, uniforms getting repossessed.

The lemmings are coming back from the sea. Some of the athletes—certainly those who fled to the WFL—are saying now that they would settle for a nice, regular, authentic paycheck.

I have always contended that when you represent an athlete, you can't go to the point where your demands hurt the team that employs him. Once you do, once you allow money to become the only priority, the industry will suffer because, in the end, it all flows from the fans.

I have always felt it was more important for *every* athlete to make a living than for a few to make astronomical sums and have entire leagues fold. The salaries have become so unrealistic that they are going to come back to haunt us. Perhaps they already have.

The greatest challenge for me has been to prepare athletes for the future. I have found it easier to prepare them financially than emotionally for that inevitable day when they have to come back to the real world.

This is why so many are reluctant to call it a career when their turn comes. Deep down they knew how much it cost them to get there, and at its longest it was a short trip. When it's over the "name" that got the athlete invited to so many parties, that got him the great job in the off-season, that made him somebody in the community, is sometimes just another name. It isn't necessary to be unlisted in the phone book anymore.

Not long ago, I attended a sports banquet honoring many of the top athletes in the nation, and a few of the great ones of the past. It was held in a small town, and on the afternoon of the event many local residents came over to the hotel where the guests were lodged to mingle with the celebrities. I happened to be lounging on a sofa in the lobby, chatting with an old gentleman who had been a figure of legend in baseball. Some middle-aged people followed by a fleet of kids bore down on us.

The kids crowded around and waved their pens and autograph pads, for reasons of their own descending on me first. "You don't want me," I said politely. "But you do want my friend here." And I placed my hand on the shoulder of the gray-haired man beside me. "Oh yeah," said one, thrusting a piece of paper and a pen at my friend while asking, "Who did you used to be?"

My friend just smiled softly, as he signed for everyone who put anything in front of him. I don't know if he was hurt or not. Maybe you get used to that type of thing.

But it was cruel. "Who did you used to be?" He used to be

the exact same person he was at that moment. A living, feeling, sensitive human being, but who now just couldn't play games anymore.

He died a few months after that. The name may mean little to today's generation, but Frankie Frisch was someone special to mine. He was a Hall of Fame second baseman, the spiritual leader of the Gashouse Gang of St. Louis, and a pennant-winning manager. He was college-educated, in an era when many in baseball did not consider brains to be an asset. But he became immortal as the Fordham Flash.

I wondered how often, he, and others like him, had heard that tactless question: "Who did you used to be?"

Of course, this condition isn't exclusive to sports.

This was brought home to me in a poignant way on another occasion, on my visit to the Soviet Union. I was taken on a tour of a graveyard. The cemeteries are different in Russia. There are no big stones or fancy epitaphs. Just a simple slab on the ground with a picture of the person buried there. So I was startled, as I walked along, when my eyes chanced across a familiar face.

Nikita Khrushchev.

No, I told myself, it couldn't be. This great Russian leader buried out here like a peasant? I called over our interpreter, a plump, matronly lady.

"Isn't that Khrushchev?" I asked.

"Yes," she said, her face blank.

"What's he doing here?" I asked. "Why isn't there some monument to his importance?"

She looked at me rather coldly and replied, "Why? He was only a man. Only another man."

And, as the Latins say, *sic transit gloria mundi*. So goes the glory of the world. Life is like that, whether you live in Russia or the United States, whether you were as powerful and meaningful to history as Nikita Khrushchev was, or the greatest athlete on the globe. Once you can't do your thing any more, once you've lost the power or the magic or the machismo, whatever it was that put you up there, the admiring public is off scouting for new blood. The poet A. E. Housman put it well:

> Runners whom renown outran,
> And the name died before the man.

In the last dozen years I have dealt with athletes from many countries. I have watched Pele perform his magic before a lunatic crowd of 200,000 in Rio de Janeiro. I have been in Spain for the finals of the world amateur basketball championships. I have heard the patrons applaud politely, as though they were enjoying the opera, during the tennis finals at Wimbledon. And I have negotiated through interpreters in Japan and Russia.

My contact with sports has taken me from ghettoes to palaces. I have met with people from just about every stratum of society: world leaders, ambassadors, senators, governors, entertainers, the captains of industry. All of this because of sport, and the reverence for athletes shared by all peoples of the world.

My job has given me a ticket to get up close to lots of tears and laughter. But on balance, as I think back over the years, I have to give a big edge to the joy of sport. I would say the happy memories have far outweighed the bad ones.

I remember the thrill of being the first to tell clients such as Barry Smith of the Green Bay Packers, Ken Huff of the Baltimore Colts, Glenn Cameron of the Cincinnati Bengals, and Darryl Carlton of the Miami Dolphins that they were first-round draft choices. Or laughing at the time John Bassett, the president of the Toronto franchise in the World Team Tennis League, got to the twentieth round of the draft with no one left on their list. Bassett, in a puckish mood, thought of a writer for the Toronto *Sun* named George Gross. "Hey," he said, "George likes to play tennis. We'll draft him."

So they did, and showing the kind of shrewd judgment for which sportswriters are justifiably famed, Gross immediately called me to negotiate his contract. I wrote Bassett a letter and we signed a contract for a dollar a year. George got a humorous column out of it.

And who could forget the three-day Polish wedding of Walt and Bron Patulski. Or the time Ron Stackhouse of the Pittsburgh Penguins invited me to his wedding and confided in me that he was apprehensive over the fact that his wife might earn more money than he did. I said, "How can that be? Is she in show business?"

"No," he said, "she's a lady dentist."

I encouraged him to go ahead with the marriage with a pure heart. I couldn't think of anything more useful to a hockey player than a wife who was a dentist.

I gratefully receive numerous wedding invitations each season. One was from Bob Gainey of the Montreal Canadiens. I inquired if his fiancée came from a large family.

"Rather large," he said.

"What do you mean by rather large?" I asked.

"Well, she has nineteen brothers and sisters," he said.

From then on, when Bob Gainey described anything as "rather large," I knew he wasn't exaggerating.

So, the memories are not always on the playing field. I have pleasant and vivid recollections of:

—circling the Indy Speedway with colorful Andy Brown, the only goalie who doesn't wear a mask and drives a race car.

—feeling the love in the home of Luis Tiant, the night after his father saw him pitch for the first time in his fifteen-year major league career. The elder Tiant's trip had been arranged by a mutual friend, Senator Edward Brooke, who personally intervened on his behalf with Fidel Castro. Luis Tiant, Sr., celebrated his seventieth birthday that night.

—remembering the look of hope on the faces of the other prisoners, while visiting with Ron LeFlore and Gates Brown, of the Detroit Tigers, both ex-convicts, at the Norfolk State Prison at Norwood, Mass.

—seeing the pressure of a million-dollar contract dramatized, the night Mickey Redmond of the Detroit Red Wings nearly fainted in my arms after an eleven-hour negotiating session.

—knowing that there are men with decent instincts in sports, such as Eddie Donovan, then of the Buffalo Braves, who encouraged a rookie named Ken Charles to go to law school, and had it written into his contract that his education would be paid by the team.

—playing golf with Joe Lazarro, the man I consider the finest athlete in the country, while he shot an 84, and I got my usual 100-plus. Lazarro is the national champion *blind* golfer. And he has nerve. He once challenged Jack Nicklaus to a match, the only condition that they play at midnight.

—watching the expressions on the faces of the fans around me, who must suspect that I'm some kind of hopeless schizophrenic, as I root tirelessly for players I represent on *both* teams at whatever game I happen to be.

—fielding the exceptionally bright and incisive questions asked of me by the "now generation" students at the University of Notre Dame Law School and the Harvard Business School.

—meeting and learning to respect Sam Pollock, the Canadiens, the man I consider the smartest general manager in sports, who is thinking three years ahead while most of them are worrying about next week.

By the same token some of the moments, some of the memories, leave a hurt that lasts a lifetime: One is to tell a client what his coach has just told you: that he's a step slower and they are going to release him; and to suffer with him through broken bones, surgery, trades and bad days and nights.

And what could be sadder than an athlete dying young? One of my clients, Don Wilson, a pitcher for the Houston Astros, died in the winter of 1975, under strange circumstances, at what should have been the prime of his career. Don was a classy fellow, thoughtful, and I felt his death deeply. He had pitched two no-hitters and had worked eight innings of another when his manager removed him for a pinch hitter, because his team trailed at the time, 1–0. In the dressing room he praised that decision. "We needed runs," he said. "I couldn't have respected him if he hadn't made it."

I will be forever saddened by the untimely death of my close friend and law associate Ross O'Hanley, former defensive back for the Boston Patriots. A gentleman in every sense of the word, he passed away at the age of thirty-three.

Some memories are meaningful in their unexpectedness. Bob Watson, a teammate of Don Wilson's, scored baseball's one millionth run, early in the 1975 season. It may not have had the social significance of, say, McDonald's billionth hamburger, but I was pleased that it happened to Bob, because it brought attention to one of the game's most underrated hitters.

It is surprising how much it all matters, the serious, the sad, the frivolous. But it does, because you grow close to them in a short time, even from a distance. Over the last decade I have represented hundreds of athletes on nothing but a handshake, and a few on less than that. Many, such as John Williams of the Los Angeles Rams and Tim Kearney of the Cincinnati Bengals and Joe Theismann of the Washington Redskins, I have never even met. We are just voices on the phone to each other. It is possible to do business this way, if the players have confidence and trust in you.

Joe, incidentally, may be the only fellow in college-football history whose name was tailored to win an award. When he arrived at Notre Dame it was pronounced *Theesmann*. An alert publicity man, Roger Valdiserri, starting rhyming it with *Heisman*. It almost worked, but not quite.

As you can see, memory is a hard closet to close! But through all my experiences I have tried never to lose sight of the fact that my job is to make the athletes' jobs easier, that the cheers of the crowd are for them, and I work best behind the scenes. Of course, at times I have been a little farther back than I would have wished.

One such occasion was April 1, 1975—as luck would have it, April Fool's Day. I flew 6,000 round-trip miles to accept an invitation to speak to the NCAA Coaches' Association, in convention at San Diego. I was to speak at 10 A.M. on Saturday morning, the last day of the meetings, which were to end at a quarter of 11, adjourning in time for the coaches to attend the NCAA basketball finals.

I followed Abe Lemons, the coach at Pan American University, one of the funniest men in sports. Abe was funny that morning, too, for his forty-five minutes and for thirty of mine. When Abe sat down, at 10:30, the audience of 3,000 coaches rose almost to a man and left the room.

I counted twenty-four people in the audience as I steeled myself to approach the lectern and give the talk I had prepared with such enthusiasm. Believe me, it takes heart to speak with purpose to an empty room. When I finished, I heard the most pathetic sound that had ever reached my ears. One handclap, as if in slow motion, echoing against the walls. It was like watching popcorn pop, one kernel at a time.

If you stay in sports long enough, you will be visited by humility. Along with the laughter and tears. It has been a happy journey, and I thank you, Earl Wilson.